OCR National
LEVEL 2
IN ICT

The author and publishers would like to thank the following for the use of photographs and/or screenshots in this book and accompanying CD-ROM. Microsoft screenshots are copyright of Microsoft Corporation, other screenshots are copyright of the relevant corporation:

2.10 bottom George Doyle/ Stockbyte/ Photolibrary.com

2.10 top © Bob Jacobson/Corbis

2.34 George Doyle & Ciaran Griffin/ Stockbyte/ Photolibrary.com

21.3 bottom George Doyle/ Stockbyte/ Photolibrary.com

21.3 top © Bob Jacobson/Corbis

21.12 reproduced with the kind permission of OCR – www.ocr.org.uk

swim.jpg © RNT Productions/CORBIS

rowing.jpg George Doyle & Ciaran Griffin/ Stockbyte/ Photolibrary.com

Orders: please contact Bookpoint Ltd, 130 Milton Park, Abingdon, Oxon OX14 4SB. Telephone: (44) 01235 827720. Fax: (44) 01235 400454. Lines are open from 9.00 - 5.00, Monday to Saturday, with a 24 hour message answering service. You can also order through our website www.hoddereducation.co.uk

If you have any comments to make about this, or any of our other titles, please send them to educationenquiries@hodder.co.uk

British Library Cataloguing in Publication Data
A catalogue record for this title is available from the British Library

ISBN-13: 978 0 340 94201 7

This Edition Published 2007
Impression number   10 9 8 7 6 5 4 3 2
Year   2012, 2011, 2010, 2009 2008

Copyright © 2007 Nicola Bowman and Ann Jones

Hachette's policy is to use papers that are natural, renewable and recyclable products and made from wood grown in sustainable forests. The logging and manufacturing processes are expected to conform to the environmental regulations of the country of origin.

Cover photo from **PETER SCOONES / SCIENCE PHOTO LIBRARY**
Typeset by Phoenix Photosetting, Chatham, Kent
Printed in Italy for Hodder Education, a part of Hachette Livre UK,
338 Euston Road, London NW1 3BH.

OCR National
LEVEL 2 IN ICT

BOWMAN AND JONES

HODDER EDUCATION
PART OF HACHETTE LIVRE UK

How to use this book and CD-ROM

A Home Standalone Edition CD-ROM is enclosed in the back of this book. Insert the CD-ROM into your computer and it will run automatically. The CD-ROM contains the pages from the book as interactive, clickable double-page spreads – click on or near an icon or filename to access it.

If you get stuck at any time, click 'Help' at the top of the screen.

The CD-ROM features:

- **Interactive pages:** all resources listed below are accessible from digital versions of the pages from this textbook.

- **Extra chapters:** the less common units (Units 8–18) are included as printable PDF files on the CD-ROM and are also fully supported by the Dynamic Learning platform.

- **Video demonstrations:** these short videos are recordings of on-screen action that will show you how to use the software discussed in the book. This icon means that there is a relevant video clip on the CD-ROM.

- **Sample files:** these are files that you can save to your computer to practice your skills on – you can also edit these files and insert them into your documents. Throughout the book, you will be instructed to open and sometimes work on these files.

- **Search function:** a comprehensive search facility is included.

The student CD-ROM in this textbook is fully compatible with the networkable *OCR National Level 2 in ICT Tutor's Resource: Dynamic Learning* (sold separately: ISBN 9780340942499). In addition to the features listed above, the networkable Tutor's Resource includes fully editable schemes of work, assignments, additional exercises and lesson plans. In addition it also includes a powerful Lesson Builder facility, allowing the teacher to group and export any set of electronic resources in a format that can be integrated into the environment of the student CD-ROM included in this book. Visit www.hoddereducation.co.uk to find out more.

CONTENTS

Unit 1

Unit Overview

By completing this unit, you will create a variety of documents, which include using wordprocessing (WP) or desktoppublishing (DTP), spreadsheet, database and presentation software. You will be able to communicate using email software and search the Internet for information which can be used in your documents.

By working through the *Skills*, *How To* and *Tasks* sections in this unit, you will demonstrate all the skills required for Unit 1 and be able to use:

- good working practices, including the organisation of files, using appropriate file and directory/folder names, and the regular backing up of files;

- features of email software;

- methods of searching for information on the Internet;

- methods of integrating different types of files into a document or presentation;

- appropriate software for different tasks;

- methods of storing, retrieving and analysing data.

The skills are based around Microsoft® Office 2003.

The *How To* sections in this unit are built around creating promotional material for an organisation that is trying to preserve mammals nearing extinction. A database holding the animal details and a spreadsheet showing the donations received will be used in relation to this project. You will be required to carry out some research on the Internet in relation to extinct animals, to collect information to be used and send/receive emails as part of this project.

1

The Tasks are built around promoting mobile phones. You will need to carry out research into new phones available, tariffs and any additional extras. A promotional leaflet will be created to highlight the new offers, and a mail merge will be produced to show these to existing customers. A spreadsheet to calculate the cheapest option for customers will be produced, along with a database to hold customer details. A presentation of the business's phones will be shown to your colleagues.

Section 1: Create folders and subfolders

Assessment objective 1: *Demonstrate good working practices with files, directories/folders and subdirectories/subfolders* is covered in this section.

Skills

Extinct Mammals has asked you to create a number of folders/subfolders that will hold the files to be used throughout this project. Extinct Mammals has been in existence for a number of years and has now created a website, www.extinctmammals.co.uk, which provides details of those animals that have become extinct over the last 50 years and those that will become extinct in the next 20 years. You have been recruited by Extinct Mammals and they have asked you to carry out some research into extinct animals, send emails and produce business documents, including a letter and flyer providing details of how individuals can help. You will create a Microsoft PowerPoint® presentation, giving details of the business; create a spreadsheet showing the donations received; and interrogate a database showing details of the different animals that have become extinct.

Remember that this assessment objective is evidenced throughout this unit of the book, and a list of tasks is provided at the end of this unit, showing the evidence to be produced for this assessment objective.

How to create a folder

A folder allows you to effectively file documents and files in a logical place. It makes sense to save all the files for a project in the same folder. To create a folder:

Open My Computer

→ Click on the usual place where you would save files

→ File menu

→ New

→ Folder

→ **Extinct Mammals1**

→ Enter

Figure 1.1 – Create folders

How to create a subfolder

A subfolder is a folder within a folder – you can have as many subfolders as you want for your project. For Extinctmammals.co.uk you will need at least four subfolders: one for the DTP/WP documents; one for the database files; one for the spreadsheet files; and one for the files downloaded from the Internet. To create a subfolder:

Click on ExtinctMammals1

→ Click New

→ Folder

→ Drafts to create a subfolder

Figure 1.2 – Create subfolders

Create three subfolders to hold the different files for word processing, database and spreadsheet, and a further folder called **MammalsDownloads**.

How to create a short cut to a program, directory and file

If you use folders/files or programs regularly, it is helpful to have these displayed on the desktop. You can create a variety of different short cuts (e.g. to a file, a folder or a program). To create a short cut from **ExtinctMammals1** to the desktop:

Right-click on the folder (directory)

→ Send to

→ Desktop (create short cut)

Figure 1.3 – Create short cut from a folder (directory)

To create a short cut to a program:

Right-click on the program icon

→ Send to

→ Desktop

To create a short cut to a file, right-click on a file and you can send it as a short cut to the desktop (as above), or you can create a short cut to the file on the same directory/folder:

Create short cut – the new file will be shown as a short cut

Figure 1.4 – Create short cut to a file

To delete a short cut

Highlight the short cut

→ Press delete

To edit a short cut

If you want to edit a short cut by changing its name on the desktop:

Right-click on the short cut

→ Rename

→ Change the filename

Figure 1.5 – Editing a short cut

How to password-protect a file

Password-protecting a file keeps it secure and allows only you or anyone who knows the password to access the file. Company financial files contain the sort of information that should be password-protected and made available only to those people who need it. To password-protect a file:

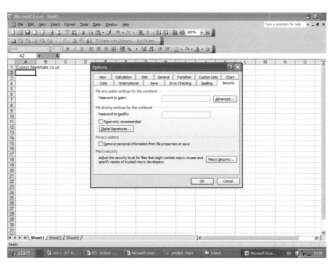

Figure 1.6 – Password-protecting a file

Open the file in the application (e.g. Microsoft Excel® file **md file.xls**)

→ Tools menu

→ Options

→ Security

→ Enter a password in the Password to open box

→ Click OK

→ Re-enter the password to proceed

→ OK

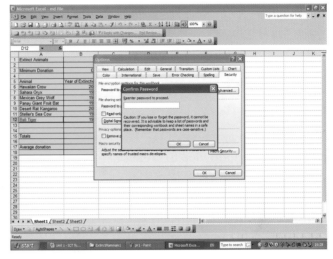

Figure 1.7 – Confirming your password

How to delete, copy and move files

It is handy to be able to move, copy and delete files in different directories if you no longer require the files, or if you want to create copies or move files to a different folder once a project is complete. To copy a file:

Open My Computer

→ Find the file you wish to copy

→ Right-click the file

→ Copy

→ Move to the folder/directory you want to copy the file to

→ Paste

To move a file:

Open My Computer

→ Find the file you wish to move

→ Right-click the file

→ Cut

→ Move to the folder/directory you want to move the file to

→ Paste

Alternatively, you can drag and drop files from one folder to another.

To delete a file:

Open My Computer

    → Find the file you wish to delete

    → Delete

How to create a backup

When creating any type of project, it is a good idea to create backups of your files. In some applications (e.g. Microsoft ® Word), you can automatically set the program to create backups of files for you, for example:

Menu Tools

    → Options

    → Save

    → Allow backup saves

To create backups regularly, create a backup of your folders and files to an external device (e.g. external hard drive or USB

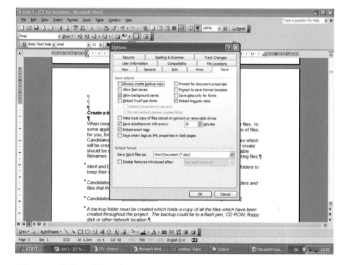

Figure 1.8 – Backup saves

memory stick). This means that if anything happens to the data on your computer, you have another copy that you can access. To create backups to an external device:

Right-click on the folder you want to create a backup of

    → Send to

    → (send to USB memory stick)

Load the memory stick to check that the folder has been copied across correctly.

Backups should be made regularly, and if you are using files often, these should be backed up daily. Some external hard drives come with software which allows you to back up the data automatically at the end of each day.

Restore files from backup

To restore files from a removable backup device, load the device into your computer. Copy the files from the backup device to your main computer area.

Search facility in operating system

To use the operating system search facility to locate and open existing files:

Click Search

→ Enter relevant criteria (e.g. all files/folders)

→ Enter filename/word/phrase or where to Look in:

→ Click Search

The files/folders should now be displayed.

Tasks

You are employed as an ICT administrator and you have been asked to review the latest mobile phone products available on the market. You should carry out your research on the Internet into new products available; the features and costs of the products; any additional accessories that are available; and whether pay as you go or a monthly contract is the cheapest option for clients who mainly send text messages.

Pass

Pass-level candidates will need to:

● Set up two directories/folders.

● Save files in appropriate locations using appropriate filenames.

● Password-protect files.

● Locate and open existing files that you have saved in your directories/folders.

● Back up files to a removable medium.

● Create short cuts to at least one directory and one file.

Merit

Merit-level candidates will also need to:

- Create an appropriate directory structure, with two main directories.

- Create at least two subdirectories, using appropriate names.

- Locate and open existing files from a range of sources.

- Provide evidence of at least one instance of deleting, copying and moving files and directories.

- Back up and restore files from a removable medium.

- Create short cuts to at least one program, directory and file.

Distinction

Distinction-level candidates will also need to:

- Create an appropriate directory structure, with at least two main directories.

- Provide evidence of at least one instance of deleting, copying, moving and renaming files and directories.

- Demonstrate the ability to password-protect files.

- Locate and open existing files, using search facilities of operating systems software.

- Create, edit and delete short cuts to at least one program, directory and file.

Remember that most of the evidence for this section of this unit will be collected throughout the whole unit.

Section 2: Search for information and send/receive emails

> **Assessment objective 2:** *Using appropriate software, select and use tools and facilities to download files/information and to send and receive email messages* **is covered in this section.**

Skills

> **Web browser:** A piece of software that allows you to view HTML files on the Internet.

Search engines

There are numerous search engines available to help you find web pages on a specific topic (e.g. Yahoo, Google and Ask). For example, if you are interested in elephants, the search engine can help you find web pages relating to elephants. Google organises information in certain ways so that it can be retrieved accurately and quickly.

Search engines allow you to quickly insert information which will retrieve the results of your search. If you want to find out about elephants, you can enter the word **elephants** into the search criteria. This is most likely to bring up thousands of entries. However, if you wanted to know about African elephants in particular, you could enter **African elephants**. Google no longer requires the word 'and' to be included in the search, and therefore will search pages for **African** and **elephant** – this search returned 1,840,000 results. Common words such as 'where' and 'how' tend to slow search engines down and therefore are usually ignored.

Instead of searching for **African elephant**, as above, you could search for **'African elephant'**, and this will only return results that include this exact phrase – this search returned 599,000 entries.

Evaluate the validity of information downloaded

Once you have downloaded the information you need to see if it is fit for purpose (e.g. if you searched for the **African elephants' habitat** and then followed one of the links to a web page), you should ask yourself the following questions:

1 Has the web page provided the information you were looking for?

2 Is the information valid – that is, how effective was the search, and how reliable is the data researched in terms of the habitat of African elephants?

3 How old is the information researched – if it is five years old, is this out of date?

4 How reliable is the source of the information – if it was a large, well-known, national organisation, would this make the information presented more reliable?

Copy and paste text and graphics from the Internet in compliance with copyright

Copyright legislation applies to information that is posted on the Internet, and therefore you should acknowledge the source of any information you find (e.g. Brown 2006, www.ictnational.com, accessed March 2007). Remember that certain types of material (especially if you want to copy anything of significant length) require permission from the copyright holder to reproduce them.

Once you have found relevant information, you might want to copy and paste this information into a Microsoft® Word document. Remember that if you are producing a document and you have copied and pasted information from the Internet, you should reformat the text so that it is all consistent and has the same font style and size.

Download graphic and text files in compliance with copyright

Remember that any files you download from the Internet are subject to copyright and should be referenced if used in any of your documents. You may also need to ask the website owner for permission to use the text and images from their website.

It is a good idea to download the text and images that you require for your project and store the material in a specific folder that allows you to find them easily in the future. In Section 1 you created a folder **MammalsDownloads**. Save any text and graphics that you have downloaded into this folder.

How to organise bookmarks/Favorites

Another way to save websites and information is into Favorites or bookmarks. It is a good idea to organise website links and create a folder specifically for each project.

Open your Internet browser and search for 'African elephants'. Follow links to different pages and find a web page that shows the suitable habitat and information related to African elephants. Save this page as a bookmark.

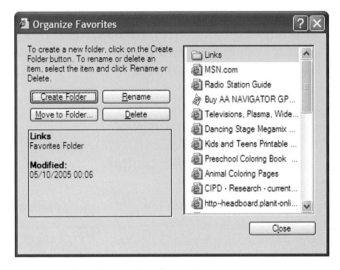

Figure 1.9 – Organise Favorites

To organise Favorites:

Click Favorites

→ Organise

→ Create folder

→ **Elephants**

→ Close

To save the web link into the Elephants folder:

Click Favorites

→ Add to Favorites

→ Select the Elephants folder

→ Click OK

→ Check that the link has been stored in the Elephants folder

Looking at the African elephants web page, answer the following questions:

Has the web page provided the information you were looking for?	Is the information valid – that is, how effective was the search, and how reliable is the data researched in terms of the habitat of African elephants?	How old is the information you researched? Is the web page dated? Is the information out of date?	How reliable is the source of the information?

For example, I did a search for African elephants and conservation and found the website www.elephants.com, which provides details of The Elephant Sanctuary. I have therefore provided an answer to the table using this website.

When you find some information on African elephants, to copy and paste it from the Web:

Highlight the text and click Edit menu

- → Copy
- → Open the Microsoft® Word document
- → Edit menu
- → Paste

Africanelephants.doc

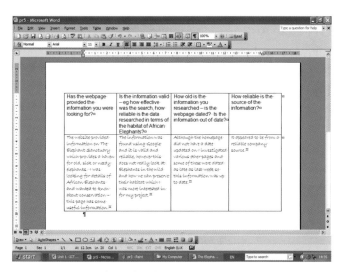

Figure 1.10 – The Elephant Sanctuary

> **Email:** The ability to send and receive messages via a computer network.

How to create email

Open Microsoft Outlook®

→ File

→ New

→ Mail Message, or click on the New Message icon

Enter an email address in the To: bar: **enquiries@ictnational.com**

Enter a subject: **Unit 1**

Type your message in the message box:

I am creating a project for Unit 1 OCR National in ICT and wonder if I could use one of the images from your website?

This is for educational purposes only.

Many thanks

Freda

Click **Send** and the message will be sent.

Figure 1.11 – Microsoft Outlook® inbox

Figure 1.12 – Example email

How to reply to an email you have received

Double-click on the message to open it

→ Click on the Reply button

→ Type the following reply message

Hi Freda

Thank you for your message – no problem – please just quote our website on your final publication, but I would be more than happy for you to use any pictures from our website.

Best wishes

Webmaster

ictnational.com

→ Click Send

Figure 1.13 – Replying to an email

How to forward email messages

Once you have received an email message, you might want to forward this to someone else for information. To forward a message:

Click on the Forward button on the Microsoft Outlook® toolbar

→ Type in the email address **jo@ictnational.com** and the title **FW: Unit** 1

→ Type the following message

Figure 1.14 – Forwarding an email

Hi Jo

ictnational.com has allowed us to use some images from its website in our project.

Freda

→ Click Send

How to attach multiple files

Files can be 'attached' to an email to send to other people – for example, you might want to send your supervisor a copy of a document you have drafted, and instead of printing this out and handing it in, you could attach it to an email and send it via email.

Figure 1.15 – Attaching files to an email

To attach files to an email:

Create a new email by clicking: New message

→ Add the email address **enquiries@ictnational.com**

→ Type a subject: **African elephants**

→ Type in the message: **I found this information which I hope you find helpful**

→ Click on the Attach files icon on the Microsoft Outlook® toolbar

Select the file from your work area

→ Click Insert

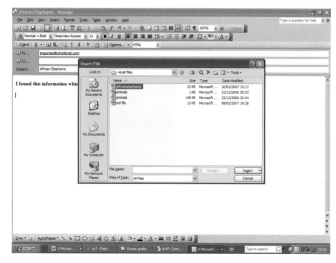

Figure 1.16 – Inserting files to attach

Check that the correct file has been attached

→ Click Send

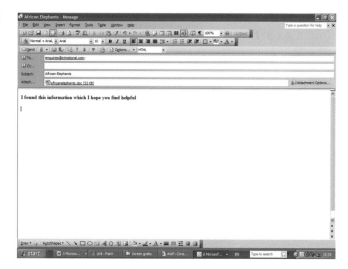

Figure 1.17 – Sending an email with attached files

How to minimise risks from receiving and opening attachments from emails

Viruses and other computer infections can be transmitted via email and, in particular, by file attachments. The safest way to deal with receiving emails is not to open any files when you do not know the person the message is from.

To open a file attachment, the safest way is to download it and save it to your computer, ensuring that you virus-scan the attachment before it is opened.

How to send email using cc and bcc

When typewriters were popular, 'cc' meant carbon copy, which indicated that the typist had placed a sheet of carbon paper between two pieces of ordinary paper, so that two copies of the document were produced. Nowadays, when using email, cc can be used if you want to send a message to one person and send another person a copy of the message. For example, you might want to send some information to one person and let another person know that you have done this – instead of sending two separate messages, the second person can be 'copied in', using cc.

'Bcc' means blind carbon copy, which indicates that the first person you have addressed the message to does not know that you have sent a copy of the message to someone else. This enables you to hide the other email addresses from all the other people you are sending the message to. For example, if I send an email message to a group of learners and do not want to disclose their email addresses to each other, I would send myself a message and bcc everyone else into the message. This keeps everyone else's email address private. To use cc or bcc:

Create a new message

→ Click on the Cc button underneath the To button in the message

→ Select the recipient from your address book and then select either Cc or Bcc and Close

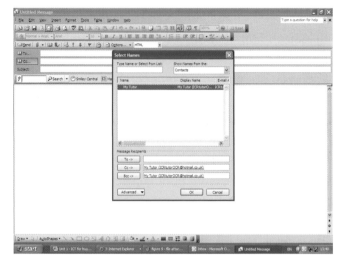

Figure 1.18 – Cc and Bcc

How to set mail to high or low priority

Emails can be set to high or low priority – this is a useful tool if you want to make a message important or if you need a speedy reply. High priority shows a red exclamation mark on messages, so that the recipient can see that this email is important. Low priority is shown as a blue arrow.

Figure 1.19 – High and low priority

To set priority, click on the red exclamation mark or the blue down arrow.

How to store, retrieve and use email addresses and details of personal contacts

It is a good idea to store the email addresses of your contacts in the Microsoft Outlook® address book. This makes it easier for you to send email messages in the future, as you can quickly look up contact details from the address book. To add an email address:

Click on the address book icon or Contacts

> → New
>
> → New Contact
>
> → OK

Enter the details shown in the figure into the address book:

> → Click Save and Close
>
> → Close the open window

To retrieve an email address from the address book:

Create a new message

> → Click on the To button on the email address and the address book will open

Select the names of the recipients

> → **My ICT Tutor**
>
> → Click OK and the email message will be sent to your ICT tutor

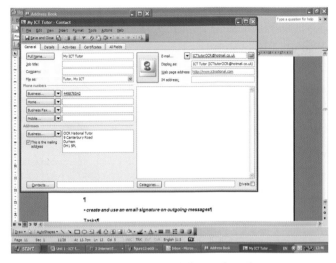

Figure 1.20 – Individual address book entry

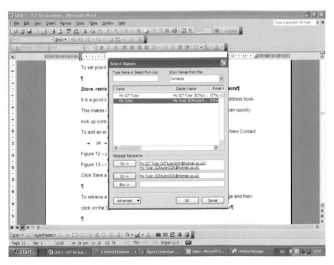

Figure 1.21 – Using the address book

How to create and use an email signature on outgoing messages

An email signature allows you to personalise each email message with your name and/or telephone number/company details, so that people know who the message is from and how to contact you. To create an email signature:

Click Tools

→ Options

→ Mail Format

→ Signatures

→ New

→ Enter a name for the signature **(ICT Signature)**

→ Enter the information you wish to appear on each message (see below)

→ Click Font to change the font style and colour

→ Click Finish

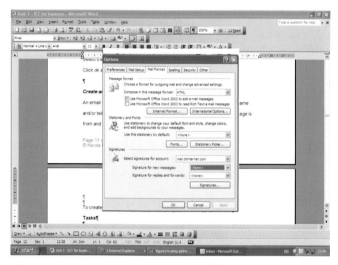

Figure 1.22 – Creating an email signature

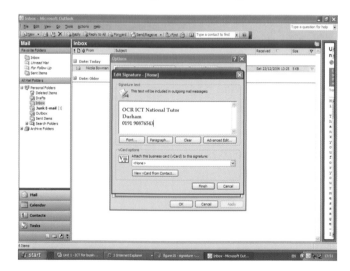

Figure 1.23 – Signature text

Tasks

Use the mobile phone scenario on page 9.

Pass

Pass-level candidates will need to:

- Use two different search engines (e.g. Google and Ask) to search for and collect information relating to the most popular mobile phones, accessories and different tariffs available, which can be used in promotional material.

- Collect copyright-free text and graphics.

- Draw up and complete a table (like the one shown here) to show a list of the websites accessed and where you have sourced information from.

Date accessed	Hyperlink	Source useful or not?

- Send an email to one of your friends, telling them about the project you are carrying out to find information about mobile phones. Attach one of the graphic files you have downloaded from the Internet and ask your friend to reply to you, commenting on the graphic that you have attached, and ask them to send you a copy of an appropriate file that they have downloaded.

- Save the file that they email to you in your folder structure relating to mobile phones.

- Reply to your friend, thanking them for their comments.

- Forward a copy of your email to your tutor and another friend, using cc or bcc.

- Ensure that each of your messages has an appropriate subject heading and text in the message.

- Write a short paragraph about the risks of opening and receiving email attachments and include this with your evidence.

Merit

*Merit-level candidates will **also** need to:*

- Comment on the trustworthiness of the information sourced (this can be added to the table, as shown).

Date accessed	Hyperlink	Source useful or not?	Trustworthiness of information source

- Store website links as bookmarks/Favorites.

- Provide evidence in the form of a document showing text/graphics that have been copied/pasted from web pages ensuring compliance with copyright.

- In an email to your tutor, summarise the risks of receiving and opening email attachments.

- When sending the message to your tutor, mark this as low priority.

Distinction

*Distinction-level candidates will **also** need to:*

- Show evidence in the form of screen prints of effective use of advanced search criteria (e.g. include 'quotes' in the search for mobile phones).

- Write a short email to your tutor, discussing the validity of the websites and provide names of the websites used. Note the trustworthiness of the sources and provide the date the information was accessed and found (this can be added to your table).

Date accessed	Hyperlink	Source useful or not?	Trustworthiness of information source	Information valid or not?

- Provide an acknowledgement list of sources of information found.

- Add at least two of your friends' email addresses and your tutor's email address to your address book.

- Retrieve these email addresses from the address book when creating the emails listed above and provide screen-print evidence to show that these were retrieved from an address book.

- Create an email signature, which will be inserted in all the emails that you send.

- Summarise the risks of receiving and opening email attachments, and in an email to your tutor suggest actions that could be taken to reduce risks.

Section 3: Create a business presentation

Assessment objective 3: *Produce a business presentation using presentation software* **is covered in this section.**

In this section, you are required to create a business presentation, showing details of the extinct animals company and how it can be promoted in order to receive donations to help with its work. The presentation will need to include the company history and details of how donations can be made.

Skills

Create screen layouts by using existing templates and by creating and positioning text and graphic frames

In Microsoft PowerPoint® you can create screen layouts using templates from within the program. You can use Slide Design or slide templates.

Within Slide Design, you can select:

● design templates;

● colour schemes;

● animation schemes.

Choose an appropriate design template or colour scheme to create a presentation without having to set background colours yourself. In this section, you are required to create a variety of business documents that could be used by the company Extinct Mammals. This unit is based around Microsoft Powerpoint®.

Figure 1.24 – Slide Design

Figure 1.25 – Slide Layout

How to set up a presentation including styles and background

Using a Slide Master ensures a consistent display and is the most efficient way to store designs, including style sheets and backgrounds. In the Slide Master you can set up the following:

- font styles/sizes;
- images;
- headers and footers;
- background designs.

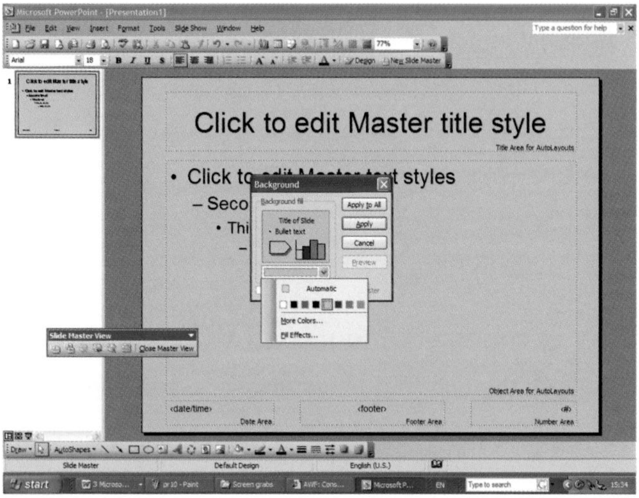

How to create a master slide

Open Microsoft PowerPoint®, which will open on a new blank slide, ready to create your own multimedia product.

View

→ Master

→ Slide Master

Figure 1.26 – Creating a master slide by adding background colours

Insert a background image or colour

→ Format

→ Background

→ Select a pale-blue colour from the dropdown arrow

→ Choose from the options available or choose More Colors or Fill Effects

→ OK

→ Apply to All

To insert a picture as an image, follow the instructions as above, but instead of selecting a colour:

Select Fill effects

>   → Picture
>   → Select Picture
>   → Choose your picture
>   → OK
>   → Apply to All

How to change the fonts and styles of text

Highlight the text in the heading box on the master slide and choose **Georgia** and **48 pt**. Apply bold and change the alignment to **left alignment**.

Change the font of the first-level bullets to: **Curlz MT** and **32 pt**. Change the font of the second-level bullets to: **Rockwell, 28 pt** and **italic**.

To insert the slide numbers:

Click in the number area on the master slide

>   → Insert
>   → Slide number
>   → Check Footer
>   → Check Slide number
>   → Apply to All

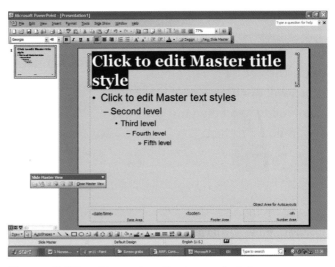

Figure 1.27 – Changing fonts and styles

(Nothing will appear to have changed, but do not worry – you will see the results later.)

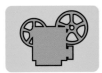

How to insert date

Click in the Date Area box, then highlighting the Date/time

- → Insert
- → Date and time
- → Choose the date format you wish to use
- → OK

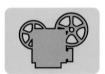

Once you have set up all the master slide elements, select **Close Master View**. If this is not visible, click on the **Normal View** at the bottom left of your screen.

You are now ready to create your multimedia presentation. Save your master slide presentation as a template.

Slide 1:

Type the information shown in the figure into slide 1.

Figure 1.28 – Close Master View menu

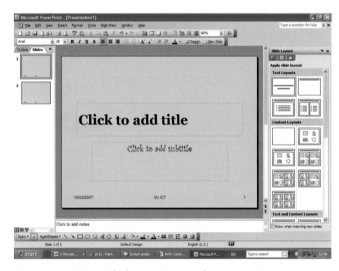

Figure 1.29 – Click on Normal View

Figure 1.30 – Slide 1

How to insert different slide types

Insert menu

→ New slide

To the right of your screen will appear the different types of slide you can insert into your presentation. The default is **Title and text**. This allows you to key in a title and then add bullet text.

Now create the following slides:

Slide 2:

Title: Extinct Elephants

Bullet: The following activities are causing the numbers of elephants to decline:

Sub-bullets: *Over-hunting*

Ivory trade

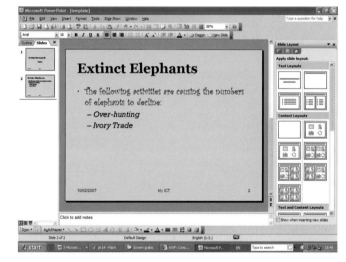

Figure 1.31 – Slide 2

Slide 3:

Title: What we are doing

Bullets: Protecting the elephants' habitat

Working with the local community to educate so that they can help protect the elephants

Developing boundaries to keep the elephants safe from human conflict

How to use text and graphics

To insert a picture:

Insert menu

→ Picture

→ Choose From File or Clip Art

→ Select the required image

Slide 4:

Title: Our Elephants

Insert the image: **elephants.jpg**

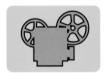

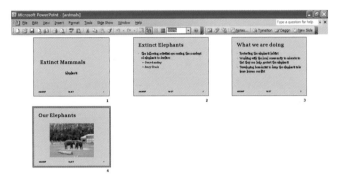

Figure 1.32 – Slides 1–4

How to edit screen content and layout (by moving or resizing frames) to achieve the required outcome

Once you have completed your presentation, you can change the layout of the slides by resizing or moving the frames. To move or resize a frame:

Select the outside of the text box/frame

→ Use the handles to resize the frame

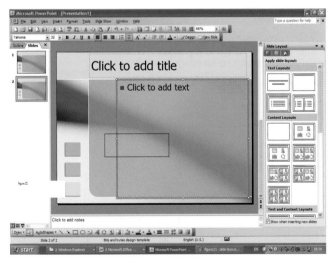

Figure 1.33 – Resize frame

Animations: effects that make text and other screen items move, appear and disappear. They can significantly enhance a presentation and focus the audience's attention on the point or points that you would like them to focus on – they can also distract if overdone.

Transition: a visual motion when one slide changes to the next during a presentation. By default, one slide simply replaces the previous one on screen, in much the same way that a slide show of photographs would change from each one to the next.

How to apply appropriate transition effects and slide animation

In Slide Sorter View, click on the transition icon from CD

→ Checkerboard Across

→ Apply to All and the transition will be applied to all slides

To apply an animation to slides 1 and 2:

Highlight both these slides and click Slide Show

→ Animation Schemes

→ Appear

To animate slides 3 and 4 with a different animation scheme:

Highlight both these slides

→ Choose Bounce from the Animation Schemes menu

How to animate your chart

After you have created your chart:

→ Custom animation

→ Add Effect

→ Entrance

→ Effect

→ In the animation task pane, select the animation effect from the list

→ Dropdown arrow

→ Effect options

→ Chart animations

→ Group chart

→ Here you can choose to animate by series, categories, or elements of either series or categories

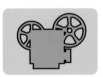

Figure 1.34 – Custom animation dialog box

How to add speaker notes and print the slides with these notes

You may wish to add speaker notes to your slides. Speaker notes can act as prompts and give you more information when you carry out your talk. To insert speaker notes:

Change to notes display by clicking View

→ Notes Page

The screen shown in the figure will appear, and you can type in the notes, as shown.

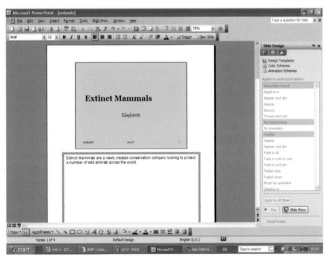

Figure 1.35 – Adding speaker notes

How to print out slides in handout form

File menu

→ Print

→ Print what: choose from Slide, Handouts, Notes Page, Outline View

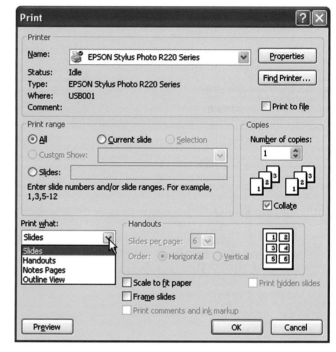

Figure 1.36 – Print dialog box

Slides: each slide will be printed on one page.

Handouts: select the number of slides per page – 2, 3, 4, 6, 9.

Notes Page: used when you have added speaker's notes – prints one slide plus notes.

Outline View: prints an outline of the text for each slide on a single page (does not show graphs, graphics, and so on – only text).

How to carry out checks (e.g. spelling/grammar, testing slide transitions)

Once you have completed your presentation, it is a good idea to check through the presentation by proofreading it very carefully. You can also spellcheck the presentation by clicking on the spellcheck icon on the toolbar.

You should also test your presentation to check that the animations and transitions work correctly. Test the presentation by running the presentation as a slide show to check that all text and images are displayed as expected and that the presentation runs smoothly.

Tasks

Use the mobile phone scenario on page 9.

Pass

Pass-level candidates will need to:

- Create an electronic slide presentation relating to Mobilephones.com, which contains (as a minimum) the company information and two slides showing a couple of mobile phone products that you have found from the Internet, plus any images that you want to show. The presentation should include at least three slides.

- The presentation will support a talk to a new colleague about Mobilephones.com – consider suitable layout and content.

- The presentation must include both text and graphics, and you can use any of the information you have downloaded from the Internet.

- The presentation should be checked using a spelling/grammar checker, and you should include a screen print to show that you have completed this.

| Merit | Merit-level candidates will **also** need to:
 - Include four slides in the presentation.
 - Add slide transitions.
 - The presentation should be checked using a spelling/grammar checker and you should include a screenshot to show you have done this.
 - Print out the presentation in handout form.

| Distinction | Distinction-level candidates will **also** need to:
 - Include five slides in the presentation.
 - Add slide transitions and animations throughout the presentation.
 - Add speaker notes to at least one of the slides.
 - Print out the presentation showing the speaker notes that have been added.

Section 4: Create a variety of business documents

Assessment objective 4: *Select and use tools and facilities in word-processing or DTP software to produce a variety of business documents* **is covered in this section.**

In this section, you are required to create a variety of business documents that could be used by the company Extinct Mammals. This unit is based around Microsoft® Word 2003.

Skills

A variety of different document types exist. Some examples are set out below.

Letter: A business letter is a written document that tends to be written in a formal manner from one person to another. Letters are usually posted.

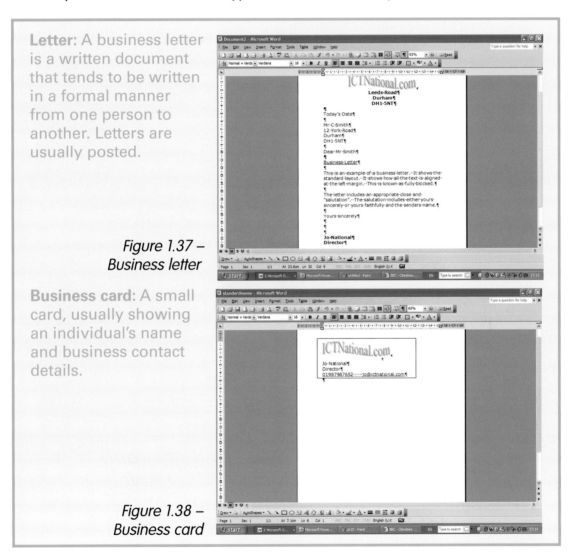

Figure 1.37 – Business letter

Business card: A small card, usually showing an individual's name and business contact details.

Figure 1.38 – Business card

Flyer: Usually a single-sheet printed advertisement.

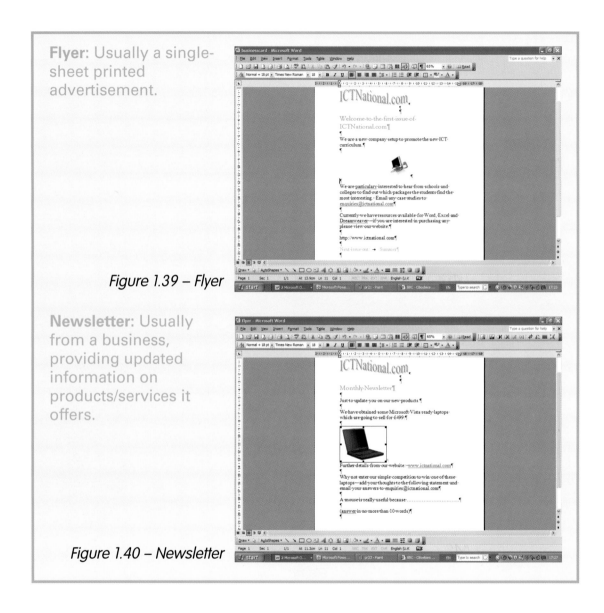

Figure 1.39 – Flyer

Newsletter: Usually from a business, providing updated information on products/services it offers.

Figure 1.40 – Newsletter

Invoice: A request for payment, issued by a business to another business or individual, detailing the amount to be paid.

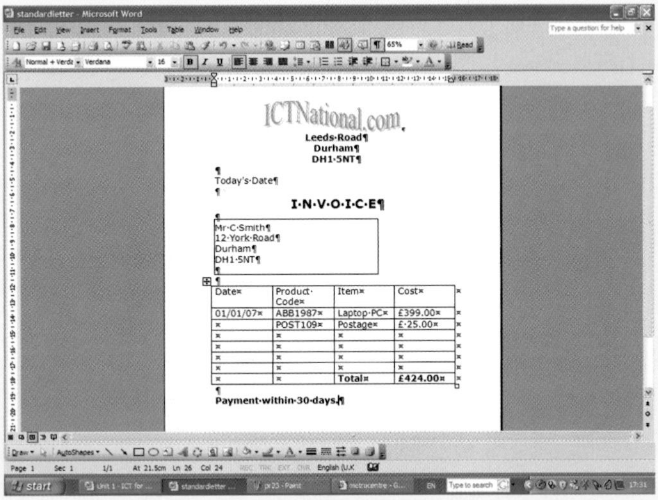

Figure 1.41 – Invoice

Memo: Usually an internal, informal document, used to send information between different departments within an organisation. Email is now replacing some memos within organisations.

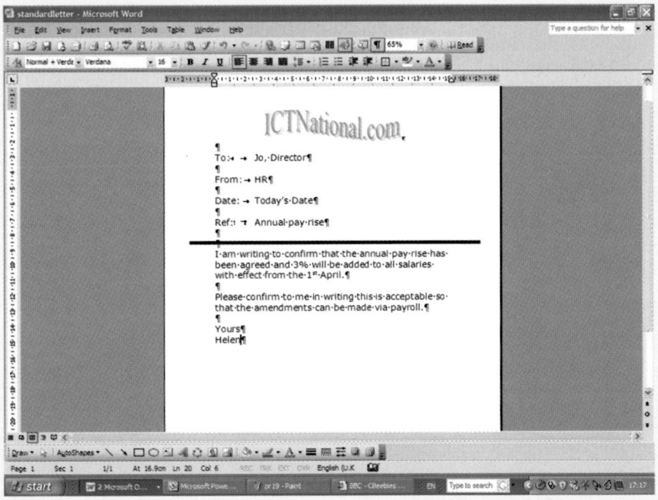

Figure 1.42 – Memo

Agenda: Lists the time, place and items for discussion for a meeting that is due to take place.

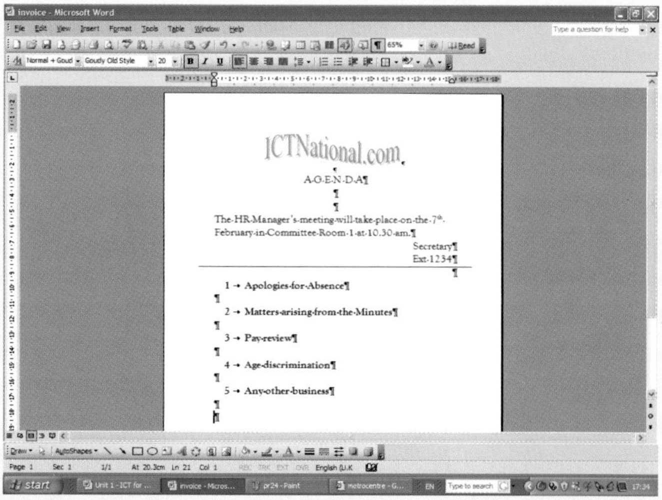

Figure 1.43 – Agenda

Report: A well-structured written document, which presents findings from some type of investigation or is an account of an event.

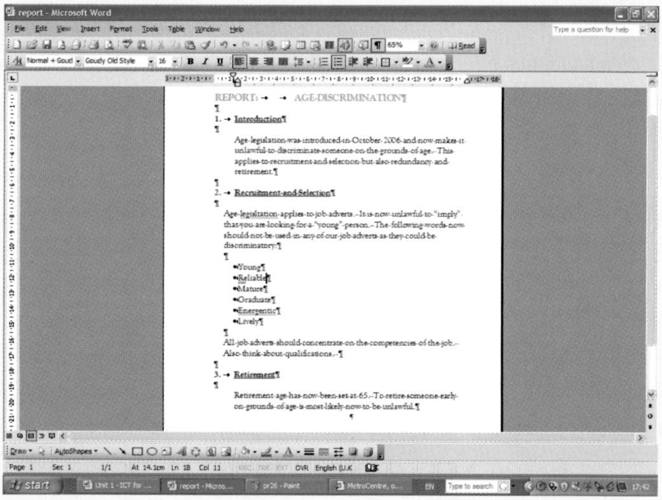

Figure 1.44 – Report

Minutes: Formal written recordings of a meeting that has taken place. Minutes will follow an organisational house style and will show the discussion that has taken place and actions agreed resulting from the meeting.

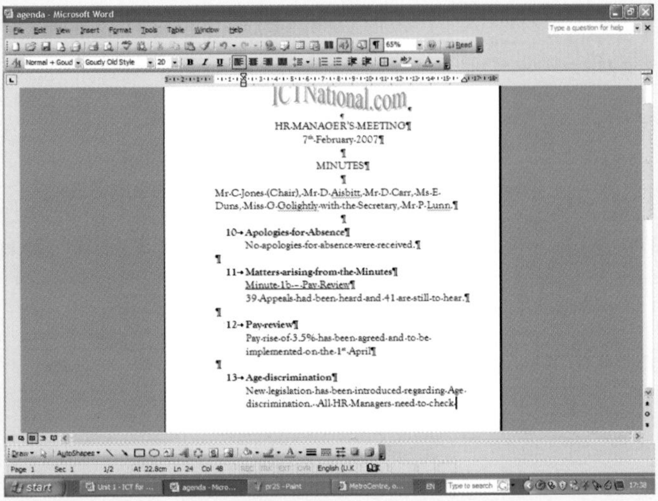

Figure 1.45 – Minutes

How to enter text, tables and images, using the keyboard, mouse or other input device

In Microsoft® Word it is quite simple to insert text into a document. Create a new document and start typing. Microsoft® Word will automatically create new lines when you type.

How to create a table

Open a new Microsoft® Word document and create the following table.

Figure 1.46 – Create a table

Table menu

→ Insert

→ Table

→ Choose 3 columns by 2 rows

EXTINCT MAMMALS		
Animal	**Year of extinction**	**Country**
Hawaiian crow	2004	America
Sahara oryx	1999	America
Mexican grey wolf	1998	Africa
Panay giant fruit bat	1987	America
Desert rat kangaroo	2001	Australia
Steller's sea cow	1982	America
Caribbean monk seal	1996	America
Bali tiger	1952	Bali
Balinese tiger	1970	Bali
Barbary lion	1945	North Africa
Schomburgk's deer	1990	China

The first row in the table has merged cells.

Highlight the first row of your table

→ Table menu

→ Merge Cells

Borders and shading has also been applied to the table.

View menu

→ Toolbars

→ Tables and Borders

Use the tables and borders toolbar to perform most of the formatting functions. After the table has been drawn up, you can use the commands you need by using a right-mouse-click on the table.

Figure 1.47 – Table borders

Draw	Erase	Line type	Line thick-ness	Line colour	Borders colour	Fill

Figure 1.48 – Table formatting

Insert table	Merge cells	Split cells	Align-ment	Distribute rows evenly	Distribute columns evenly	Auto-Format

To merge cells:

Highlight the cells to be merged

> → Table menu

> → Cells menu

To split cells:

Highlight the cells to be split

> → Table menu

> → Split Cells

To add borders:

Highlight the cells where the border is to be added

> → Click on the toolbar icons to add borders

Add borders and shading as shown in the Extinct Mammals table above.

How to format documents

The easiest way to change the font size, style, line spacing or alignment of a document is to create styles. Once you have created a style, you can then amend it and apply this to any text you wish to have this style, instead of having to change all the text separately.

By setting the top four boxes of the New Style figure shown here, you can set the text style, alignment, enhancement and paragraph spacing from the initial dialog box, using the Formatting area.

To create a new style:

Format menu

> → Styles and Formatting
> → New Style
> → Give the style a name (e.g. body text)
> → Change the font face
> → Change the font size
> → Change the alignment
> → Change the line spacing
> → Click OK

To create a style for bullets:

Format menu

> → Styles and Formatting
> → New Style
> → Give the style a name (e.g. bullet text)
> → Numbering
> → Set the bullets/numbers as required

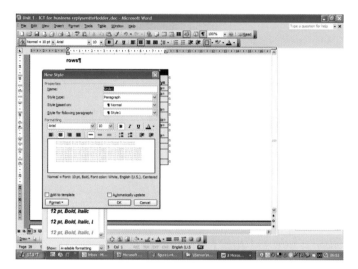

Figure 1.49 – New Style

How to insert headers and footers

Headers and footers enable information to appear automatically on every page. Headers and footers can include text, dates and document information (e.g. filename).

To insert a header and footer:

View menu

> → Header and Footer

→ (and then choose from)
insert page numbers

→ insert date

→ insert filenames

→ insert text

→ choose layout of different
sections

→ choose page numbers
starting at any number.

How to edit documents using insert, delete, cut, copy and paste functions

Once you have created your document, you might want to delete some of the text or make some amendments.

To delete text:

Highlight the text to be deleted

→ Click on the Delete/Del button on the keyboard

To cut text:

Highlight the text to be cut

→ Click on the Cut button on the toolbar

To copy text:

Highlight the text to be copied

→ Click on the Copy button on the toolbar

→ Move the cursor to where the information is to be copied to

→ Click on the Paste button

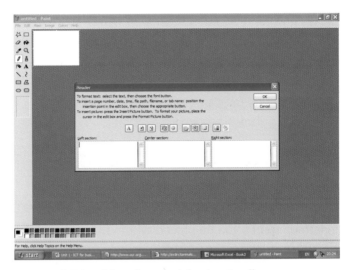

Figure 1.50 – Header and footer toolbar

Figure 1.51 – Standard toolbar showing cut, copy, paste buttons

How to import tables created in other software

The table can be imported or copied/pasted from Microsoft Excel® into Microsoft® Word. The easiest way is to open Microsoft Excel® and the file.

Open the Microsoft Excel® file **animals.xls**:

Highlight the data to be copied

→ Select Copy

→ Click in Microsoft® Word where the table is to be inserted

→ Click Paste

How to insert images created in other software

Inserted images can be placed within the text and they can be used to add features (e.g. maps, photos).

Place your cursor at the position you wish to insert an image

→ Insert menu

→ Picture

→ From file

→ **elephants.jpg**

Pictures can also be inserted from Clip Art, by selecting Clip Art instead of From File.

You can resize your image, but you should ensure that you keep the aspect ratio of the image (the proportions) the same:

Hold down the Shift key and left-click on a corner of image

→ Drag the image to the desired size – this will adjust both the height and the width proportionally

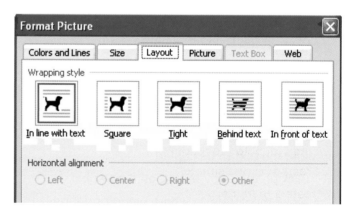

Figure 1.52 – Layout tab

You may wish to position the image more precisely in the text.

Double-click on the image and a dialog box will appear

→ Select the Layout tab and you can change the way that text wraps around the image and how the image is placed within text

How to insert a graph or chart created in other software

You can copy and paste the chart into Microsoft® Word or you can import it. To import the graph/chart:

Insert menu

→ Object

→ **chart.xls**

→ Click OK

→ Resize your graph/chart

How to change text to column display

Highlight the text

→ Format menu

→ Columns

→ Select the number of columns to be included in the document

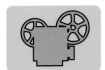

How to carry out a mail merge

A mail merge is useful when you want to merge information from a data file, such as a spreadsheet or database, and send to more than one person. Mail merge labels can be printed or letters can be produced, which look individual to the reader but are created by one simple click.

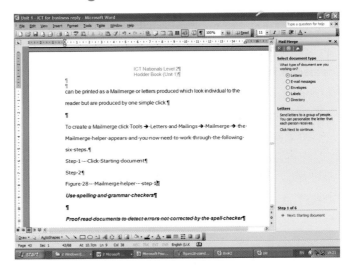

Figure 1.53 – Mail Merge helper

To create a mail merge:

Tools menu

→ Letters and Mailings

→ Mail Merge

→ Mail merge helper appears

You now need to work through the following six steps:

1 Click Starting document

2 Select Use the current document, if you are going to type a new letter, or Start from existing document, if you want to open a document you have previously typed

→ Click Select recipients

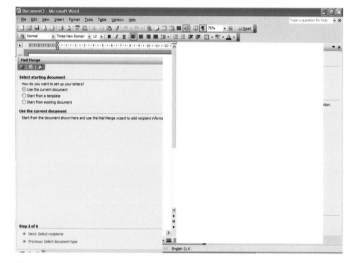

Figure 1.54 – Select starting document

3 To use an existing list (e.g. database/spreadsheet file):

Click Browse

→ Open the data file **names.xls** and select **sheet1**

→ Click OK

→ OK

→ Click Write your letter

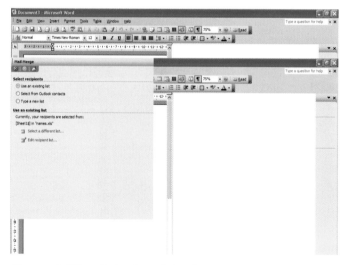

Figure 1.55 – Select recipients

4 Write your letter and insert the merge fields

→ More items

→ Match fields

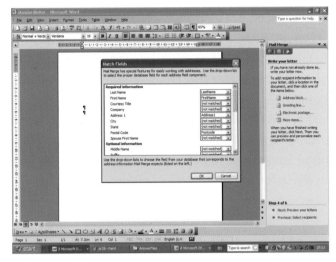

Figure 1.56 – Match Fields

Insert menu

→ Insert all required fields

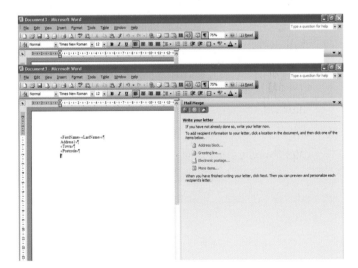

5 Select Preview your letters, and click to preview

→ Click Complete the merge

6 Click Print, to print out all the mail merge letters, or Edit individual letters, to edit your letters

→ Merge 'All' to new document

→ OK

Figure 1.57 – Insert fields

Your mail-merged letters will now be displayed.

How to use spelling and grammar checkers

Once you have completed a document, it is a good idea to check the spelling and grammar to ensure that it is correct. To use the spelling/grammar checker in Microsoft® Word, click on the spelling and grammar icon on the toolbar. Change any spellings that are incorrect.

Remember, the spellchecker cannot pick up words that you have inserted incorrectly but spelt correctly (e.g. 'coy' instead of 'copy'). It is extremely important that you work through the documents you have produced and proofread these very carefully. It is also a good idea to ask someone else to proofread the document for you once you have read it, to check for any errors you may have missed.

Tasks

Use the mobile phone scenario on page 9.

Pass

Pass-level candidates will need to:

- Create a business letter for mobilephones.com which includes a company logo. The letter will need to be sent to customers who are already on the mailing list (**names.xls**), providing details of the newest top three phone models and their tariffs however, for a pass you need to complete the mail merge.

- Create a flyer showing details of the three new phones. Add suitable text and images that you have found on the Internet and that you have obtained from another source (e.g. a CD). The flyer will need to show the company logo and include column displays.

- Both documents need to use the same house style, which should have the same font styles and font sizes throughout.

- Create a business card for mobilephones.com

- The documents should be checked using a spellchecker.

Merit

*Merit-level candidates will **also** need to:*

- Create a three-page report, discussing the new mobile phones and the new technology that is now available (e.g. GPRS, Bluetooth, Internet, mini PDA).

- The report should also include a table and a graph imported from spreadsheet software. You will create these in Unit 6: Spreadsheets.

Distinction

*Distinction-level candidates will **also** need to:*

- Create a standard business letter and create a mail merge with the **names.xls** spreadsheet, to tell customers on the spreadsheet about new details of mobile phones.

- The report will need to include suitable fields (e.g. filename, page numbers, date and document information, such as when it was last printed/saved).

- The document must be proofread. You should make any necessary changes to ensure that it is error-free and looks professional.

Section 5: Create a business spreadsheet

Assessment objective 5: *Create and use a simple business spreadsheet* **is covered in this section.**

Skills

In this section, you will create a simple spreadsheet that can be used by the company Extinct Mammals.

Open Microsoft Excel® and key the following data directly into the first workbook:

Extinct Animals					
Minimum donation	£10				
Animal	**Year of extinction**	**No. of donations**	**Total donation**	**Target**	**Above/ below target**
Hawaiian crow	2004	248		250	
Sahara oryx	1999	351		350	
Mexican grey wolf	1998	876		650	
Panay giant fruit bat	1987	221		200	
Desert rat kangaroo	2001	943		1000	
Steller's sea cow	1982	478		500	
Bali tiger	1952	23		800	
Totals					
Average donation					

How to enter text/numeric data

Text and numbers can easily be inserted into a spreadsheet. You should proofread the text and numbers carefully. To change the fields to number fields with no decimal places:

Format menu

> → Cells

> → Number

> → 0 decimal places

How to insert and delete rows and columns

To insert new rows:

> → Insert menu

> → Rows

To delete rows:

Highlight the row to be deleted and totally removed

> → Edit menu

> → Delete

How to create formulae involving arithmetic operators

You can create the formulae using the following arithmetic operators within Microsoft Excel® to calculate a variety of different sums:

+ this allows you to add one or more numbers together;

? this allows you to subtract one or more numbers from each other;

* this allows you to multiply numbers together;

/ this allows you to divide numbers by each other.

How to create simple functions

● **Sum:** calculates the sum of different numbers in a range of cells e.g. =sum(A1:A10)

 Tip: To add cells in a continuous row or column, you can use the AutoSum button on the toolbar e.g. A1:A6 (if data is not in a continuous row or column, you would use the =SUM formula)

● **AVERAGE:** calculates an average across a number of cells e.g. =AVERAGE (A1:B3)

- **MAX:** returns the maximum number over a range of cells e.g. =MAX (B1:C10)
- **MIN:** returns the minimum number over a range of cells e.g. =MIN(B1:C10)
- **MEDIAN:** returns the median, or the middle number, in a set of numbers e.g. =MEDIAN(B1:C10)
- **MODE:** returns the mode, or the most frequently occurring number, in a range of data e.g. =MODE(B1:C10)
- **COUNT:** counts the numbers in a range of cells e.g. =COUNT(B1:C10)

  Tip: If you wish to count the number of text items in a range of cells, you would need to use the function =COUNTA(B1:C10)

- **COUNTIF:** counts the number of cells that meet specific criteria e.g. counts the number of items that need to be reordered, such as =COUNTIF(B6:B18, 10)

Relative cell: A reference displayed in the spreadsheet formulae as, for example, A4, and when it is replicated down a column it becomes A5, A6, A7, etc.

Absolute cell: A reference displayed in the spreadsheet formulae as, for example, A4. The '$' makes both the column and row references within the cell absolute (i.e. they do not change) when it is replicated. 'Absolute' can refer to just a column $A4 or row A$4.

Using the Microsoft Excel® file **md file.xls**, carry out the following calculations:

1 Calculate the **Total Donation** by multiplying the **No. of donations** by the **Minimum donation** – remember to use an *absolute* cell reference.

2 Add a new row to the spreadsheet: **Bali tiger, 1952, 23**.

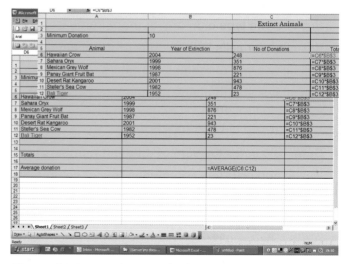

Figure 1.58 – Making calculations

3 Create an IF statement to show whether the number of donations is above or below target.

4 Calculate the average number of donations that have been received using =AVERAGE

Save the file as **mammals1**. The figure shown here provides some expected answers.

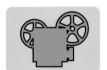

How to format cells: text (font, style, size, alignment), numbers (decimal places, percentages, currency, date/time), borders and shading

Open the file **mammals1**. To change the font of text within the spreadsheet:

Highlight the title of the spreadsheet **Extinct Animals**

→ Format menu

→ Cells

→ Font

→ Century 14 pt

To change the background colour of cells:

Highlight the cells to which the colour should be applied

→ Fill Color

→ Yellow – the fill colour will colour the highlighted cells

To add cell borders:

Highlight the cells A1–C12

→ Click on the border icon

→ Select the type of border required (e.g. outside, inside, all)

→ Repeat for cells D1–F12, expected answers 1–60

How to merge cells

A heading, for example, can be merged and centred across a number of cells, to make it stand out or to ensure that the data is shown in full. To merge cells:

Highlight the title **Extinct Animals**

→ Click on the merge and center icon

Change data

Data can be changed so that different figures can be obtained. Within a spreadsheet you can make predictions, for example to see if the school tuck shop is making a profit.

The company Extinct Mammals has noticed that the minimum donation should be increased and have asked you to make some predictions; the spreadsheet can be used to test out these different variables before making a final decision.

In this section, we will employ an absolute cell reference in the spreadsheet to be used in the calculation to make the predications.

How to print data from a spreadsheet

Data can be printed in full or a selection of data can be printed.

To print the data in full:

Ensure that all the columns are wide enough

→ Click on the print icon

To print a selection of data:

Highlight the data to be printed

→ File menu

→ Print

→ Selection

→ Click OK

How to set the orientation, headers, footers and other options to print

To change the orientation of the worksheet:

File menu

→ Page Setup

→ Click on either Portrait or Landscape

→ Click OK

To add headers and footers:

File menu

→ Page Setup

→ Header/Footer

→ Click either Custom Header or Custom Footer

→ Enter the details

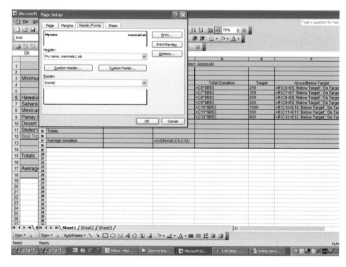

Figure 1.59 – Header and footer

How to work with a spreadsheet

Using the **mammals1** spreadsheet:

1 Format the cells so that the **Total donation** is shown as currency.

2 Change the font size of all the cells except the title to 12 pt.

3 Centre the column headings by clicking on the centre icon.

4 Print out the spreadsheet showing the figures.

5 Change the **Minimum Donation** to **£15** and see how this changes your figures.

6 Add a password to the spreadsheet:

Tools menu

→ Options

→ Security

→ Key in a password to modify

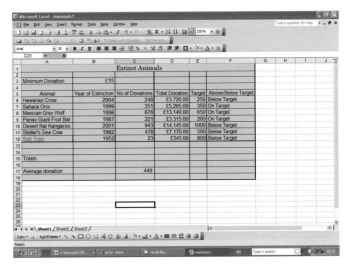

Figure 1.60 – Extinct Animals

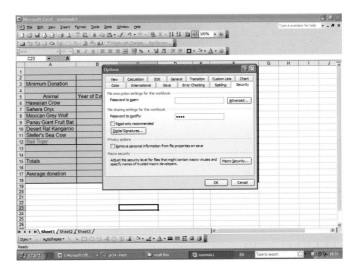

Figure 1.61 – Adding a password

7 Print out the spreadsheet showing figures and annotate the printout, showing the changes you have made.

8 Change the orientation of the spreadsheet worksheet to landscape and print one page:

File menu

→ Page Setup

→ Landscape

→ Fit to: 1 page(s) wide by 1 tall

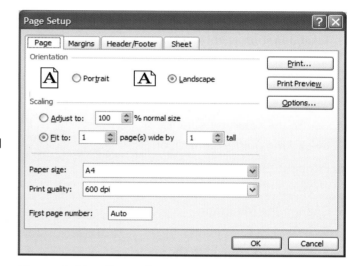

Figure 1.62 – Page Setup

9 Add your name as a header and the filename using an automatic field.

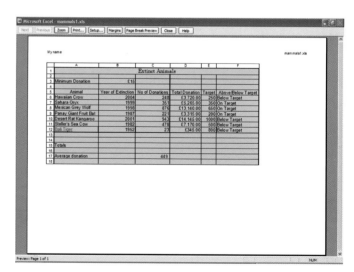

Figure 1.63 – Header/Footer

10 Set the print options so that gridlines and row/column headings are printed.

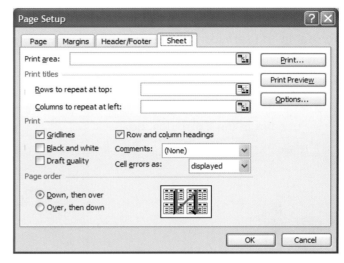

Figure 1.64 – Print options

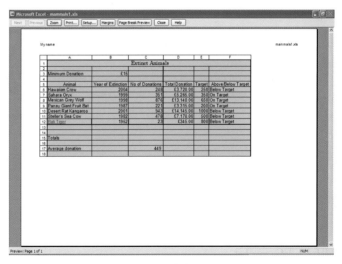

Figure 1.65 – Final spreadsheet

How to print the formulae used

To change the spreadsheet to show the formulae:

Tools menu

→ Options

→ Put a tick in the 'Formulas' box

→ Click OK

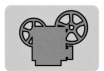

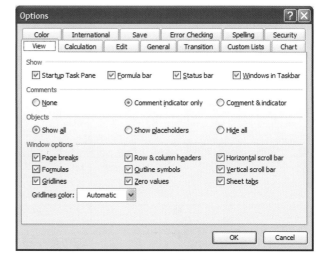

Figure 1.66 – View formulae

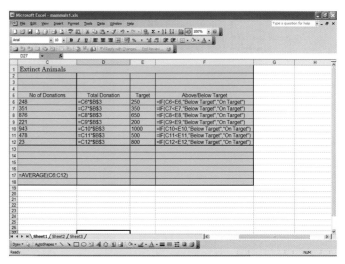

Figure 1.67 – Spreadsheet showing formulae

Tasks

Use the mobile phone scenario on page 9.

Pass

Pass-level candidates will need to:

- Create a very simple business spreadsheet, using a limited number of calculations (e.g. SUM and AVERAGE).
- The functions/formulae will work.
- Enter sufficient row/column headings to make the spreadsheet reasonably easy to understand.
- Apply some formatting.
- There will be evidence that some of the data has been changed to obtain different results.
- Print out your spreadsheet.

Merit

*Merit-level candidates will **also** need to:*

- Edit the spreadsheet by inserting/deleting rows.
- Add title
- Reprint the spreadsheet, highlighting the changes and showing how this has affected the totals.
- Formula printouts will be included.
- Preview and print out your spreadsheet, using appropriate page orientation and number of pages.

Distinction

*Distinction-level candidates will **also** need to:*

- Include the appropriate use of more than one function.
- The spreadsheet will be formatted effectively, using a range of format options.
- Use appropriate headers and footers and set other print layout features appropriately.
- Formula printout(s) will be included.
- Print out your spreadsheet, using appropriate page orientation and number of pages.

Section 6: Manipulate a database

> **Assessment objective 6**: *Select and use tools and facilities in database software to enter, sort and search for information for business purposes, using a realistic business database provided by the centre is covered in this section.*

Skills

Extinct Mammals has provided you with a Microsoft® Access™ database **animals.mdb**, which you can manipulate. A database is a useful piece of software that allows you to easily search for records that meet specific criteria.

In this unit, you will be using Microsoft® Access™ 2003.

A business database, such as a client database, is used to:

- enter and edit data;
- run queries to search for specific data;
- run reports;
- create forms.

How to enter, edit and delete data to keep it up to date

You will be required to enter, edit and delete data in the existing database. Remember to be careful when amending data within the database – once you have deleted data, it can no longer be retrieved.

Open the **animals.mdb** database and make the following amendments:

● Enter the following new record:

| Red gazelle | 1936 | Algiers |

● Amend the following record:

| Sahara oryx | 2001 | America |

● Delete the following record:

| Balinese tiger | 1970 | Bali |

It is a good idea to take a screenshot showing the amendments.

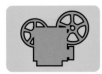

How to sort data

Select the column of data to be sorted

→ Click A–Z for ascending or Z–A for descending – all data will now be sorted

Using the **animals.mdb** database, sort the **Animal** field into *ascending* order. Save and close the table.

To sort more than one field in the database, it is easier to create a query and sort the data into ascending or descending order within the query.

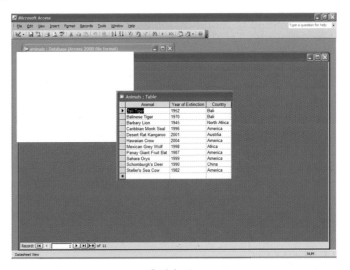

Figure 1.68 – Sorting fields

Create a new query and sort the **Animals** and the **Year of extinction** into ascending order.

How to search for data using queries, including searching on more than one criterion

Simple queries can be created within the database to search for and find specific results that match a given criteria – for example, you might want to search for all 'red' cars in a database. Microsoft® Access™ then returns the results showing all the 'red' cars.

Multiple queries can be created to find more than one item within a database – you could search for 'Ford' and 'red' to return the results showing all 'red Ford' cars. However, you can also use multiple queries in the same field (e.g. 'Ford' and 'BMW'), and Microsoft® Access™ will return the results showing all Ford and BMW cars.

Complex queries (not, between, and)

Complex queries look at more than one field. They are made up of two or more simple queries joined together by logical operators, such as AND, OR and NOT, for example 'Ford' and 'BMW'.

The table below shows the logical operators that can be used in Microsoft® Access™.

NOT	WHERE **NOT** (Author = Jones) This will search for all records where the author is NOT Jones.
AND	WHERE Author = Jones **AND** Date = 1999 This will search for all records where the author is Jones AND the book was published in 1999.
OR	WHERE Author = Jones **OR** Date = 1999 This will search for all records where the author is Jones OR the book was published in 1999.

Example range operators to be used in queries

The table below shows the range operators that can be used in Microsoft® Access™.

Operators	Description
>	Greater than
<	Less than
>=	Greater than or equal to
<=	Less than or equal to
<>	Not equal to

Wildcard or like queries

The asterisk (*), per cent sign (%), question mark (?), underscore character (_), number sign (#), exclamation mark (!), hyphen (-) and brackets ([ ]) are wildcard characters. These can be used in queries and will search for criteria that starts with, includes or ends with a wildcard character.

How to create a simple query

Create a query and search for those animals that were in the country **America**.

Click Queries

→ New

→ Design View

→ OK

→ Select the table

→ Add

→ Close

Transfer all the required fields to the bottom half of the database screen by double-clicking on each field name. Enter the criteria, for example **America**, and then only the animals from **America** will be displayed.

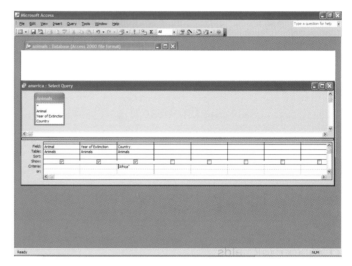

Figure 1.69 – Simple query

How to create a multiple query on more than one field

Create the query as indicated above, and at the criteria stage enter **Africa** or **America**.

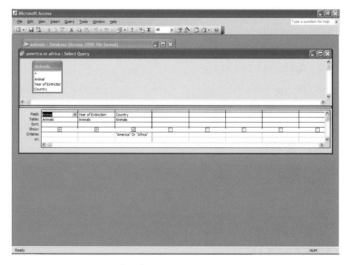

Figure 1.70 – Multiple query

How to print out data using reports in different formats

To print out a table:

Open the table

→ Select Print Preview to check that data is displayed in full

→ Click print icon

How to create a report

Reports

→ New

→ Report Wizard

→ Africa and America query

→ OK

→ Select all fields

→ Next

→ Next

→ Next

→ Columnar

→ Next

→ Compact

→ Enter the title **American and African Mammals**

→ Finish

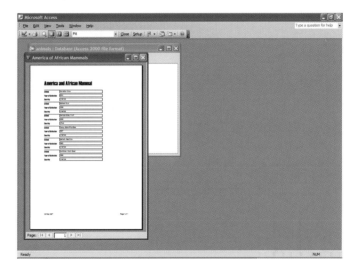

Figure 1.71 – Report

Tasks

Using the mobile phone scenario on page 9, create a relational database that includes at least 20 products for sale by mobile phones.com in one table. Or you can use the names.xls file and import the data into a database as you do not need to create a database

Pass

Pass-level candidates will need to:

- Enter, edit and delete data in the database.
- Produce screenshots to show the changes you have made to your database.
- Create and use at least one simple query (i.e. using a single search criterion, such as customers in one town).

Merit

*Merit-level candidates will **also** need to:*

- Sort data on at least one field.
- Create and print out a report for a specific need (you will need to annotate the report, showing how it meets a specific need) – you could use the query you created above and produce a report.

Distinction

*Distinction-level candidates will **also** need to:*

- Use the data to meet a wide range of business purposes.
- Create and use another query, including more than one criterion.
- Create a report in table format.
- Create a report using address labels.

Additional tasks

Now that you have completed the project, you will need to produce evidence for Assessment objective 1.

| Pass |

Pass-level candidates will need to:

- Show that you have organised your files during the completion of this project.

- Produce annotated screenshots of the folders you have created and the filenames used, and to show the files that have been found and opened.

- Produce an annotated screenshot showing a short cut to at least one folder and file that you have created.

- Show evidence of backing up your files – this folder should be saved on a removable medium (e.g. flash pen, CD-ROM, floppy disk or alternative network location).

| Merit |

*Merit-level candidates will **also** need to:*

- Include screenshots that show evidence of:

    1 the folders and files that have been deleted, copied, moved;

    2 folders and files that have been renamed;

    3 search facilities to locate and open existing files;

    4 files that have been restored from a removable medium;

    5 short cuts created to at least one program.

| Distinction |

*Distinction-level candidates will **also** need to:*

- Edit and delete short cuts.

Unit 2

Unit Overview

This unit will help you develop knowledge relating to the planning and creation of a multimedia website that is fit for purpose. You will develop the skills to plan, design and implement a simple website. You will develop an understanding of common concepts and features relating to the creation of web pages, web page formatting and website structure. You will be able to format pages to create a house style, including creating hyperlinks, tables and forms. You will also develop skills to include interactive elements.

By working through the *Skills*, *How to* and *Tasks* sections in this unit, you will demonstrate all the skills required for Unit 2 and be able to:

- design a multimedia website;
- create a multimedia website;
- create hyperlinks;
- create interactive elements;
- create a user form for capturing user feedback;
- test your website and act on the findings;
- evaluate your website.

Examples in this unit are based on Macromedia Dreamweaver®.

For this unit you will need to create a simple website of at least five pages. There should be evidence of:

- planning;
- design;
- testing;
- use of a template;
- creating the web page.

70

On the web pages you will need to:

● insert hyperlinks – both internal and external;

● use tables.

Throughout the How to sections, you will be working on a theme of creating a new website for a local school, to advertise both the school and the new sports facility.

For the Tasks sections, you will be working on the theme of creating a new website for a local band. This website can be of your choosing.

Section 1: Design a multimedia website

Assessment objective 1: *Design a multimedia website* **is covered in this section.**

Skills

You have been asked to produce a website for a local school to advertise its new sports facilities. You can research other websites and collect details, information, graphics and multimedia components, which will help you when you create your own website.

The proposal

You will need to write a proposal for a five-page website. A **proposal** is a written document, setting out ideas for the planned website. The proposal should include:

1 An outline of why the website is being produced – for example, if you are creating a website for a school or college, your outline is likely to include:

● to increase enrolments and parent/student communication.

2 The purpose the website will serve – for example:

- location of the school;
- map and directions to the school;
- a portal for information about the school and students;
- up-to-date details on daily features;
- news and a facility to receive views;
- community events calendar;
- photographs of the school buildings and facilities (e.g. swimming pool, sports centre).

3 Who the website is intended for – for example:

- staff;
- students;
- parents;
- governors;
- other interested parties.

4 The plan for the website – for example:

- content;
- layout (including navigation system placement);
- styles (fonts);
- image placement;
- hyperlinks;
- hot spots/image maps;
- interactive form layout and links;
- number of pages.

5　How the website will be tested – for example:

- beta tester used – other users test and report back on errors/omissions.

6　A site map, including the links and pages in the website.

7　What resources will be needed – for example:

- PC or Mac;

- Internet connection;

- software to be used;

- Internet service provider (ISP).

See layoutplan.doc

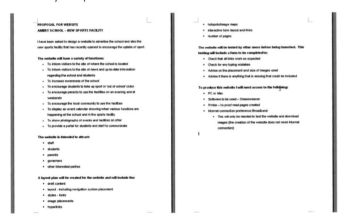

Figure 2.1 – Proposal

Site map

You will need to draw a **site map**. A site map is a visual model of the pages in a website; it can show a diagram of the entire site's contents. Similar to a book's table of contents, the site map makes it easier for a user to find information on a site, without having to navigate through all the pages in the website. Site maps can be textual or visual; visual sketches can be easier to follow.

For a textual example, visit:
www.qub.ac.uk/home/TheUniversity/Location/Maps/WebsiteMap/

For a visual example, visit:
www.hud.ac.uk/hhs/teaching_learning/educaitah/map.htm

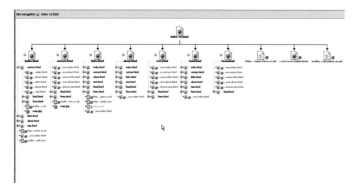

Figure 2.2 – Site plan

House style

To ensure that the website has a professional and consistent look, it is advisable to use a house style. A **house style** will specify the formatting of all the pages in the website, such as font attributes (font sizes, font types, font colours, hyperlink colours), background images and metatags. The font attributes should be saved in a cascading style sheet (CSS), and this CSS should be used on each page to ensure consistency. The font attributes are created and then saved as a CSS file format. An example of the content of a CSS file is set out below:

```
1
2   <!--
3   body,td,th {
4       font-family: Arial, Helvetica, sans-serif;
5       color: #0033CC;
6   }
7   body {
8       background-color: #99FFFF;
9       background-image: url();
10  }
11  h1 {
12      font-size: 24px;
13      color: #0000CC;
14  }
15  h2 {
16      font-size: 18px;
17      color: #0033FF;
18  }
19  h3 {
20      font-size: 14px;
21      color: #0099CC;
22  }
23  -->
24
25
```

Figure 2.3 – CSS file

h1 [color: #000000; font-family: Times New Roman; font-size: 45pt; text-align: Center; font-weight: bold }

h2 [color: #0000FF; font-family: Arial; font-size: 18pt; text-align: Left; font-weight: bold }

h3 [color: #0000A0; font-family: Arial; font-size: 14pt; text-align: Justify }

Visit: www.cam.ac.uk/cambuniv/style/ for an example of what a house style consists of and why.

Collect and store components from other websites

Search out other websites, looking at a variety of sites that have been created to show similar content to the site you are going to develop.

Check out the following sites to capture images or copy text and stories for your site:

www.olympic.org/uk/sports/index_uk.asp

http://news.bbc.co.uk/sport/

www.uksport.gov.uk/

www.culture.gov.uk/about_us/sport/default.htm

www.youthsporttrust.org/

www.teachernet.gov.uk/teachingandlearning/subjects/pe/

www.iconbazaar.com

You may save components to use, such as:

- images;
- text;
- animations;
- interactive elements;
- video;
- sound.

You must acknowledge the source of any components that you use on your own website. The easiest way to store this information is by using a simple table, such as that shown here:

Date	Source	Location	Filename	Copyright
21 Dec	Icon bazaar	www.iconbazaar.com	home.gif	ALL CONTENT copyright © 2006 IconBAZAAR LLC. World rights reserved.

How to create a CSS

In a blank page of your website:

File menu

> → Save As
>
> → Choose the folder you have created for your website
>
> → Save as file
>
> → Style Sheets [*.css]
>
> → Filename = **School**
>
> → OK

To open the CSS Styles palette:

Click on the window to the right of the screen

> → CSS Styles
>
> → Right-click on the window to create a new style
>
> → New

Figure 2.4 – CSS style sheet styles

You will see a pop-up box. Write the name of your style (**.h1**). (Remember, *always start your styles with a full stop* – you can add your initials to make the style your own.)

Create your own custom style by choosing the font type, size, weight, colour, and so on

> → OK

You have created a style. Repeat these steps to create .h2 .h3 .h4 and so on. Save and close the open style sheet.

The code for your style could look like the one shown here, depending on what you choose for your styles.

How to import a CSS to your web page

With a page open, (this can have text and layouts on it, or be blank):

In the Properties panel

→ Style

→ CSS

→ Attach Style Sheet

→ Choose your style sheet

How to assign your style to text

Highlight the relevant text in your document

→ In the Properties panel

→ Style

→ Choose your style

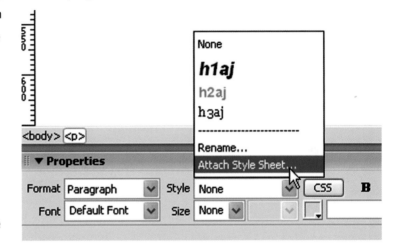

Figure 2.5 – Attach Style Sheet

Tasks

You have been asked to produce a website for a local band, to give details of their gigs, music and band members. You can research other websites, and collect details, information, graphics and multimedia components, to help you when you create your own website. The website must have a form for fans to ask questions and get responses from the band or from the fan club secretary.

Pass

Pass-level candidates will need to:

- Produce and plan a brief proposal – a minimum of half a page of A4.

- State a purpose of the website.

- State the target audience.

- Show details for at least five web pages.

- Produce a site plan (this will only be one A4 page).

- Produce page plans for each of the five web pages.

- Ensure that there is a house style, including the colour scheme and navigation to be used, and the positioning on each page of text, images, tables, and so on.

- Demonstrate evidence of linking pages.

- Collect relevant material for your website:

  1 You may download multimedia components from the Internet for use in your website, but you must identify all source material.

  2 You must show evidence that you have checked the copyright of all downloaded materials (i.e. who is the owner of the downloaded materials?).

  3 You may create multimedia components yourself, using skills you may already have or those you have learned as part of Units 4, 20, 21, 22 and 23.

Merit

*Merit-level candidates will **also** need to:*

- Produce and plan a detailed proposal.

- Ensure that the house style is suitable.

- Ensure that the layout detail is suitable.

- Demonstrate more than one way of linking pages.

Distinction

*Distinction-level candidates will **also** need to:*

- Produce and plan a comprehensive proposal.
- Ensure that the house style is accurate.
- Ensure that the layout detail is accurate.
- Include colours, links and multimedia components.

Section 2: Create web pages

Assessment objective 2: *Create multimedia web pages* is covered in this section.

Skills 1: File management

You will need to set up a suitable folder structure for the website, using subfolders and appropriate filenames for all files (web pages, images). You will also need to keep copies of your work on a suitable backup device (e.g. USB memory stick, removable hard disk/drive, CD-ROM).

Remember the following important points for your folder structure:

- All images must be stored in an **images** subfolder.
- Text source documents are stored in a separate folder.

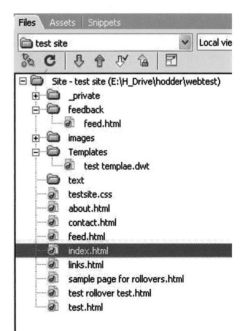

Figure 2.6 – Site plan 1

● Templates are stored in a different area of the website.

● CSS files are attached to web pages and stored in your website folder.

How to create a folder and subfolders, and back up work

Open your user area through Microsoft Windows® Explorer or My Computer.

To create a folder:

→ File menu

→ New

→ Folder

→ Enter a suitable folder name

→ Enter

To create a subfolder:

Double-click to open an existing folder

→ File menu

→ New

→ Folder

→ Enter a suitable folder name

→ Enter

To back up a folder to a memory stick:

Insert the memory stick into a USB port

→ Click on the main folder name

→ Drag to

→ Drive for your memory stick

To back up work to a CD-ROM:

Insert a blank, writable CD into the CD drive

→ Open My Computer

→ Click the folders that you want to copy to the CD (to select more than one folder, hold down the Ctrl key)

→ Under File and Folder Tasks, click Copy this folder

→ In the Copy Items dialog box, click the CD drive

→ Click Copy

→ In My Computer, double-click the CD drive

→ Under Files Ready to be Written to the CD, select the folder(s) you want to write to CD

→ Under CD Writing Tasks, click Write these files to CD

→ Microsoft Windows® displays the CD Writing Wizard

→ Follow the instructions in the wizard

Alternatively, if you have Nero CD-writing software (or similar), use this to write data to a CD as a backup.

You will need to provide screenshots of your folder structure, of backing up work and to show the file types and sizes created.

How to take a screenshot

To ensure that you can show evidence of your folder structure, you should take a screenshot of the computer screen showing the folders and files.

Open the required folder or subfolder

→ Press Alt + Print Screen

→ Open a new or previously saved text document (e.g. Microsoft® Word/Notepad)

→ Edit

→ Paste

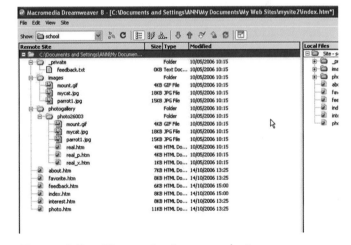

Figure 2.7 – Site content screenshot

An example of a screenshot, displaying site content, is shown here.

Skills 2: Create a multimedia website

Defining the website

Once you have set up your folder structure, you will need to set up a folder system for your website in Dreamweaver. It will then maintain a link to that folder. It is important that you do not move or delete this folder, because the link will then be lost. At the beginning of a new session, you may need to re-establish the link.

Template pages or CSS

When creating a website, each page should have a standard appearance so that visitors can recognise your pages and navigate your site easily. It is therefore practical to create a master page or template.

The master page or template will not form part of the site, but will give you a foundation on which to build each of the pages. As outlined in Section 1 of this unit, the following could be created as a master page or template to produce a basic page layout:

- colours;
- background images;
- logos;
- embedded CSS file;
- metatags;
- navigation system;
- standard content.

To create a template in Dreamweaver, create a web page and use this as your template.

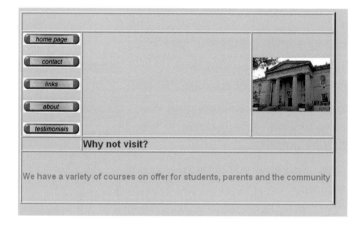

Figure 2.8 – Table layout 1

The use of tables for content layout in Dreamweaver

Tables are used to lay out the page content because:

- they grow with content;
- images can be positioned more accurately;
- navigation systems can be created to standard width and height (where images of different sizes are used).

Figure 2.9 – Table layout 2

Figure 2.10 – Table layout 3

House style (text attributes)

You need to establish that the text format and colours used on your website will be pleasing to your viewers and complementary to your web content.

Import/insert text and graphics

You are not required to create all the content for your website – you can import from other software/websites, or use images and text that you have created in other units. You must proofread the text and correct any spelling mistakes, to ensure that errors on your website are minimised.

Range of different components

You need to use a range of different components in your website, such as images, animations, interactive elements, video and sound. These can be created at this stage or may have been created in other units.

Optimise images

You will need to optimise images used on your website to ensure that the file size is kept to a minimum, reducing download time.

Websites you can visit to download images

www.amazing-animations.com/
www.freeimages.co.uk/galleries/sports/index.htm
www.barrysclipart.com/

How to define a website in Dreamweaver

Launch Dreamweaver

→ Select the Site menu

→ New Site

→ Enter your website folder name (e.g. schooltest)

→ Next

→ Select the top radio button for No, I do not want to use a server technology

→ Next

→ Select the top option to Edit local copies on my machine, then upload to server when ready

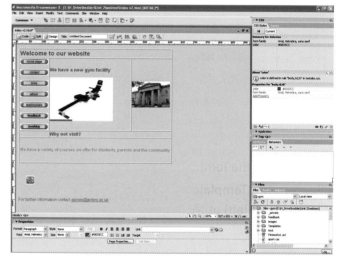

Figure 2.11 – Dreamweaver screen

→ Below this, click the folder icon

→ Browse to your user area to locate your website folder

→ Select the folder

→ Click Open

→ Select

→ Next

For How do you connect to your remote server?

→ Click the dropdown and select None

→ Next

→ A summary of your site will be displayed

→ Click Done

Select the Site panel on the right of the Dreamweaver page and check that you have the source files correctly in your website – double-click on your website folder to check the folder structure.

To make sure that your website looks consistent throughout, you need to create a master page or template on which all web pages in the site will be based. When producing the template, you must stick to the guidelines you set in the house style in Section 1 of this unit. This template page will be used to create the home page (index.html) and other pages in the website, so be sure that you create the master page or template correctly.

How to create a new template in Dreamweaver

Select the Assets panel on the right. If this is not displayed:

Click on the Window menu

→ Assets

→ Select the Templates button

Click the New Template button (second from left) at the bottom of the Assets panel

Name your template (e.g. **school template**)

→ Enter

Double-click on the template name in the Assets panel; Dreamweaver will open it in a separate document window. The title bar will display your template name followed by **.dwt** (this is a Dreamweaver file extension).

Select the Files tab

→ Select the Refresh icon

→ You will see your saved template in your website

Figure 2.12 – Templates button

Figure 2.13 – New template button

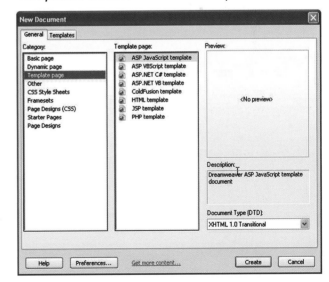

Figure 2.14 – Template

Set up the standard content that will be on all the pages of your website (e.g. navigation system, copyright notice). Save your template.

How to insert tables into Dreamweaver

In the Layout bar, select the Table tab.

Figure 2.15 – Table button

- Select the number of rows and columns you wish to display (you can change this easily later if it is not right).
- Select the overall size of your table (again, this can be changed if not right initially).
- Select the border thickness and any cell padding and spacing.
- Once you have set up your table, click OK.

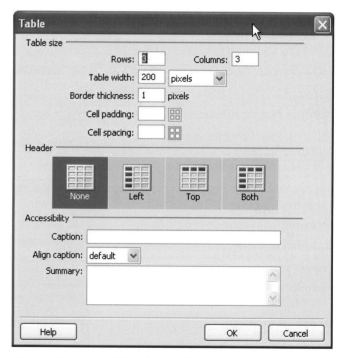

Figure 2.16 – Table dialog box

Cell padding: the internal margin within a cell.

Cell spacing: the space between each cell.

How to insert content into your table

- Images
- Text
- Navigation buttons
- Links
- Video
- Sound

This is a very simple process:

Insert

→ Image

→ Select image

→ OK

Key in text or

→ Insert

→ File

→ Select text file or

→ File

→ Import

→ Word document

→ Select text file

→ OK

Place the video clip in your site folder and link to the clip or embed it in your page.

To link to the clip:

Enter text for the link (e.g. Download Clip)

→ Select the text

→ Click the folder icon in the Property panel

→ Browse to the video file

→ Select it

Select the text or image you want to use as the link to the audio file

→ In the Property panel, click the folder icon to browse for the audio file or

→ Type the file's path and name in the Link text box

→ Key in text to be used for link

→ Highlight text

→ In the Properties panel key in or Select the link in the Link dialog box

If image or text is to be used as a link:

Select the image or text

→ In the Properties panel at the bottom of the screen, key in or Select the link in the Link dialog box

How to set text attributes

See house style and CSS in Section 1 of this unit. You created your text styles as part of your CSS template. This holds information on each style attribute:

h1 [color: #000000; font-family: Times New Roman; font-size: 45pt; text-align:

Center; font-weight: bold }

h2 [color: #0000FF; font-family: Arial; font-size: 18pt; text-align: Left;

font-weight: bold }

h3 [color: #0000A0; font-family: Arial; font-size: 14pt; text-align: Justify }

Visit www.cam.ac.uk/cambuniv/style/ for a reminder of what a house style consists of and why.

How to optimise images to make the file size smaller

● **Choose the correct file format:** A .gif file format loses no pixel data when it is compressed, whereas a .jpg file format loses some pixel data in order to make the file size smaller. Therefore .jpg gives a smaller file size, but a lower-quality image.

● **Choose the correct colour depth:** The more colours in your graphics, the more file space for the colour information. GIF files can use as many as 256 colours, or 8-bit colour, or as few as 2 colours, known as 1-bit colour. But 256-colour images can be 24-bit images – in these cases you need to reduce to 8-bit colour (taking down the colour can reduce the file size by one-third).

● **Choose the correct resolution:** If you are producing a graphic to be used solely on a computer, you can use a lower resolution as computer screens display at 72 dpi (dots per inch) – you will get the same result at a lower resolution, and therefore a smaller file size.

Preparation for tasks

The web pages themselves should be produced using the plans created in the Section 1 Tasks.

Final web pages must be printed from a web browser. These will be produced after Sections 3, 4 and 5 have been completed. Evidence of hyperlinks, interactive elements and form components in printed format must be produced.

Screenshots will be acceptable if design choices make the printouts unsuitable for use with A4 paper – multiple screenshots will be required to show the pages in their entirety.

Figure 2.17 – Home page

Figure 2.18 – Contact page

Figure 2.19 – Links page

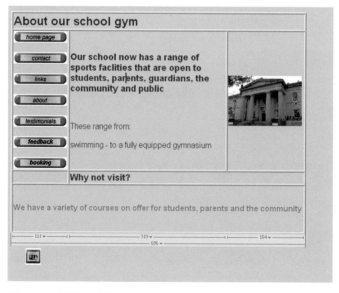

Figure 2.20 – About page

Figure 2.21 – Testimonials page

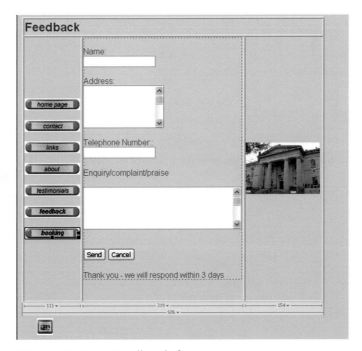

Figure 2.22 – Feedback form

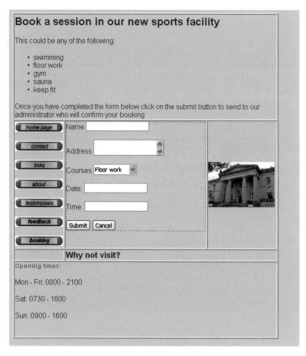

Figure 2.23 – Booking form

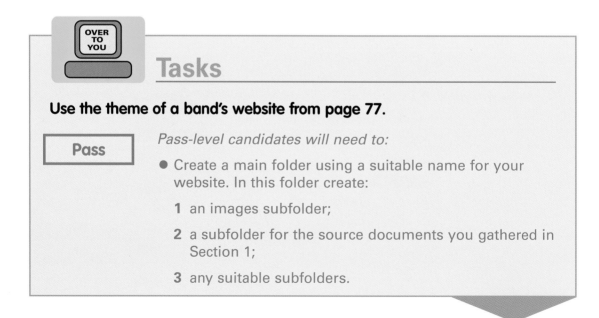

Tasks

Use the theme of a band's website from page 77.

Pass

Pass-level candidates will need to:

- Create a main folder using a suitable name for your website. In this folder create:

  1 an images subfolder;

  2 a subfolder for the source documents you gathered in Section 1;

  3 any suitable subfolders.

Move any source files and images into the correct folders.

- Produce screenshot(s) of your folder structure. Save the screenshot documents.
- Use a basic template.
- Ensure that the meaning of the web pages is clear.
- Show evidence of the page navigation method used for all pages.
- Insert at least five different images across the five pages.
- Print all five web pages from a browser.

Merit

*Merit-level candidates will **also** need to:*

- Use appropriate styles, using either a template or a cascading style sheet.
- Show evidence of some tables used to present layout of web pages.

Distinction

*Distinction-level candidates will **also** need to:*

- Use a cascading style sheet to produce high-quality web pages.
- Use tables throughout.
- Have minimal textual errors.
- Use a good range of suitable images.
- Show evidence of image optimisation by screenshot(s).
- Ensure that screenshot(s) will clearly show that image size has been altered for all files used.
- Ensure that images will be of excellent quality and scaled in proportion.
- Use a method of navigation to all pages.
- Ensure that whole pages are displayed when printed.
- Produce evidence of backup procedures – evidenced by screenshot(s).

Section 3: Create hyperlinks

Assessment objective 3: *Create functioning hyperlinks* **is covered in this section.**

Skills

You will need to set up a variety of hyperlinks to:

● link at least five web pages;

● link to other websites;

● link to an email address.

A hyperlink may be a:

● word;

● button;

● graphic;

● hot spot/image map.

When text is a hyperlink, the text is displayed in a different colour and may also be underlined. A text hyperlink that has already been visited (clicked on) is usually displayed in a different colour. The most common hyperlinks in text format are those displayed on search engines (e.g. Google) when looking for information on the Internet, for example: *www.bbc.co.uk*

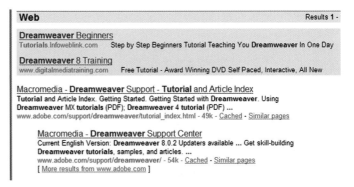

Figure 2.24 – Google search engine

A hyperlink is also a common element found on most web pages. When clicked with a mouse, it automatically opens a file or web page in your web browser.

A navigation system on a website can be in the form of buttons (graphics), with hyperlinks to the other pages in the website, or it could be text in a table.
Images/graphics can be used as links; a photograph could be used as a link to more images or thumbnails of images, for example.

Hot spots/image maps are areas defined by the designer of the website to be clickable areas on the web page. These areas do not have to be the whole image, but may be only a selected area.

How to create a navigation system, including hyperlinks

Figure 2.25 – Navigation system

Before beginning this exercise, you may wish to open your template or attach your CSS file created earlier.

● On a new blank page in Dreamweaver, insert a table of six rows and three columns.

● Add the image **homeb.gif** to your web page in the second row of the table in column one.

● Add the image **aboutb.gif** to your web page in the third row of the table in column one.

● Continue adding the following images in the first column: **contactb.gif**, **linksb.gif**, **testimonb.gif**.

Select the first button

→ In the Properties panel at the bottom of your screen

→ Link: key in **index.html**

→ Alt: key in **Home page**

● Continue adding the links and alternative text to each of the navigation buttons:

1 aboutb.html – About us

2 contactb.html – Contact us

3 linksb.html – Various links

4 testb.html – Testimonials

● You have now created a navigation system with hyperlinks – at this stage you may not have created all the pages, but as you do, these will link to the navigation system.

● Save this web page as **index**.

How to create a hyperlink and image map

Continue to work on the web page created above.

● Add the image **homepb.gif** to your web page, below the table.

● Click on the image to select it.

● In the Properties panel at the bottom of your screen, click on one of the three hot-spot tools: rectangle, circle or polygon.

● Use the tool to draw out the shape you want on the image map on your image.

Figure 2.26 – Image map 1

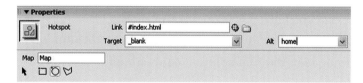

Figure 2.27 – Image map 2

● In the Properties panel for the hot spot
  → Key in the page or select the page your hot spot is to link to
  → **index.html**
  → Select the Target: blank
  → Add the Alt text: **home** (this Alt text will display even if the image is not displayed on the viewer's computer)

● This will create a link from the icon at the bottom of your page to your home page.

How to create a hyperlink from text to websites or email addresses

Continue to work on the open web page.

● At the bottom of your web page, below the table and home button graphic, key in: **For further information contact** (key in your own email address here)

● Highlight your email address

→ On the Common bar

→ Email link

→ Check the content of the dialog box

→ OK

● If you look at the Properties panel at the bottom of your screen, you will see that the link appears as: **mailto:youremailaddress**

You are now going to create a hyperlink from an image to another website. Insert the image **rowing.jpg** in one of the cells to the right of the navigation system.

Click on the image

→ In the Properties panel at the bottom of your screen, click in the Link box

→ Key in **http://www.fitness-superstore.co.uk/**

→ add the Alt text: **rowing machine**

→ This link will take the viewer from your website to a site that sells fitness equipment

You can also change the image's physical size in this dialog box. (Refer to Unit 21 to see how to optimise your images.) If you want to, you could create an image map/hot spot on the image rather than selecting the whole image as the link.

Figure 2.28 – Row link

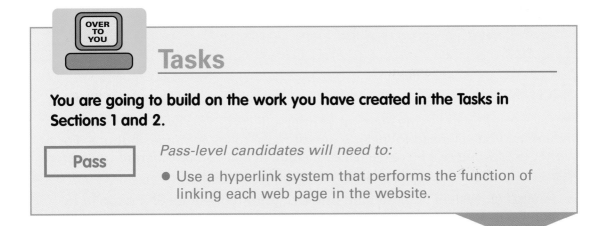

You are going to build on the work you have created in the Tasks in Sections 1 and 2.

Pass

Pass-level candidates will need to:

● Use a hyperlink system that performs the function of linking each web page in the website.

- Link all five pages together.
- Use links to external websites.
- Use a consistent system of hyperlinks.
- Show evidence of your hyperlink function and structure by screenshots.

Merit

*Merit-level candidates will **also** need to:*

- Use a hyperlink system consistently.
- Use at least one email link.
- Use one hot spot/image map.
- Use a fully functional and clearly structured system.

Distinction

*Distinction-level candidates will **also** need to:*

- Use a comprehensive hyperlink system consistently.

Section 4: Create interactive elements

Assessment objective 4: *Create interactive elements* **is covered in this section.**

Skills

You will need to add some element of interactivity to your website. As a minimum, you will need to include one or more rollover images/buttons. For a higher grade, you will be expected to include at least three different rollover objects and one further interactive element. This could be:

- navigation system (e.g. method of moving from one area of a website to another);

- rollover objects (images or buttons), such as images that change either shape, colour or image as the mouse passes over them;

- movies;

- sound;

- Macromedia Flash® objects (e.g. animations created in Flash – moving images or drawings);

- JavaScript, Java, ASP/ASP.NET, CGI scripting, other (e.g. programming language to create web aspects that sometimes cannot be created using an editor (e.g. Dreamweaver).

How to create a navigation system, including interactive elements (rollovers)

There can be four states:

1 **Up image:** how the image will appear before it has been clicked on.

2 **Over image:** how the image appears when the mouse pointer is moved over the Up image (the image may go lighter or darker, depending on how you set up the graphic).

3 **Down image:** how the image appears once it has been clicked on.

4 **Over while down image:** how the down image appears when the mouse is moved over it.

You do not have to use all four of these interactive element states – you may only wish to use one or two.

- Open a web page.

- You are going to insert the following images as rollover buttons:

   homeb.gif → homeb2.gif

   aboutb.gif → aboutb2.gif

   contactb.gif → contactb2.gif

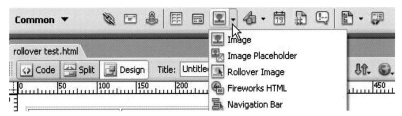

Figure 2.29 – Image button

● From the Common bar:

Select the Images dropdown arrow

→ Select the Navigation system option

The Modify Navigation Bar dialog box will appear.

● Complete each section:

Element name: **home**

Up image

→ Browse

→ select **homeb**

Over image

→ Browse

→ select **homeb2**

Alternate text

→ Key in **home page**

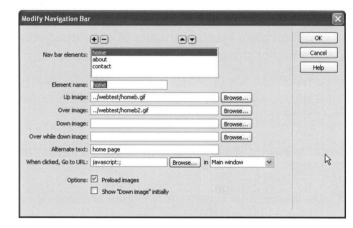

Figure 2.30 – Modify Navigation Bar

● Click on + symbol to add another element to the navigation system. Repeat the instructions above to complete each section for each of the elements (three elements). You should now have three elements in your navigation system dialog box.

● You can also add the links to each element:

In the box, When clicked, Go to URL

→ Browse

→ In the second dialog box, URL

→ Select web page link or

→ If not created yet, key in link

→ OK

→ OK

● You have now created a rollover navigation system using two images with slightly different colours; these also link to the pages.

Figure 2.31 – Rollover Button

- Save your web page.
- Click on the Preview/debug in browser button on the task bar, and test your buttons. Do they change to show the mouse roll over?

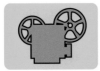

How to create a rollover image

You may wish to create an image that changes as the mouse is rolled over it. This could be one image on the initial viewing, but when pointed at with the mouse it changes to a different or related image.

- Open a web page.
- You are going to insert the following images as rollover images:

  school.jpg

  recept.jpg

- On your web page:

  From the Common bar, select the Images dropdown arrow

  → Select the Rollover image option Browse

  → image 1 = **school**

  → image 2 = **recept**

  → Alternate text = school

  → OK

- Test your rollover using the Preview/debug in browser button on the task bar. Do the images change?

- Save your web page.

Figure 2.32 – Rollover images

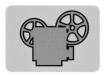

How to link a short video clip to your web page

You may wish to add a video clip to your web page, to provide a little more interest for the visitors to your site.

- Place the clip in your site folder (these clips are often in the AVI, WMV or MPEG file format) – the file you will use is **fireworks1.avi**
- To link to the clip, enter text for the link, such as **Download firework display here**: Select the text
  - → Click the folder icon in the Property panel
  - → Browse to the video file
  - → Select **fireworks1.avi**

How to link a sound to your web page

You may wish to include sound on your web page to add interest to your site. There are several different file formats you can add (these include WAV, MIDI and MP3). The sound files need to be of good quality, but bear in mind the file size and how this may arrive through different browsers and hardware.

The most effective way to include sound is to allow visitors to your website to choose whether they wish to listen to the audio or not. This is done by creating a link on your web page that visitors can open should they choose to do so, or by adding user controls with play and pause options.

Highlight the text or image that you wish to use as a link to your audio file

  - → In the Property panel, click on the folder icon
  - → Link
  - → Select your audio file **gym.wav**

How to embed a sound that plays when the page opens, using script

Having a sound play when a page opens is easy and reliable. Place the following code in the text area of your code view:

embed src="gym.wav" autostart="true" hidden="true" loop="true"> </embed>

If you want the sound to play only once, change **loop="true"** to **loop="false"**. (*You must paste the sound in code view*.) Once you have added a sound, it will be represented on the page by the plug-in jigsaw puzzle piece icon.

How to add a Flash text to your web page

Another option you may wish to consider is adding Flash text. Here, you create the text you wish to display on your web page, along with the colours for the initial viewing and the rollover viewing.

- On your web page, from the Common bar, select the Flash text option.
- Key in the text you wish to be present on your web page.
- Select the colours for both the text (the first box) and the rollover colour – you can also choose the font, size, attributes and style here.

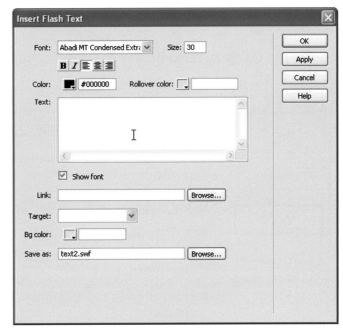

Figure 2.33 – Insert Flash Text

- You can even set up a link to other pages, or websites – this will depend on what you want the text to do.
- Save your web page.
- Click on the Preview/debug in browser button on the task bar and test your Flash text. Does it change when the mouse is rolled over?

How to add play controls to your web page, using script

You embed a sound or video, along with controls that your reader can use to start or stop the sound, or to change volume:

<embed src="gym.wav" autostart="false" loop="false" width="144" height="60">
</embed>

Tasks

You are going to build on the Tasks in Sections 1, 2 and 3.

Pass

Pass-level candidates will need to:

● Add at least one rollover image or interactive button to your website – this can be downloaded from the Internet.

● Identify all interactive elements and hyperlinks on each printout.

Merit

*Merit-level candidates will **also** need to:*

● Add at least two different rollover images or interactive buttons to your website – these can be downloaded from the Internet.

● Have a consistent approach for button rollovers on all pages.

● Add one additional interactive element to your website – either a Flash object or user controls to video or audio.

Distinction

*Distinction-level candidates will **also** need to:*

● Add at least three different rollover objects.

● Add additional interactive elements to your website – a Flash object and user controls to video or audio.

● Use a limited amount of scripting (although this may not work as intended).

Section 5: Create a user feedback form

Assessment objective 5: *Create a user form for capturing user feedback* is covered in this section.

Skills

Your website is nearly complete. It is useful if visitors to your website can contact you, and if you are able to collect data about visitors and receive feedback from users.

Forms can be used in many ways:

- to collect information;
- to give feedback;
- to request information;
- to book items (e.g. courses, trips, etc.);
- to order products.

Forms can be part of a web page or can be a web page themselves.

Forms need to be set up to collect data and send it on to a mailbox or collection point. This needs to be set up as part of the form, but it is not seen by visitors to the website.

Forms are made up of different elements:

- **Text boxes – single-line:** the user can input a single line of text (e.g. their name).
- **Text boxes – multi-line:** the user can input multiple lines of text (e.g. their address).
- **Radio buttons:** the user can choose only one option from the ones given.
- **Check boxes:** the user can make multiple selections.
- **Dropdown selection menus:** the user can select an option from a dropdown menu.

- **Submit and reset buttons:** once the form has been completed by the user, they can submit (send) or reset (cancel/clear) the form and contents.

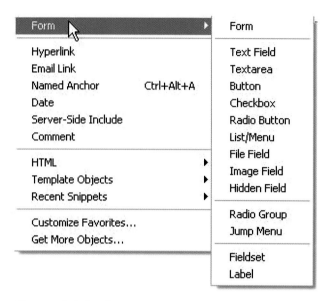

Figure 2.34 – Form menu

Before beginning this exercise, you may wish to open your template or attach your CSS file created earlier.

You will need to create a new web page on your site. This web page will contain a table or an interactive form. If you create a booking web page, you have been provided with buttons, to be inserted on each page. Buttons have also been provided for a feedback web page.
bookingb.gif
bookingb2.gif (this is the rollover image of bookingb)
feedbackb.gif
feedbackb2.gif (this is the rollover image of feedbackb)

You may wish to show the location of the centre – a map has been provided (**map.jpg**). This can be used on any web page.

How to create a table

- First, you must insert a table, deciding how many columns and rows you may need (you can add more as you enter data, if needed)

  Insert menu

  → Table

  → A table will appear with the columns and rows you requested

- By using the Amend Table menu, you can:

  1 merge cells;

  2 split cells;

  3 delete rows/delete columns;

  4 insert rows/insert columns.

- Plan your form layout before you start to insert elements – what purpose do you want the form completed for?

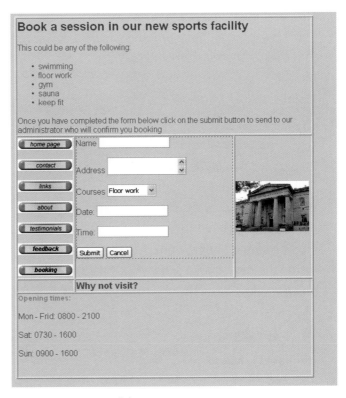

Figure 2.35 – Table

- Make sure that you have space on your form for at least:

  1 name;

  2 address;

  3 courses.

For example, if you were creating a form for a gym, you could provide options to select, such as: swimming, floor work, gym, sauna or keep fit.

How to create a form

- First you must insert a form area
  – this is where all the elements
  that make up your form will be
  placed.

  Insert

  → Form

  → A red box will appear

- Plan your form layout before
  you start to insert elements –
  what purpose do you want
  the form completed for?

  Insert a single-line text box
  inside the red box:

  Insert menu

  → Form

  → Text Field

  → Label = **Name**

  → OK

  → Enter

Figure 2.36 – Form entry point

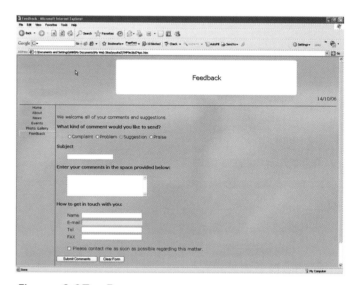

Figure 2.37 – Form

In the Properties panel, you can change the character length of input, but at this stage
leave as the default.

Insert a text area:

Insert menu

→ Form

→ TextArea

→ Label = **Address**

→ OK

→ Enter

Figure 2.38 – Form properties

Again, at this stage leave as the default.

Insert a dropdown menu:

Insert menu

→ Form

→ List/Menu

→ Label = **Courses**

→ OK

→ Enter

Again, at this stage leave as the default.

● You could also add check boxes or radio buttons:

Insert a checkbox:

Insert menu

→ Form

→ Checkbox

→ Label = **yes**

→ OK

Insert a radio button:

Insert menu

→ Form

→ Radio button

→ Label = **yes**

→ OK

Insert a Submit button:

Insert menu

→ Form

→ Button

→ Label = (do not put anything here)

→ OK

→ Enter

Insert a Reset button:

Insert menu

> → Form
> → Button
> → Label = (do not put anything here)
> → OK
> → Enter

(Do not worry that this button also says 'Submit' – you will change this later.)

● Now you are going to set the Properties on each element you have added.

Click on the Name box

> → In the Properties Panel, select the character length you are going to allow your box to be
> → **40** (this will normally accommodate a person's name)

Click on the TextArea box

> → In the Properties Panel
> → Num Lines = **6**

Click on the List/Menu

> → Right-click
> → The List Values box appears
> → After you key in each subject, click on the + sign to add to the list
> → Once you have entered all subjects
> → OK

For example, if you were creating a form for a gym, your list/menu could include:

Swimming

Floor work

Gym

Sauna

Keep fit

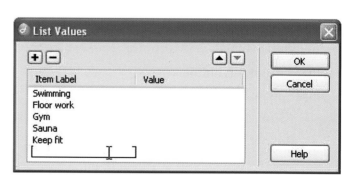

Figure 2.39 – List Values

- You are going to change the second Submit button to Reset.

  Click on the second Submit button

    → In the Properties Panel, change the Value to Reset

    → Change the Action to Reset form

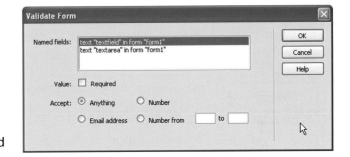

Figure 2.40 – Submit properties

- You can validate your form (i.e. ensure that it cannot be submitted without the correct elements being completed by the user).

  Select Window

    → Behaviors

    → Select the tab Tag

    → Click on the + icon

    → Choose Validate Form

    → In the pop-up window that appears, select the Text field

    → Value = Required

    → Accept = Anything

    → OK

Figure 2.41 – Validate Form

- Check the validation by previewing in browser – you will notice that the area you have asked to be completed has changed colour.

- Depending on whether you have attached your CSS or used your template, you may now wish to format the web page.

Tasks

Building on the work you have completed in the Tasks in Sections 1, 2, 3 and 4, you are going to create a feedback form.

Pass

Pass-level candidates will need to:

- Create a form in the layout of a table that can be printed out and filled in.
- Ensure that the layout of the form is functional and has at least four areas to be completed manually by a user.
- Give instructions that the form should be completed and printed.
- Produce evidence (screenshots/hard-copy printouts) of the above.

Merit

*Merit-level candidates will **also** need to:*

- Create a form that can be filled in online.
- Use a range of form techniques, with a minimum of four elements: radio buttons, check boxes, text boxes and dropdown menus.
- Include a Submit button.
- Ensure that the form is well laid out and mainly working.
- Give instructions that the form should be completed and submitted online, using the Submit button.
- Produce evidence (screenshots/hard-copy printouts) of the above.

Distinction

*Distinction-level candidates will **also** need to:*

- Add a Reset button (optional).
- Ensure that the form is fully functional.

Section 6: Testing your website

> **Assessment objective 6: *Test website* is covered in this section.**

Skills

You have designed your website in the Task in Section 1, and created it in the Tasks in Sections 2, 3, 4 and 5. Now it is time to test your website, to see if it meets all your design plans. You are testing to make sure that:

- what was in your proposal has happened;
- the structure of your file management is correct and functions;
- all your page links work and go where they should;
- the email link works correctly;
- the links to external websites work correctly;
- all your images are displayed fully;
- your navigation system works as it should;
- your site has a consistent look – colour scheme, house style;
- rollover objects do what is expected;
- movies work when selected;
- sound works as expected;
- Flash objects function as expected;
- forms created capture the correct data;
- forms are well laid out and appropriate to the task;
- your website is suitable for your target audience;
- your website has met its purpose;
- your website is easy to use.

Testing is a valuable part of the design of a website. The best way to capture the testing process is by creating a test table. A test table will include all the elements being tested and could look something like the one shown here.

Date tested	Action type	Object type	Expected	Error	Links	Action to take
18 Oct	Mouse down	Navigation button	Change colour	No change	HTML page	
18 Oct	Mouse over	Graphic	Image change	Image change but incorrect image appears	Graphic	
18 Oct	Email link	Text link	Launch email package	No error	Email address	

All elements of the website must be tested.

Tasks

You are going to build on the work you have produced in the Tasks in Sections 1, 2, 3, 4 and 5.

Pass

Pass-level candidates will need to:

● Create a test table to test your website.

● Conduct a comprehensive range of tests (four areas).

● Make notes of any errors found.

● Provide evidence of testing.

- Produce evidence of errors found (screenshots or printouts).

Merit

*Merit-level candidates will **also** need to:*

- Conduct a comprehensive range of tests (five areas).
- Use annotated code or screenshots showing *before* and *after* changes, where appropriate.

Distinction

*Distinction-level candidates will **also** need to:*

- Conduct a comprehensive range of tests (six areas or more).
- Produce a test table that will indicate action(s) that are required to solve problems.

Section 7: Evaluate your website

Assessment objective 7: *Evaluate own website* is covered in this section.

Skills

Having planned, designed, created, tested and amended your website, it is now time to evaluate your work.

You should be looking for and reporting that the purpose of the website was met and that the audience identified would have found the website:

- readable – use of font, font size, colour, language;
- usable – navigation method, ease of use;
- accessible – issues with screen readers, nested tables, use of ALT tags for images.

You should also discuss your strengths and weaknesses, identified throughout the development of the unit and the unit outcomes. You should provide examples from your website and evaluation comments on the website. You should give examples of your strengths and weaknesses and how you may address these in future. The evidence could be in the form of a short presentation or an evaluation report.

EVALUATION OF MY WEBSITE

The website purpose:
- To inform visitors to the site of where the school is located
- To inform visitors to the site of news and up-to-date information regarding the school and students
- To increase awareness of the school
- To encourage students to take up sport in 'out of school' clubs
- To encourage parents to use the facilities on an evening and at weekends
- To encourage the local community to use the facilities
- To display an event calendar showing when various functions are happening at the school and in the sports facility
- To show photographs of events and facilities on offer
- To provide a portal for students and staff to communicate

Suitability for purpose
I feel the website met the purpose – it had areas of interest and interactivity for visitors to contact the school. It gave options of booking sports activities on-line.

Audience
My audience was internal and external – I feel that I could have added more colours to encourage students to view, but the colours I choose were subtle to attract the adult population in our community.

Readability
I feel that the data was readable and I checked for spelling mistakes. Information was given in bulleted lists to make reading easier.

My strengths
I knew my subject and had collected enough information before starting my project. I had collected images and visited other websites to get ideas before I started to design my website.

My weaknesses
I know the package I used can do more, but I did not have the skills or time to discover more. I also had problems with my timings as I got into my project and learning the software, I nearly ran out of time when it came to creating the website.

Usability
I feel the website is very useable with clear links to ensure the visitor can navigate easily.

Accessibility
I need to look back at my website and use more accessible options so that people with poor vision can also navigate through my website, this can be done by using Alternative text on images, which I have done, but did not try out without displaying images as I ran out of time.

Figure 2.42 – Evaluation report

Tasks

Now you have completed producing and testing your website, you need to evaluate how the development to final production has worked. Working on the Tasks in Sections 1, 2, 3, 4, 5 and 6, evaluate your work, giving examples. Prepare a presentation, providing examples of your work, to be delivered to your peers.

Pass

Pass-level candidates will need to:

- Produce a brief evaluation of your work, giving examples. This could be a presentation or an evaluation report, but whichever method you choose, your evaluation should cover:

  1 the website purpose;

  2 suitability for purpose;

  3 audience;

  4 readability;

  5 your strengths;

  6 your weaknesses;

  7 usability;

  8 accessibility.

Merit

*Merit-level candidates will **also** need to:*

- Produce a detailed evaluation of your work, giving examples and supported with printouts taken from your website.

- Your evaluation should cover thoroughly all aspects listed above (for Pass-level candidates).

Distinction

*Distinction-level candidates will **also** need to:*

- Produce an extensive evaluation of your work, giving examples and supported with printouts taken from your website. Your evaluation should cover thoroughly all aspects listed above (for Pass-level candidates).

Unit 3 Digital imaging

Unit overview

This unit will help you develop the knowledge, skills and understanding of computer graphics. By working through the *Skills*, *How to* and *Tasks* sections in this unit, you will demonstrate all the skills required for Unit 3 and be able to:

- describe and evaluate a range of bitmap and vector images;
- plan the production of graphic images for a client;
- source and store components for graphic products;
- record the sources of computer graphics and consider relevant legislation;
- use appropriate software tools to create, edit and combine graphic images;
- present work to a client for a specific purpose, using suitable format for display.

Examples in this unit are based on Adobe Photoshop® 7.0.

For this unit you will need to create:

- a combination of graphic images;
- rough sketches detailing some key areas: lines, text, shapes, colour, component parts, paper size and paper orientation;
- source table to include: location, date of collection, filename, file size and copyright;
- screenshots of graphic tools used (not needed for every item, but giving a wide range of both bitmap and vector tools).

There should be evidence of:

- research;
- planning a range of graphic images (two or three);

- design of both vector and bitmap images;
- reporting on the purpose.

The work produced will need to be presented in a suitable format. This could be:

- a slide presentation;
- reports;
- printouts.

You will need to demonstrate the following skills:

- researching, collecting and describing a range of existing bitmap and vector images found on the Internet, scanned or taken by digital camera;
- evaluation of the graphics, focusing on their purpose (what message they convey) and use for the target audience;
- consideration of image size – both physical dimensions and file size;
- use of both vector and bitmap tools;
- presentation of the work to a client, using a suitable format.

Throughout the How to sections, you will be working on a theme of creating new images for a local school to advertise both the school and the new sports facility.

For the Tasks sections, you will be working on the theme of creating a new website for a local band. These images can be of your choosing.

Section 1: Describe and evaluate a range of bitmap and vector images

> **Assessment objective 1:** *Describe and evaluate a range of bitmap and vector images* **is covered in this section.**

You have been asked to create a digital image to be used in a variety of media, advertising new sports facilities. Before you start producing any images, you need to collect a range of bitmap *and* vector images from two different sources.

Skills

You will need to research a selection of published materials, evaluating the design. You may wish to produce a simple table to track your research. This table could include:

1 Range of sources researched:

- newspapers;
- magazines;
- advertisements;
- posters;
- maps;
- diagrams;
- plans;
- Internet;
- digital photographs.

2 Source of materials images printed on:

- packaging;
- labels;
- signs.

3 Images viewed on screen:

- digital artwork;
- buttons;
- navigation means.

An example table is shown here.

Date	Range of sources researched	Source of materials images printed on	Images viewed on screen	Image found	Source of images	Physical size and/or file size	Saved
4 Aug	Magazine	Adverts for cars		Colour image in magazine	What Car	900 x 1100	Scanned and saved as bitmap images
	Newspaper			B&W image in paper	Daily Mail	850 x 1000	

You may wish to visit the following websites to gather information and images:

www.activeplaces.com/
www.sport.ed.ac.uk/
www.aber.ac.uk/~pedwww/
www2.warwick.ac.uk/conferences/whatwedo/sportsfacilities/

Vector images

Vector graphics are made up of multiple individual objects. Each object can be defined by mathematical statements and has individual properties such as colour, fill and outline. Vector graphics are resolution-independent – they can be output to the highest quality at any scale/size.

Vector images are not restricted to a rectangular shape like bitmaps. Vector objects can be placed over other objects, and the object below will show through. When you place a bitmap image over another coloured object (e.g. background), it has a rectangular box around it, which will show as white on a background colour.

A disadvantage of vector images is that they are unsuitable for producing photo-realistic images, as they are made up of solid areas of colour or gradients and do not show the subtle tones needed on photographs.

Vector images can be converted to bitmaps. This process is called rasterising. You will need to specify the output resolution and size of the final bitmap. It is important always to save a copy of the original artwork in its native vector format before converting it to a bitmap, as you cannot change it back.

Common vector-based formats are CGM (computer graphics metafile) and WMF (Windows metafile). WMF is the default graphics format used by the Microsoft Windows® clipboard.

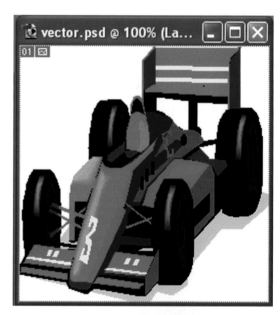

Figure 3.1 – Vector image

Bitmap images

Bitmap-based images are comprised of pixels (dots) in a grid. Bitmap images have a fixed resolution – resizing will lose image quality. Common bitmap-based formats are JPEG, GIF, TIFF, PNG, PICT, PCX, PSD and BMP. Most bitmap images can be converted to other bitmap formats. Bitmap images tend to have much larger file sizes than vector graphics and they are often compressed to reduce their size. Although many graphics formats are bitmap-based, bitmap (BMP) is also a graphic format.

You will need to comment on the suitability of at least two graphics, reviewed from two different sources, describing their purpose. You should indicate the size of the graphics, both physical and file size. You will also need to evaluate the use of the graphics, focusing on:

- the intended audience;

- the intended purpose of the graphics;

- the suitability of the graphics;

- the effectiveness of the design;

- the message conveyed and the graphics' effectiveness;

- the medium used.

The information and files saved could be produced in a table, like the one shown on page 12.

Figure 3.2 – Bitmap image

Date	Source	Type	Intended audience and its suitability	Purpose of graphic	Message conveyed and effectiveness	Medium used	Physical size and file size	Effectiveness of design
5 Sep	Website: www.activeplaces.com	Animated gif	Anyone wishing to take up sports This graphic gives the right message for the intended audience	Show facilities and activities	Help people get active Encouraging and engaging	Web page with links	101 KB 278 x 187	Very clear and concise message given with the image Not too many colours used Does not detract from the message

Tasks

You have been asked to collect a variety of images to be used to promote a new music band. Look at a range of websites, magazines and digital images, viewing images or graphics that could be used for this purpose. These graphics will be used on a variety of media – both electronic and paper-based – so you must consider the size (both physical and file) and the suitability of the graphic.

Visit the following websites for evaluation:

www.partysounds.co.uk/go/a-z-bands.php

www.ukbands.net/

www.viscountentertainment.co.uk/bands.htm

Look at a range of magazines and journals or newspapers that have music themes.

Pass

Pass-level candidates will need to:

- Collect and display a range of graphics from two different sources.
- Describe the purpose of the graphics.
- Discuss the suitability of the graphics.

Merit

*Merit-level candidates will **also** need to:*

- Collect and display a range of graphics from three different sources.
- Describe the target audience for the graphics.
- Give details on the size of the graphics and discuss.

Distinction	Distinction-level candidates will **also** need to:
	● Discuss the message the graphics convey (if any).
	● Discuss if the graphics are effective or not.
	● Discuss details of the size of the graphics.

Section 2: Plan to produce a range of graphic images

Assessment objective 2: *Plan the production of graphic images for a client* is covered in this section.

Skills

You are now going to create your own graphics. You will need to set out the following:

● the intended audience;

● the intended purpose of the graphics;

● the message to be conveyed;

● the medium to be used;

● where the graphics will be used;

● the size – both physical and file size;

● the resolution of the images in relation to quality and file size;

● the format of the file sizes;

● a deadline to complete the work.

This may be created in a table format, like that shown on page 127.

Date	Source	Intended audience	Intended purpose of the graphics	Message to be conveyed	Medium to be used	File size, including format	Physical size	Resolution	Deadline
15 Oct	Graphic from CD and own drawing	People who will use the sports facility	Advertise the activities that take place	A good place to visit – with good sports resources	On a website and in a paper-based publication	153 KB JPEG for web – could be slow to download For printed matter the same graphic would be 389 KB and therefore not suitable for downloading (speed)	507 x 371	150 ppi This will produce a good-quality graphic for the web This graphic would be better at 300 ppi for print	15 Nov

You must refer to information collected in Section 1 while you are researching graphics currently in use in a variety of media.

You will need to produce a plan for your graphics, identifying key areas. You should produce rough sketches, which may be annotated with the following:

- use of lines (e.g. style and thickness);
- use of text (e.g. font, size, colour);
- use of basic shapes;
- use of colour;
- component parts (e.g. resolution, size, colour mode);
- paper size and orientation.

See **exampleimageplan.doc**

File types

Graphics come in a variety of file types, each to be used in different ways for different audiences and output means:

1 **TIFF** is a very flexible format. The details of the image storage algorithm are included as part of the file. Most graphics programs that use TIFF cannot be compressed. Consequently, file sizes are quite large.

2 **PNG**, in contrast with common TIFF usage, looks for patterns in the image that it can use to compress file size. The compression is reversible, so the image is recovered exactly.

3 **GIF** creates a table of up to 256 colours from a pool of 16 million. If the image has fewer than 256 colours, GIF can produce the image exactly. Sometimes GIF uses the nearest colour to represent each pixel.

4 **JPEG** works by analysing images and discarding the types of information that the eye is least likely to notice. It can achieve astounding compression ratios, even while maintaining very high image quality. It stores information as 24-bit colour.

5 **RAW** is an image output option available on some digital cameras. The disadvantage is that there is a different RAW format for each manufacturer, so you may have to use the manufacturer's software to view the images.

6 **BMP** is an uncompressed format.

7 **PSD** is a proprietary format used by graphics programs. Photoshop's files have the PSD extension. These are the preferred working formats as you edit images in the software, because only the proprietary formats retain all the editing power of the programs. These packages use layers, for example to build complex images, and layer information may be lost in the non-proprietary formats, such as TIFF and JPEG. However, make sure that you save your end result as a standard TIFF or JPEG, or you may not be able to view it in a few years when your software has changed.

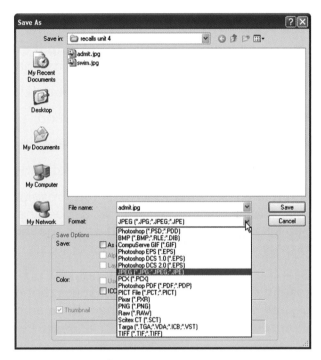

Figure 3.3 – File types

An example of file sizes for the same digital image in different formats are shown in the table.

File type	Size
TIFF, uncompressed	901 KB
JPEG, high quality	319 KB
JPEG, medium quality	188 KB
JPEG, web quality	105 KB
JPEG, low quality/high compression	50 KB
JPEG, high compression	18 KB
PNG, compression	741 KB
GIF, compression, but only 256 colours	131 KB

Resolution

Resolution is the measurement of output quality of an image. A variety of terms are used when discussing output measurement:

- **ppi:** pixels per inch – screen resolution;
- **dpi:** dots per inch – printer resolution;
- **spi:** sample per inch – scanning resolution;
- **lpi:** lines per inch – halftone resolution.

Often images are referred to as high-resolution (hi-res) or low-resolution (low-res). A high-resolution image would be one intended for print, generally having 300 spi or more. A low-resolution image refers to those only intended for screen display, generally having 100 ppi or less.

Scanner and digital camera manufacturers often refer to two different types of resolution when listing product specs: optical resolution and interpolated (or digital) resolution. Most scanners have an optical resolution of 300 dpi, but an interpolated resolution of up to 4800 dpi.

Optical resolution: the physical resolution at which a device can capture an image. This term is used most frequently when discussing the resolution of optical scanners and digital cameras.

Interpolated resolution: indicates the resolution that the device can produce through interpolation.

Interpolation (sometimes called resampling): an imaging method to increase or decrease the number of pixels in a digital image.

Tasks

Continuing with the theme of a new band for your graphics, produce rough sketches for a range of different types of graphics. You will be creating a minimum of two graphics to be used electronically, and others to be used in printed materials. These sketches should be annotated with the key features you are going to use – you should also include a table covering the following information:

- source;

- intended audience;

- intended purpose of the graphics;

- message to be conveyed;

- medium to be used;

- file size, including format;

- physical size;

- resolution;

- deadline.

Pass	*Pass-level candidates will need to:*
	● Plan the use of the graphics.
	● Identify some key features of the graphics, and discuss.
	● Describe the target audience for the graphics.
	● Describe the purpose of the graphics.

Merit

*Merit-level candidates will **also** need to:*

- Refer to ideas gained in your research undertaken in the Tasks in Section 1.

Distinction

*Distinction-level candidates will **also** need to:*

- Set a deadline for the production of the work.
- Discuss where the graphics are to be used.
- Produce rough sketches for different types of graphic.
- Take into consideration the graphic size, and discuss.
- Discuss the resolution of the graphics.
- Discuss the file format of each of the graphics.

Section 3: Find and save components of graphics

Assessment objective 3: *Source and store components for graphic products* is covered in this section.

Having completed your research on graphics available, and planned your own graphics, it is now time to find/create and save graphics ready for use. It is advisable to create a table to log the graphics you have saved; this information will also be used as evidence for Section 4.

Skills

You will need to find and store graphics from the following categories:

- computer graphics;
- digital camera;
- scanner.

Computer graphics

These can be images you have found on the Internet or on a Clip Art gallery from the Internet or a CD. You will need to consider:

- image quality;
- saved format;
- output format;
- output size.

Digital camera

These will be images stored from pictures taken with a digital camera. You will need to consider:

- image quality;
- saved format;
- transfer speeds;
- output format;
- output size.

Scanner

These could be images you have found and scanned, or images you have drawn and scanned. You will need to consider:

- scanning software;
- resolution;
- file sizes;

- saved format;
- transfer speeds;
- output format;
- output size;
- storage device.

Create a table to save the data for each image you find, covering the following information (this will also be evidence for Section 4):

- date;
- source;
- image quality;
- file size;
- saved format;
- resolution;
- output format;
- output size;
- transfer speed;
- scanning software;
- storage device.

How to download images from a digital camera

You must have the camera or graphics software loaded onto your PC before you can download images. Examples of graphics software are Photoshop and ThumbsPlus.

Insert your card into your PC and follow the instructions. Your software will display the card's library on screen, and this will allow you to select and save your images.

How to scan an image and save it to a file

All scanners work in a similar way (the software must be installed on the PC). Place your image (e.g. from a text book) on the glass, activate your software and follow the instructions. This could be through Photoshop:

File menu

→ Import

→ Twain

→ follow through dialog boxes

Save your image in a suitable format.

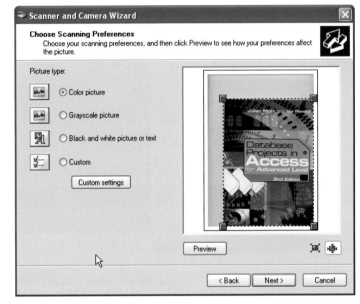

Figure 3.4 – Image capture

Figure 3.5 – Image capture – confirmation of image saved

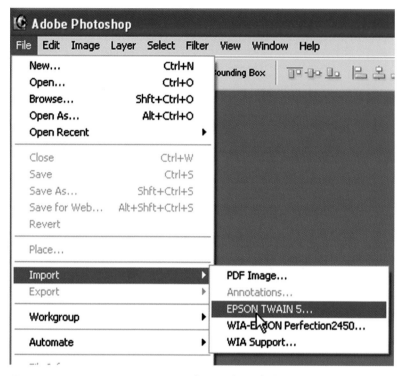

Figure 3.6 – Image capture through Adobe Photoshop

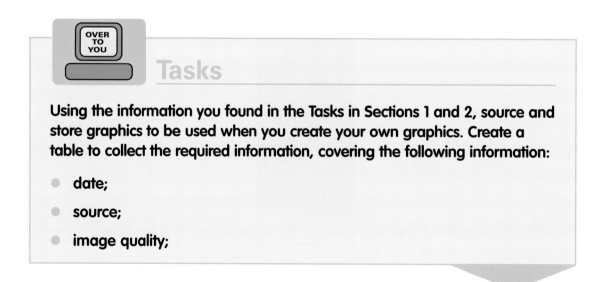

Tasks

Using the information you found in the Tasks in Sections 1 and 2, source and store graphics to be used when you create your own graphics. Create a table to collect the required information, covering the following information:

- date;

- source;

- image quality;

- **file size;**

- **saved format;**

- **resolution;**

- **output format;**

- **output size;**

- **transfer speed;**

- **scanning software;**

- **storage device.**

Pass

Pass-level candidates will need to:

- Source and store graphics from two of the listed categories (some graphics may not be appropriate):

  1 Internet;

  2 CD-ROM;

  3 Clip Art library;

  4 Digital camera – take your own photographs for use later;

  5 Scanned images from books, journals, magazines.

Merit

*Merit-level candidates will **also** need to:*

- Source and store graphics from three of the categories listed above (for Pass-level candidates) (most graphics will be appropriate).

Distinction

*Distinction-level candidates will **also** need to:*

- Source and store graphics from all the categories listed above (all graphics will be appropriate).

Section 4: Keep records of computer graphics, including copyright information

> **Assessment objective 4:** *Record the sources of computer graphics and consider relevant legislation* **is covered in this section.**

Linking this section to Section 3, you should create a data table to store information about the images you have found and saved.

Skills

Create a table, like the one shown here, to store information about the images you have found and saved.

Date	Source	Location	Filename	File size (KB)	Purpose of the graphic	Copyright Y/N
7 Mar	Scanner	h:scanner\aj	book1.gif	2	Image of the latest sports book to advertise the book	Would have to seek copyright from publisher
7 Mar	Camera	h:camera\aj	house1.jpg	24	Photo of a house to show the area	No copyright as this was my own picture
7 Mar	Internet	h:internet\aj	sport1.jpg	72	Image of a runner to be used on media publicity	Would have to seek copyright from publisher

Copyright Law

All images (except your own drawings and photographs) will be protected by copyright. You need not get permission to use the images you have collected in this instance, but reference to the relevance of copyright law will need to be considered. For information on copyright law, visit: www.copyrightservice.co.uk/copyright/p01_uk_copyright_law

Tasks

You are now going to record the source of graphics you have saved. Using a table, record the following information about your graphics:

- **date saved;**

- **source of image;**

- **location of image;**

- **filename saved as;**

- **file size (KB);**

- **purpose of the graphic;**

- **is there copyright?**

Also, write a short report on copyright law and the importance of copyright with regard to using images from a variety of sources, explaining when an image has copyright and when it does not.

Pass

Pass-level candidates will need to:

- Keep a record of the source of computer graphics.
- Use a table to record this information.

*Merit-level candidates will **also** need to:*

- Keep a detailed record of the source of computer graphics.

- Discuss the detailed record, which should enable others to locate some of the files.

- Discuss the need to be aware of copyright law.

Distinction

*Distinction-level candidates will **also** need to:*

- Keep an accurate record of the source of computer graphics.

- Discuss the detailed record, which should enable others to locate most of the files.

Section 5: Use software tools to create and combine graphic images

Assessment objective 5: *Use appropriate software tools to create, edit and combine graphic images* is covered in this section.

You have now evaluated, collected, recorded and saved a variety of graphic images. Using these images, you are now going to create your own images.

Skills

Images you have saved may not represent the whole product you are wishing to show on your final graphic. You may wish to create one image using several parts of images you have saved. You may wish to add to the images collected, using a variety of graphic tools available in your software – these can be either vector (v) or bitmap (b) or both (v/b):

- drawing/painting (b);
- geometric/freehand shapes (v/b);
- lines/arrows (v);
- rotate/flip (b);
- colour adjustments (v/b);
- fills (v);
- layers (v/b);
- opacity/transparency (v/b);
- group/ungroup (v);
- shadows (v);
- adjust image size (v/b);
- cut, copy, crop and paste (v/b);
- use brush types and shapes (b);
- filters (b);
- move and position elements (v/b);
- alignment and order (v);
- stroke thickness (v);
- insert and manipulate text (v);
- gradients (v).

You will need to show clear development of graphics and provide an explanation of the processes undertaken in producing them. This will be a paragraph of text.

You will also need to save the new graphics in an appropriate file format that can be used at a later stage.

In Photoshop, there is a set of graphic tools down the left side of your screen – the shape toolbox – as shown in the figure.

Figure 3.7 – Photoshop shape toolbox

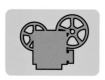

How to add a gradient fill background in colours of your choice

Select the gradient option from the shape toolbox

→ Select the colours you wish to fill from and to

→ Drag your mouse across the artwork, holding down the left button

→ Your gradient fill will follow the direction of your mouse

You can select the type of fill you wish to use from the menu that will appear at the top of your screen, as shown in the figure.

Figure 3.8 – Gradient tools

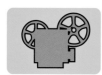

How to create text

Select the text tool from the shape toolbox

→ Click on your screen

→ Key in your text

→ Choose the text style and size from the menu that appears at the top of your screen

How to rotate

Select the move tool from the shape toolbox

→ Select the frame holding the text

→ Edit menu

→ Free Transform

→ Move your image

Warp text tool

Figure 3.9 – Text toolbar

You can use the text tool to create your text in any font, colour and size to suit your artwork. Using the warp text tool on the toolbar will change the shape of your text. Experiment with each of the Layer Style options:

Double-click on the layer to open the Layer Style options dialog box

→ Experiment with Styles options until you find an option you like

→ Experiment with Blending options, again, choosing an option you like

→ OK

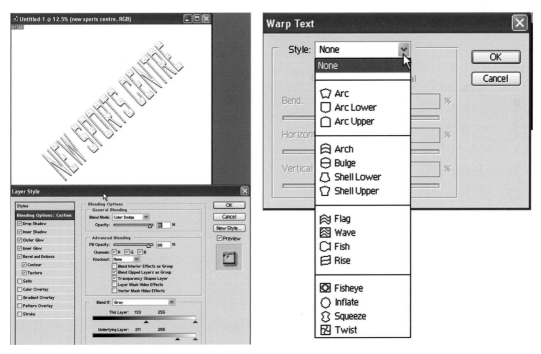

Figure 3.10 – Example of text Layer Style options

Figure 3.11 – Example of warp text

How to crop an image

Open an image you have saved – for this example an image has been provided.

File

  → Open

  → **swim.jpg**

  → Using the rectangular marquee tool, draw out over a part of the image you wish to keep

  → Edit – You should now see just the section you have cropped

Figure 3.12 – Rectangle shape options

How to draw shapes

Right-click on the shape tool rectangle and choose the custom shape

  → Add some stars to your background

  → Choose a complementary colour for the stars

  → Draw three or four stars

  → Double-click on the layer palette

  → Select Bevel and Emboss

  → Choose a variety of options

  → Experiment

  → OK

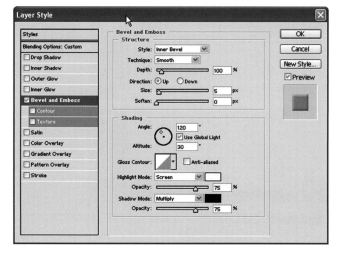

Figure 3.13 – Bevel and Emboss layer shape options

How to modify shapes

Using the shapes toolbox, create a graphic shape using the rectangle tool

→ Convert this to a layer by double-clicking in the layer box

→ Select OK at the dialog box

→ Double-click on the layer to open the Layer Style options dialog box

→ Experiment with each of the Styles options until you find an option you like

→ Experiment with Blending options, again, choosing an option you like

→ OK

Try using the pattern option and select a background pattern – changing the opacity if necessary.

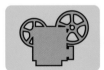

How to draw lines and arrows

Right-click on the rectangle tool

→ Select line tool

→ Click and drag your mouse to draw a line

→ Use the icons that appear at the top of your screen to modify the thickness of the line

If you wish to add arrowheads to your line, before you draw your line, at the end of the icons on your toolbar you will see a dropdown arrow – click on this and you can add arrowheads to either or both ends of your line.

How to change the brush

Use the same way as shapes and lines.

How to change the colour of an image

Open the image **admit.jpg**. The wood is too orange and needs toning down to look more like wood.

Select

→ Image

→ Adjustment

→ Hue and Saturation

Adjust the scales until you reach a correct wood colour.

How to change the opacity/transparency of an image

With the image selected

→ Layer

→ Layer Style

→ Blending Options

→ Enter the value in the Opacity text box or drag the Opacity slider

(*You cannot use opacity on the background layer.*)

Layers/group

You can work on one element without disturbing others by using layers. You can lock layers to prevent accidental changes, hide them to get a clear view of other elements within your graphic, and link them to move them as a group. The layer palette also makes it easy to apply blending modes, adjustment layers and layer effects.

You can use layers to change the alignment and order of your images, as well as to move and position the various elements on your graphic.

How to adjust image size

Select image

> → Image

> → Image size

> → OK

 **How to use the clone tool to remove unwanted content (filter)**

Open the image **carbeach.jpg**. The image has an aerial that has to be removed before the image can be used in any publicity materials.

- Using the marquee, select as much of the area as possible (the aerial is in the top right of the picture).
- To use the clone stamp tool, use Alt + click, and select part of the sky that matches the colour you wish to use over the aerial.
- Copy the sky detail and cover the aerial so that it blends in.
- Continue working with the clone stamp tool to remove the whole aerial.

You will need to use the marquee and the clone stamp as a minimum to remove unwanted content.

How to set opacity/transparency

- Open an image.
- Create a new layer in the layer palette.
- In the new layer, create a rectangular marquee over part of the image.
- Using a colour and the paint bucket tool, fill the rectangle with solid colour.
- In the layer palette you can change the opacity – change this to 50% to see your image appear through the rectangle.

Figure 3.14 – Rectangle over image – no transparency

Figure 3.15 – Opacity/transparency set

How to group/ungroup

- Using the drawing tools, create some shapes on your page. Using the fill option, create some images with colour – each layer will become a new layer of your overall image.
- In the layer palette, link each of the layers you wish to group together.
- Using the move tool, move all the linked shapes to a new location.
- Ungroup by deselecting the link option.

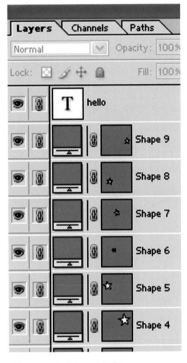

Figure 3.16 – Linking layers

How to add shadows

Having created a shape using one of the shape tools, or text using the text tool, you can give emphasis to this by adding a shadow.

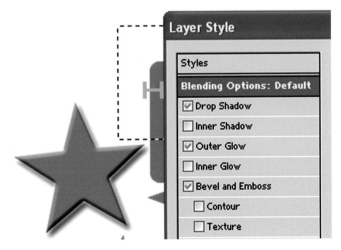

Figure 3.17 – Shadow added

Select the image you wish to add shadow to

→ In the layer palette, double-click to activate the Layer Style dialog box

→ Select the option Drop Shadow, Outer Glow, and so on

How to align and place in order

Drag the layer up or down in the layer palette. Release the mouse button when the highlighted line appears where you want to place the layer.

Select a layer

→ Choose Layer

→ Arrange and choose a command from the submenu

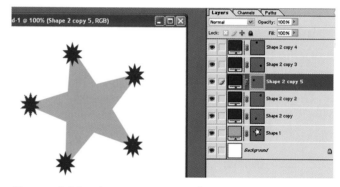

Figure 3.18 – Image – no order

The background layer is always at the bottom. Therefore, the Send to Back command places the selected item directly above the background layer.

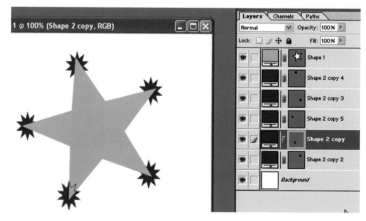

Figure 3.19 – Image with images ordered

Tasks

You are now going to create your own graphics, based on your research and sourcing as in Sections 1 to 4. This could be graphics you have collected, mixed with your own designs. These graphics could be from the following sources:

- digital camera;
- scanner;
- Internet;
- CD-ROMs;
- Clip Art gallery.

It is expected that you will add to any images you have collected to create new images, incorporating features from your graphics software.

Pass	*Pass-level candidates will need to:*

- Create graphics using a limited range of vector and bitmap tools.
- Show evidence of development by providing a brief report with supportive printouts.

Merit	*Merit-level candidates will **also** need to:*

- Create graphics using a range of vector and bitmap tools.
- Ensure that the graphics will be fit for purpose.
- Annotate the graphics to explain the processes taken.
- Save most of the graphics in an appropriate format.

Distinction

*Distinction-level candidates will **also** need to:*

- Create graphics using a wide range of vector and bitmap tools.
- Annotate the graphics to explain and justify the processes taken.
- Save all the graphics in an appropriate format.

Section 6: Present your work to the client

Assessment objective 6: *Present work to a client for a specific purpose, using a suitable format for display* is covered in this section.

You have now finished your artwork and the final part is to present the work you have created in a suitable format so that it can be viewed by others. This could be on a slide show, using Microsoft PowerPoint®, as printouts or as a digital portfolio (or any combination of these).

Skills

You should consider the file sizes of your artwork. Another consideration is the actual physical size if you are to print out the work – do you have a printer that can print out the size you have created? Think about the colour of your printouts – do you have a colour printer? (If you used opacity, you will need to show this in a colour printout.)

You need to create a portfolio to present your artwork; this could be paper-based or electronic/digital.

See **my artwork.ppt**

Tasks

The easiest method of presenting your artwork would be to create a digital portfolio, but this may not be suitable for your viewers, as they may not have the software you have used. As Microsoft PowerPoint® is an industry-standard piece of software, you have been asked to present your graphics and text using this program.

Pass

Pass-level candidates will need to:

- Present your work in a suitable format.
- Discuss that you have considered the size – both physical and file size.

Merit

*Merit-level candidates will **also** need to:*

- Discuss the graphic resolution.
- Discuss the file type you have created your graphics as (e.g. GIF, JPEG).

Distinction

*Distinction-level candidates will **also** need to:*

- Justify the use of the medium used to present the work.
- Discuss the graphic colour mode.

Unit 4

Design and produce multimedia products

Unit overview

This unit will help you develop the knowledge, skills and understanding of producing and using a multimedia product. By working through the *Skills*, *How to* and *Tasks* sections in this unit, you will demonstrate all the skills required for Unit 4 and be able to:

- review several existing multimedia products;
- design a multimedia product;
- source and store suitable multimedia elements;
- create the multimedia product;
- seek feedback and suggest improvements.

Examples in this unit are based on Microsoft PowerPoint® 2003.

For this unit you will be creating a portfolio including all the elements below. All work must be your own work, but may include witness statements. You will need to create:

- a storyboard;
- a report covering the purpose;
- a multimedia product;
- written report(s);
- feedback from users.

There should be evidence of:

- research;
- planning;
- design (house style);
- a navigation system;

- acknowledgement of the source of text, photographs, drawings, Clip Art, video, animation, sound, and so on.

The output you create will need to be presented in a suitable format; this will be:

- a slide presentation;
- printouts of each screen;
- annotated printouts;
- evidence of some user interaction.

You will need to demonstrate the following skills:

- researching and reviewing existing examples of different multimedia products;
- planning and designing a multimedia product;
- use of a range of suitable and appropriate techniques in creating a multimedia product.

Throughout the How to sections, you will be working on a theme of creating new multimedia products for a local school, to advertise both the school and the new sports facility.

For the Tasks sections, you will be working on the theme of creating new multimedia products for a keep fit centre. This media can be of your choosing.

Section 1: Review multimedia products

Assessment objective 1: *Review several existing multimedia products* **is covered in this section.**

You have been asked to create a multimedia presentation advertising the new sports facilities. Before you start producing any media, you need to research different multimedia products. You should be looking at media products from a variety of sources (as listed in the Skills section). You are looking for media products that show sporting activities, gyms, outdoor activities and games.

It has been decided that a presentation providing full information about each of the activities available in the sports facility would be a useful medium; this will play in the reception area of the school. The presentation will also be published on the school website.

There should be a standard format that is used across the whole presentation, including a colour scheme to be used throughout. You will also use a school logo (you may have created this in a different unit).

When reviewing other products, be aware of the graphics used, the colour schemes, font types and sizes, timings, and the good and not so good features used – and keep all these in mind for when you produce your presentation.

Skills

You will need to research at least three different multimedia products. These can be from the following:

● interactive multimedia websites (e.g. www.olympic.org/uk/sports/index_uk.asp; www.bbc.co.uk/);

● educational computer games (e.g. www.yourchildlearns.com/owlmouse.htm);

● recreational computer games (e.g. www.freegames.ws/games/freegames07.htm);

● online and CD-ROM/DVD presentations (e.g. www.bluegrotto.com/);

● commercial advertisements on CD-ROMs/DVDs.

When reviewing, you may wish to produce a simple table to track your research; this table should:

● identify the intended audience – who is the multimedia product aimed at?

● identify the good and not so good features – colour scheme; use of text and graphics; timing/speed; user interaction;

● state the aims of the multimedia product – who is it for? what is it advertising/informing? who uses it? what media are used?

● describe how the aims are met;

● if the aims are not met, explain why not;

● suggest any possible improvements.

(Do not forget that your research and reviews must inform your choices in the design and development of your own multimedia product.)

The table is an example of a reviewing check sheet (you may create your own) – you will need to repeat this three times with different media.

Date 14 January	Source Internet www.bbc.co.uk	Type Interactive multimedia website
Intended audience	People interested in finding out more about things from the BBC. The site includes information on programmes, backgrounds to programmes, competitions. It has interesting facts, weather and different sections.	
The aims of the media product	Keep people interested. Encourage people to click further into the site. Used to advertise the BBC and its radio and TV. Generally a static website, with a small amount of animation. Two different methods of searching offered, one with a search box and one with A–Z searching. Colour scheme not too bright, but enough to be interesting.	
Were the aims met? If so, how?	It did encourage me to click on links to see what else was available. Following a search to education, there were video clips to watch.	
Were the aims met? If not, why not?	There was no link to education, even though the BBC advertises that they have a website for education. I needed to search for education before I found it.	
Good features	Simple to use, not fussy, clean appearance – light blue.	

	Each link leads to more interesting and colourful pages.
Not so good features	I was looking for education when I should have looked for learning. When I used the link for learning, it brought up more information than the search for education did, but it did not bring up the video links. The audio links did not work, and there was no error message, so I did not know what the problem was. I got a message with advice about looking at the site's Audio help, but could not find the Audio help screen easily.
Any possible improvements	Add more info to menus at top of screen, maybe with popular links as well as the ones already there. Have a button available when error messages say 'Look on...' to make it easier.

Tasks

Using the topic of a keep fit centre, research and report on three different multimedia products to inform your choices when you create your multimedia product.

Pass

Pass-level candidates will need to:

- List and explain the good and not so good features of three different multimedia products based on the theme of keep fit. These could be:

  1 animations from a website (e.g. of a fitness centre or sports hall);

2 items from computer games – either home games or educational games (e.g. that focus on sports as a theme);

3 CD-ROMS or DVDs that have presentations (e.g. about keeping fit);

4 free CDs/DVDs that are given away, or online adverts (e.g. health centres).

Merit

*Merit-level candidates will **also** need to:*

● Give a detailed explanation of the good and not so good features of at least three multimedia products.

● Identify the aims of the multimedia product.

● Suggest possible improvements to the multimedia products discussed.

Distinction

*Distinction-level candidates will **also** need to:*

● Give a thorough explanation of the good and not so good features of at least three multimedia products.

● Identify the audience for the multimedia product.

● Suggest a range of valid improvements to the multimedia product to help meet the aims.

Section 2: Design a multimedia product

> **Assessment objective 2:** *Design a multimedia product* **is covered in this section.**

Skills

Building on the research from Section 1, plan the design and layout of your multimedia product for the new keep fit centre. You should create a design brief so that your product is well laid out and covers all the requirements, including the following:

- Linking the research to your design (e.g. the good and not so good you found in your research – consider colour, text, images, etc.);
- Plans for your product (e.g. site map/plan – this may include the number of pages/screens and the links between these);
- Stating the navigation system to be used between pages/screens (e.g. hyperlinks: image links, text links, document links, web links);
- Sketches of layout, considering house style (styles used);
- Storyboard (more detailed description of content placements for each page/screen);
- Definition of the purpose of your product;
- Definition of the target audience;
- (optional) a flowchart to map your links and order of pages/screens.

See **exampledesignbrief.doc**

Tasks

Using the research from Section 1, plan the design and layout of your multimedia product for the new keep fit centre.

Follow the links below for examples of websites that have multimedia elements about sports facilities:

- www.activeplaces.com/ – select 'Start your Search here';

- www.sport.ed.ac.uk/ – select 'CSE for Yourself';

- www2.warwick.ac.uk/conferences/whatwedo/sportsfacilities/ – select 'Virtual Tours', then 'Radcliffe Tours' and run the image gallery;

- www.mastersport.co.uk/soccerskills.htm – a static site but with images of actions;

- www.olympic.org/uk/index_uk.asp – a variety of multimedia based around the Olympics;

- www.sevenoaksart.co.uk/rugby.htm – downloadable animations of sports equipment.

You should create a design brief so that your product is well laid out and covers all the requirements.

| Pass |

Pass-level candidates will need to:

- Discuss the purpose of the multimedia product.

- Discuss the audience for the multimedia product.

- Produce a basic layout plan for the multimedia product.

- Use a house style (e.g. create three styles of text; consider the colour of the background; use a consistent approach to inserting text and graphics).

- Use a navigation system (e.g. hyperlinks, text, images, URLs, email, document links).
- Create a simple storyboard, covering the main elements of the multimedia product.

Merit

*Merit-level candidates will **also** need to:*

- Produce a detailed plan for the multimedia product.
- Create a storyboard, covering the main elements of the multimedia product.
- Ensure that the design has a clear structure.

Distinction

*Distinction-level candidates will **also** need to:*

- Discuss thoroughly the purpose of the multimedia product.
- Discuss thoroughly the audience for the multimedia product.
- Use an effective navigation system.
- Create a storyboard covering all elements of the multimedia product.
- Produce a well-structured design.

Section 3: Find and save elements for use in multimedia

> **Assessment objective 3:** *Source and store suitable multimedia elements* **is covered in this section.**

Skills

You are asked to collect and store a range of multimedia elements to make up your own design for the new sports facility. You may have collected some during your research stage in Section 1 or your design stage in Section 2. You are going to use these in Section 4 when you create your own multimedia product.

You can create or collect each of the following to be used in your multimedia product:

- text;
- photographs;
- graphics, including drawings and Clip Art;
- sound clips – you may save these from a variety of sources (e.g. CD, Internet);
- any elements you have created or possess;
- animations – you may download these from a variety of sources on the Internet;
- video clips – you can download these from a variety of Internet sites, or you may have a video you have been provided with or have made yourself.

For any of the above that you use, and which you have not created yourself, you must acknowledge the source; this could be in the form of a simple table, like the one shown here.

Date	Item	Source	Saved as

Tasks

You have to collect and store a range of multimedia elements to make up your own design for the new keep fit centre.

Pass

Pass-level candidates will need to:

- Source and store multimedia elements, including text, images and sound.

- Reference the source of your multimedia elements – you could use a table to record the following information: date, item, source, saved as.

Merit

*Merit-level candidates will **also** need to:*

- Source and store multimedia elements, including text, images, sound and animation.

- Acknowledge most of the sources.

Distinction

*Distinction-level candidates will **also** need to:*

- Source and store multimedia elements, including text, images, sound, animation and video.

- Provide accurate acknowledgement of all sources.

Section 4: Create a multimedia product

Assessment objective 4: *Create a multimedia product* **is covered in this section.**

Skills

There are many tools available in multimedia packages. As you are to produce a presentation using Microsoft PowerPoint® 2003, you could use some of the following to enhance your presentation of graphics and text:

- backgrounds;
- range of multimedia elements (e.g. sound, animations – downloaded or created, on one slide or on the master slide so it appears on each slide);
- transitions (how each slide moves from one to another – a variety of options is available);
- hyperlinks (text, images, URLs, email, document links, return to start);
- user interaction – does the user need to click or use the space bar to progress through the presentation, or will this be automated?
- alternate pathways (e.g. the user can select how they wish to view the presentation – this could be a menu slide at the beginning, with each of the slides shown with links, enabling the user to look at just the areas they select);
- hide/show – a presentation that may have certain slides that would not be shown to every audience (e.g. pupils may see a slightly different presentation to parents), and this can be achieved in one show by hiding slides or customising the show and saving as a customised show.

Text files and image files have been provided for practice, but you do not have to use these – you may create, use and copy any text and images to create your own multimedia product for practice purposes:

admit.jpg

run.bmp

rungrey.bmp

swim.jpg

school.jpg

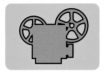

How to set up a presentation, including styles and background

Using a Slide Master ensures a consistent display and is the most efficient way to store designs, including style sheets and backgrounds. In the Slide Master you can set up the following:

- font styles/sizes;
- images;
- headers and footers;
- background designs.

Open Microsoft PowerPoint® – it will open on a new blank slide, ready for you to create your own multimedia product.

View menu

→ Master

→ Slide Master

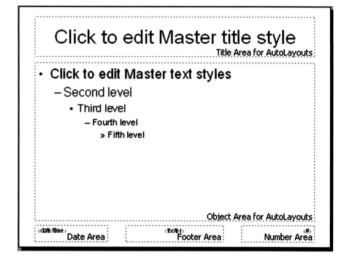

Figure 4.1 – Slide Master

How to insert slide numbers

Insert menu

→ Slide number

→ Check Footer

→ Check Slide number

→ Apply to All

(Nothing will appear to have happened, but you will see what has changed later.)

How to insert date

Click in the Date Area box – highlighting the date/time

→ Insert menu

→ Date and time

→ Choose the date format you wish to use

→ OK

How to insert a background image or colour

Format menu

→ Background

→ Select the dropdown arrow

To insert a colour:

Choose from the options available

→ Choose More colors or Fill effects

To insert an image as background:

Select Fill effects

→ Picture

→ Select Picture

→ Choose your picture

→ **rungrey.bmp**

→ OK

→ Apply to All

Figure 4.2 – Background fill

How to change the fonts and styles of text

Select the text you wish to change; using the text toolbar, select:

● font;

● size;

● enhancement – bold, italic, underline, shadow;

● alignment – left, centre, right.

Once you have set up all the Master Slide elements, select **Close Master View**. If this is not visible, click on the **Normal View** button at the bottom left of your screen.

Figure 4.3 – Close Master View

You are now ready to create your multimedia presentation. Save your Master Slide presentation as **sports**.

How to insert different slide types

Insert menu

→ New slide

To the right of your screen will appear the different types of slide you can insert into your presentation. The default is Title and text – this allows you to key in a title and then add bullet text.

Insert menu

→ New slide

→ Choose a Title and text slide layout

You are going to produce a navigation slide – this slide will take your view from the menu to a specific slide. On slide 2, using the number list, create a list of the following:

1 Welcome

2 Map

3 Message.

You need to create all your slides before you can activate this list

● Slide 1: your introductory slide – this will be followed by the three slides above;

● Slide 2: your menu list above;

● Slide 3: Welcome – add some text in the text area below the heading;

● Slide 4: Map – add a map or give directions on how to find the sports facilities;

● Slide 5: Message – provide a message (this could be about opening times of the facility).

On slide 2, which has your three-item menu:

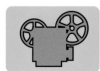

1 Highlight the text and number **Welcome**

→ Insert menu

→ Hyperlink

→ Slide

→ Choose slide 3

Repeat this for each of the other two menu items and slides. You have now created an alternative pathway for your viewer to use your presentation.

When using this method, you must consider that each slide should also have a hyperlink back to Slide 2, to assist the viewer to return to the menu slide – you can use a graphic or text and hyperlink back to Slide 2.

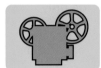

How to insert a media clip

Insert menu

  → New slide

  → Choose Title, Text, Media

→ Double-click on the media icon

→ Choose a media clip from the available list or insert one that you have saved

How to animate your chart

Once you have created your chart:

Custom animation

  → Add Effect

  → Entrance

  → Effect

  → In the animation task pane, select the animation effect from the list

→ Dropdown arrow

→ Effect options

→ Chart animations

→ Group chart

→ Here you can choose to animate by series, categories or elements of either series or categories

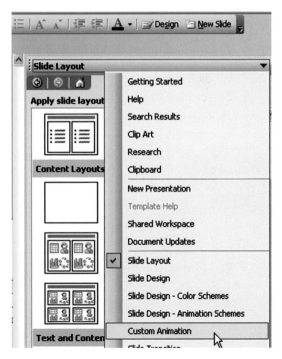

Figure 4.4 – Custom Animation

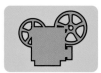

How to add animations to a slide

Slide Show

→ Animation Schemes

→ Choose from Subtle, Moderate, Exciting

→ Select Play to view how your animation will appear

→ You can then choose whether to Apply to all slides or Apply to this slide only

You can choose other elements on your slides and select options for animations, but do not overdo these effects – this can make the presentation too 'busy' for viewers and they may miss the point that you are making.

How to add transitions to a slide

Slide Show

→ Slide Transition

→ Choose a design

→ Choose a speed

→ Choose a sound

→ Choose how to advance your slides during the presentation

→ Select Play to view how your transitions will appear

→ Choose whether to Apply to all slides

How to insert a hyperlink

Highlight the relevant text on your slide

→ Insert menu

→ Hyperlink

→ Existing File or Web Page

→ Key in the web address

→ OK

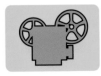

How to insert a link to another file

Highlight the relevant words

→ Insert menu

→ Hyperlink

→ Existing File or Web Page

→ Choose the file

→ OK

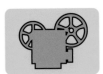

How to add sound

You have now created a multimedia presentation – the only thing missing is sound. As you may have noticed when you set up your transitions, you can add sound to your transition effects. Add some sound to any slide, if you have not already done so. You can add sound from either your PC or the Internet:

Insert menu

→ Movies and Sound

→ Sound from Clip organiser

→ Choose

→ Right-click

→ Insert

Alternatively, you can add any media sound clip you may have:

Insert menu

→ Movies and Sound

→ Sound from file

→ Choose your file

→ Right-click

→ Insert

How to produce different print options

File menu

→ Print

→ Print what:

choose from Slide, Handouts, Notes Page, Outline View

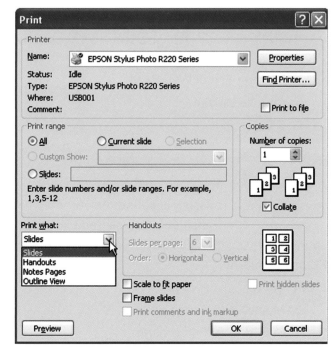

Figure 4.5 – Print dialog box

● **Slides**: each slide will be printed on one page each.

● **Handouts**: select the number of slides per page – 2, 3, 4, 6, 9.

● **Notes Page**: used when you have added speaker's notes – prints one slide + notes.

● **Outline View**: prints an outline of the text for each slide on a single page (does not show graphs, graphics, etc. – only text).

Tasks

Create a multimedia product to introduce the new keep fit centre. You should include a media clip and a wide variety of slide content. You will need to create five slides:

● **Slide 1: Title slide;**

● **Slide 2: Menu slide;**

● **Slide 3: Title and text;**

- **Slide 4: Title, text and media (video, audio, animation);**

- **Slide 5: Title and chart.**

Pass

Pass-level candidates will need to:

- Produce the multimedia product using some form of pathway through the product: alternative pathways, hyperlinks, multimedia effects, transitions.

- Include an option to allow the user to step through the presentation (e.g. a menu page showing different sections of the presentation).

- Produce a multimedia product containing text, images and sound.

- Annotate your printouts, indicating which elements you have used.

- Discuss in a report if the features you used turned out as intended.

Merit

*Merit-level candidates will **also** need to:*

- Produce the multimedia product making good use of pathways through the product: alternative pathways, hyperlinks, multimedia effects, user interaction, and so on.

- Ensure that most elements work as intended.

- Produce a multimedia product containing text, images, sound and animation.

Distinction

*Distinction-level candidates will **also** need to:*

- Produce the multimedia product making effective use of pathways through the product: alternative pathways, hyperlinks, multimedia effects, user interaction, and so on.

- Ensure that all elements work as intended.

- Produce a multimedia product containing text, images, sound, animation and video.

Section 5: Gain feedback and suggestions for improvement

> **Assessment objective 5**: *Seek feedback and suggest improvements* **is covered in this section.**

Skills

Once you have created your presentation, it is advisable to test it with your peers or a supervisor. This could be by questionnaire, feedback sheet, interview or checklist.

The easiest way to collect feedback is to create a feedback sheet/questionnaire that can be completed by the reviewer as they view your presentation. You can then ask one or more people to view your media product and provide you with feedback. Using a feedback sheet gives you consistency in the feedback, helping you to focus on changes that need to be made prior to the media product being used/launched.

Before giving the feedback sheet and media product to peers or supervisors, use the sheet yourself to evaluate your own presentation.

Suggestions for a feedback sheet are presented here, but you may ask as many questions as you feel is appropriate for your presentation.

Did you notice any spelling mistakes?	
Was the message conveyed?	
Were the colours correct?	
Did the timings work?	
Did you have time to read the content before the next slide was shown?	

You do not need to make any of the changes suggested in the feedback, but merit- and distinction-level candidates will need to suggest valid improvements that could be made.

Tasks

Now you have completed your presentation, you need to evaluate it yourself and test it with your peers or supervisor/user.

You will need to collect the feedback in an appropriate format – this could be a sheet that you create and give to each tester with your presentation.

What you are looking for is that the presentation is free from errors, the intended message is conveyed, the timings work, the option to move through as the user wishes is available and working correctly, any automated features work, and if video and audio were inserted, that they work as expected.

You need to collate this feedback; you do not need to implement any suggestions for improvement, but this will help you to gain a higher grade. What you should do is discuss the suggestions given and provide detail of how you would change the presentation, based on the feedback.

Pass

Pass-level candidates will need to:

● Seek feedback from a test user or from peers.

● Suggest possible improvements that could be made to the multimedia product.

Merit

*Merit-level candidates will **also** need to:*

● Seek feedback from a test user or peers, and through self-evaluation.

● Suggest valid improvements that could be made to the multimedia product.

Distinction

*Distinction-level candidates will **also** need to:*

- Seek a range of feedback from a test user or peers, and through detailed self-evaluation.

- Suggest valid improvements that could be made to the multimedia product and provide details of how these improvements could be achieved.

Unit 5

Unit overview

This unit will help you to develop the knowledge, skills and understanding of the process of planning, drafting, developing and creating a desktop-published document.

By working through the *Skills*, *How to* and *Tasks* sections in this unit, you will demonstrate all the skills required for Unit 5 and be able to:

- plan a document to meet a given brief;
- create and apply style sheets;
- use graphics tools to create basic shapes;
- develop images for inclusion in a completed document;
- prepare publication for final print.

Examples in this unit are based on Microsoft® Publisher 2003.

For this unit you will need to plan, design and produce a desktop-published document, including text and images. You will need to create:

- an 8-page A4 document OR a 16-page A5 document;
- no more than two A4-page sketches – considering house style, layout and design elements;
- a report outlining the stages between production of a proof copy and the final product ready for production by a commercial printer.

There should be evidence of:

- research;
- planning – to include a timescale for completion;
- design;
- reviewing for accuracy – making changes where necessary.

The pages you create will need to show evidence of:

- styles, to include: text formats and paragraph layouts;
- use of drawing tools: basic shapes – squares, triangles and circles;
- alteration of the order of objects: layered and grouped objects.

You will need to demonstrate the following skills:

- use of desktop-publishing features and drawing tools;
- consideration of the timescale for production.

Section 1: Plan a document from a design brief

Assessment objective 1: *Plan a document to meet a given design brief for a document of at least eight A4 pages or equivalent* is covered in this section.

You have been asked to create a brochure advertising a new sports facility. The facility will have a range of activities: swimming pool, gymnasium, tennis and badminton courts, keep fit area and a variety of different classes (e.g. Pilates, yoga).

Before you start producing any documents, you need to design the layout of the publication carefully, so that it is well laid out – this will become your design brief.

Skills

You will need to research a selection of published materials, evaluating their design and layout. You may wish to produce a simple table to track your research; this table should include the elements shown in the example provided here.

Date	Organisation	Document	End user	Design of publication	Layout of publication	Intended audience	Intended message
8 Jan	College	Prospectus	Prospective learner	Colourful	Clear and to the point – giving full information	16–20 year olds	Join our full-time courses

You should use this information when producing your own plan for your publication, considering the design and layout. Your plan should be in a report format and should take into account the following:

1 Link the research to your design:

  ● easy to understand;

  ● clear and to the point;

  ● conveying the message needed to encourage visitors.

2 Basic plans for your publication:

  ● content – both text and image;

  ● number of pages;

  ● content of each page;

  ● will there be an index or a table of contents?

3 Sketches of layout (this need only be for a couple of pages) – consider the following:

  ● styles used (house style): use at least three different font styles;

  ● text and image layouts: the placement of text and images throughout;

  ● identification of software choice to be used for production of publication;

- sketches of the page of your publication: produce at least two sketches, showing alternative designs;
- choice of final design;
- timeline of production of publication: this could be in table format.

Date		
18/9–2/10	Research	Conduct research into a variety of documents, looking for those with a similar theme to what I am going to produce; collect evidence; annotate what things are good to use in my design.
9/10	Planning	Decide on colour scheme, text styles and images, based on research
9/10–16/10	Produce sketches	Sketch a layout and design brief to help with the production of the document – produce two different designs to decide which would be best.
16/10	Design layout	Consider the house style to be used, what should go on the front page and contents page; whether it will have an index page and a questionnaire.
6/11	Produce document	Produce a draft of the document – proofread to check for any omissions or errors.
13/11	Send to printers	Correct all errors and omissions; prepare for outside printer; print one copy for self and one copy for printer.

How to sketch a layout plan

The following are examples of layout plans for three different documents.

The first example shows a hand-drawn plan, giving the measurements of the page, the font to be used, how the text will flow and the design of the pages, including margins, columns and gutters. This diagram is a drawing that has been annotated.

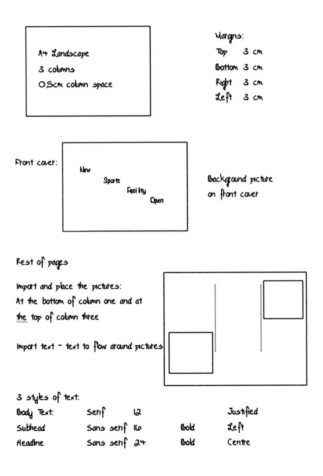

Figure 5.1 – Layout plan

The second example shows an actual layout, including text and image, and how they flow, with columns and gutters showing an outline of where the text will flow and where the heading is to be positioned. This diagram includes text and images.

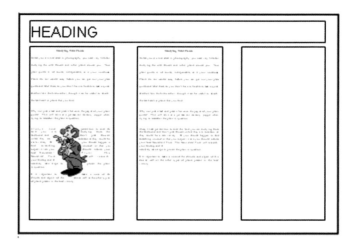

Figure 5.2 – Layout plan 2

The third example shows a layout including text flow and image placement, with columns and gutters showing an outline of where the text will flow and where the heading is to be positioned. This diagram is a line drawing.

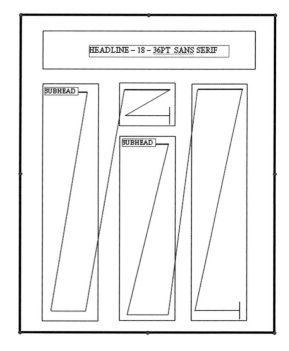

Figure 5.3 – Layout plan 3

Tasks

You have been asked to create a brochure advertising the keep fit gym. The gym will have a range of activities: swimming pool, gymnasium, tennis and badminton courts, keep fit area and a variety of different classes (e.g. Pilates, yoga).

Review a range of publications (e.g. newspapers, magazines, websites, books, journals) and decide on what you like best and what you dislike. Decide which features you would like to include in your work, and what influences your decision.

Pass

Pass-level candidates will need to:

- Collect research on example publications from a range of different sources.

- Describe the organisation and the end users of the publication (you may wish to use a table here).

- Link the research to your own design plan.

- Produce a basic plan, to include:

  1 at least two different layout sketches, showing different solutions to the design brief – these need not be a full design, but should consider house style and layout (no more than two A4 pages per layout sketch); once you have produced these two alternative design layouts, report on which one you have chosen to use and why;

  2 identification of choice of software;

  3 final design plan;

  4 a consideration of the timescale of production.

Merit

*Merit-level candidates will **also** need to:*

- Independently collate research on example publications from a range of different sources.

- Produce design plans that meet the requirements of the design brief, and also include timescales of production (these might not be realistic).

Distinction

*Distinction-level candidates will **also** need to:*

- Independently collate research on example publications from a wide range of different sources.

- Clearly link the research to your own design plan.

- Produce comprehensive design plans that fully cover the design brief, and also include timescales of production.

Visit the following websites for examples of desktop-publishing design and layout:

http://desktoppub.about.com/cs/basic/a/desktopdocument.htm

http://desktoppub.about.com/od/layout/Page_Layout_Techniques.htm

www.bestdtpdesign.com/samplejob.htm

www.typography-1st.com/typo/prnc-des.shtml

Section 2: Create styles

Assessment objective 2: *Create styles* is covered in this section.

Skills

Using the design plan created in Section 1, you are going to create your styles in the desktop-publishing software, and for this unit we are using Microsoft® Publisher 2003.

Text styles include a variety of features, but you must always consider the reader of your document, and the styles used must be legible. Consider the style of font and the size of the font used. To use a very small font size and an unclear font will make your publication less readable.

Good examples		Poor examples	
Heading	**HEADING**	Heading	HEADING
Body text	Body text body text body text body text body text body text body text body text body text	Body text	Body text body text body text body text body text

Figure 5.4 – Good and bad examples of fonts

Font face

Serif

A font that has serifs is known as a serif font. The ends of each stroke making up the characters have detail added. For example:

Times New Roman T

Sans serif

A font that has no serifs is known as a sans serif font. (Sans comes from the French *sans*, which means 'without'.) Each character is without detail at the ends. For example:

Arial A

Font size

Characters can be any font size, from 6 to 100.

Font emphasis

- **Bold**: darkening of the text – making it stand out more than other text.
- *Italic*: slanting of text – making it look different, but not always making it stand out.
- UPPER CASE: the use of Initial Capitals or all CAPITALS can give emphasis to text – especially in headings.

Alignment

Text can be aligned in four different ways, to give definition to different styles.

- Left – general use on documents:

  Lorem ipsum dolor sit amet, consectetuer adipiscing elit.
  Donec convallis. Fusce adipiscing. Cras felis diam, eleifend ac,
  mattis aliquet, fringilla sed, dui. Cum sociis natoque penatibus et magnis dis parturient montes, nascetur ridiculus mus. In luctus. Praesent id nunc.

- Right – used mainly for lines of text or headings:

  Lorem ipsum dolor sit amet, consectetuer adipiscing elit.
  Donec convallis. Fusce adipiscing. Cras felis diam, eleifend ac,
  mattis aliquet, fringilla sed, dui.

- Centre – used for lines of text, headings, or paragraphs:

  Lorem ipsum dolor sit amet, consectetuer adipiscing elit.
  Donec convallis. Fusce adipiscing. Cras felis diam, eleifend ac,
  mattis aliquet, fringilla sed, dui.

- Justified – sometimes used when documents are produced in columns:

  Lorem ipsum dolor sit amet, consectetuer adipiscing elit. Donec convallis. Fusce adipiscing. Cras felis diam, eleifend ac, mattis aliquet, fringilla sed, dui. Cum sociis natoque penatibus et magnis dis parturient montes, nascetur ridiculus mus. In luctus. Praesent id nunc.

Leading

Leading (pronounced 'ledd-ing') is the space between lines of text in a document. You can adjust the leading in all desktop-publishing software packages. The term 'leading' comes from the original form of typesetting, which used lead strips to space lines of text. Here are some examples:

- 0.75 leading:

  Lorem ipsum dolor sit amet, consectetuer adipiscing elit. Donec convallis. Fusce adipiscing. Cras felis diam, eleifend ac, mattis aliquet, fringilla sed, dui.

- 1.25 leading:

  Lorem ipsum dolor sit amet, consectetuer adipiscing elit. Donec convallis.

  Fusce adipiscing. Cras felis diam, eleifend ac, mattis aliquet, fringilla sed, dui.

- 1.75 leading:

  Lorem ipsum dolor sit amet, consectetuer adipiscing elit. Donec convallis.

  Fusce adipiscing. Cras felis diam, eleifend ac, mattis aliquet, fringilla sed, dui.

Paragraph spacing

This is the spacing between each paragraph of text, and is set in a similar way as leading between lines of text.

Indents and tabulations

Text can be indented to provide clearer definition for the reader. This type of indent is used to inset whole paragraphs from the rest of text. Text can also have just the first line indented. Tabulations are also used when laying out text in columns, although it is more usual nowadays to use tables for the same function.

| Example tabs | Example tabs | Example tabs |
| Example tabs | Example tabs | Example tabs |

Bullets

Bullets are another feature used to emphasise a list of text within a document. A symbol is placed before each piece of text, with a space between the symbol (bullet) and the text.

- Example bullet.
- Example bullet.
- Example bullet.

Creating styles

To create styles within a document you must first set up a new style. You then tag each piece of text you wish to adopt this style. The reason for using styles is to ensure conformity in your document, and also to help when any changes to the style are required. If styles have been tagged to texts, then changes are simple – you change the style and any text that has been tagged will automatically update to the new style.

How to create a style

Launch Microsoft® Publisher:

Select the Format menu

→ Styles and formatting

→ Styles and formatting window opens on the left of your document

→ Select Create new style

→ Enter the style name you wish to create

→ Select option Font

→ Select the font type from the dropdown list

→ Select the font style from the list

→ Select the font size

→ You can even change the colour of the text in this dialog box

→ OK

Figure 5.5 – New Style

To set the alignment of the paragraph, in the New Style dialog box:

Select Paragraph

→ Set the indentation of the text

→ Set the paragraph spacing and the leading

→ OK

If you are creating a bulleted text style:

Select Bullets and numbering from the New Style dialog box

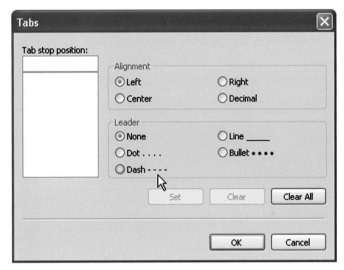

Figure 5.6 – Tabs

→ Choose the bullet you wish to use

→ Select the font size for the bullet

→ Choose the indentation between the bullet symbol and the text

→ OK

You will need to create a new style for each style you wish to use in your publication – follow instructions above. Once you have created all your styles, click OK – your styles will now be saved and ready to use.

How to modify a style

In your Styles dialog box, you should see all the styles that you have created. By clicking on the style, a dropdown list appears, which gives you the option to modify, rename or delete the style.

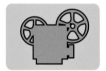

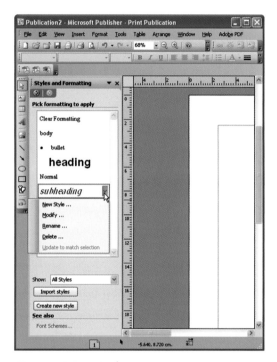

Figure 5.7 – Styles

Tasks

Building on your research from Section 1, and the scenario of the keep fit gym (see page 185), you are going to create styles for your publication.

Pass

Pass-level candidates will need to:

- Create three styles.
- Ensure that each style includes **at least one aspect** from **each** of the following:
  1 font (e.g. face, size, emphasis, alignment or leading);
  2 paragraph spacing (e.g. left-align body text, centre heading);
  3 indents or tabulations.

Merit

*Merit-level candidates will **also** need to:*

- Ensure that each style also includes a **full range** of **each** of the items listed above (for pass-level candidates).
- Make sure that the styles are mainly fit for purpose.

Distinction

*Distinction-level candidates will **also** need to:*

- Ensure each style also includes a **full range** of **each** of the following:
  1 indents or tabulations;
  2 bullets.
- Make sure that the styles are fit for purpose.

Section 3: Use desktop-publishing tools

> **Assessment objective 3:** *Select and use tools in desktop publishing* **is covered in this section.**

You have been asked to produce an eight-page document, with both text and images placed appropriately, advertising the new sports facility.

Page 1	Front cover with image
Page 2	Contents
Page 3	Introduction to organisation
Page 4	The range of facilities available – including images
Page 5	Opening times and costs – this could be a table of information
Page 6	Continuing the range of facilities and images
Page 7	Conclusion – this may have comments from people who support this facility or people who used it when it first opened Finally, it should end with something like 'Why not visit us today?' Maybe offer a discount voucher
Page 8	A questionnaire to be completed – asking questions such as: Would you use this facility? What time would you like to see the facility open from and to? What activities would you most likely take up? Any other questions you feel are relevant... Add an address to send the questionnaire back to or state 'hand in at reception desk'

Skills

There are many tools available in desktop-publishing packages – many are similar across a range of different software packages. In Microsoft® Publisher 2003, you could use some of the following to enhance your publication.

Placing of text

- Using landscape or portrait layout.
- Setting margins, columns and gutter (column spacing).
- Using styles effectively.
- Using columns to display text and images more effectively.
- Arranging text and images.
- Changing the colour of text.
- Text flow between pages and columns.
- Using bulleted lists.
- Rotating text.
- Using specialist characters – dropped capitals for beginning of paragraphs.

Placing of images

- Inserting Clip Art.
- Arranging images in layers.
- Changing the colour of images.
- Cropping and scaling of images – to ensure that the images fit where you wish to place them.

In the example shown here, the images have been resized and different wraparound options chosen. The text has been linked between three text frames to provide a flow of text across three columns. Styles have been created and applied (tagged) to the heading and to the body text. A background image of text has been placed on the master slide as a watermark.

Figure 5.8 – Example layout of a document with text and images inserted

Text files and image files have been provided for practice, but you do not have to use these – you may create, use and copy any text and images to create your own document for practice purposes:

practice1.txt

admit.jpg

run.bmp

practice2.txt

sports.txt

swim.jpg

housing.txt

school.jpg

virus.txt (contains spelling errors)

computer.jpg

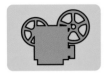

How to set up landscape or portrait layout

Select File menu

→ Page Setup

→ Orientation

→ OK

Here you can also choose to select different paper sizes and types. For the purpose of your task, you only need to select Full Page A4, which is the default option.

How to set up margins

Select Arrange

→ Layout guides

→ Margin guides

→ Amend the setting to be in line with your design

→ OK

How to set up columns and text flow

First, set up the page with gridlines to display columns – this makes it easier to draw out your text boxes on the page.

Layout guides

→ Grid guides

→ Columns

→ Key in the number

→ Make sure that there is a gutter (this is the space between the columns)

→ OK

Your page should now display blue lines indicating the columns on your page. Using the text box tool, draw out a text box over the first column, and repeat for each column on your page.

You now need to link the text boxes so that your text flows.

● Select the first text box by clicking in it.

● On the toolbar at the top of your screen there is a linked chain Create Text Box Link – your mouse pointer now changes to a jug.

● Click on the next text box in the sequence you wish your text to fill.

● Repeat this for each text box (you can even do this from page to page, to ensure that your text flows across text boxes and pages).

How to create more than a one-page document

Once you have set up the main parts of your document, before you insert any text and images that are specific to only one page, you can insert a new page copying all the elements on your first page.

Make sure that all the elements on your first page are what you want on each page, then:

Insert menu

→ Page

→ After current page

→ Duplicate all objects on this page

→ OK

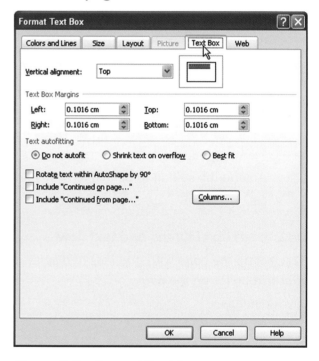

Figure 5.9 – Format Text Box

How to rotate text

Draw a text box using the text box tool on the left of your screen, or

→ Select Insert menu

→ Text Box

→ With your mouse, click and drag out the size of box you want on your page

→ Keep your text box selected

→ Select Arrange

→ Rotate or Flip

→ Green circles will appear – you can now click and drag your text box to any position, rotating the contents

How to change colour

Do this on your styles as part of the text set-up.

How to use dropped capitals

Dropped capitals are only used on the first character of a paragraph – do not overuse these. Generally, only the first character in a story is selected.

Highlight the character you wish to change

→ Menu Format

→ Drop Cap

→ Choose the style you wish to insert

→ OK

You can remove the drop cap the same way, if you no longer wish to display your text in this format.

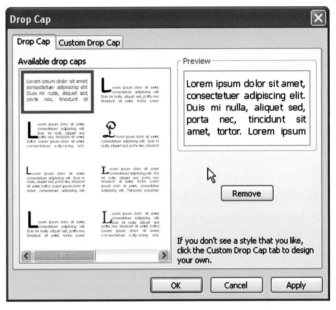

Figure 5.10 – Drop Cap

How to insert an image

Insert menu

→ Picture

→ From file

→ Choose your image from your file location

Insert a Clip Art image

Insert menu

→ Picture

→ Clip Art

→ Choose an image

How to crop and scale images

On the Picture toolbar:

Figure 5.11 – Picture toolbar

- The crop tool is two pairs of scissors facing each other.
  When using this, you will not resize your image, but will reduce or increase the space around your image. You can use this tool to crop out part of your image. This only works on the square frame of your image. *(You cannot crop Clip Art.)*
- To lighten or darken your image, use the more or less contrast circles, or the more or less brightness buttons.
- To change the colour, select the bars colour: here you can choose Automatic, Grayscale, Black and White or Washout.
- To change the text wrap options, select the text wrap button (this is a picture of a black dog against a background of text): here you can choose Square, Tight, Through, Top and Bottom, None or Edit Wrap Points.

How to arrange images and layers

Once you have images and pictures on your page, you may wish to:

- group;
- rotate;
- align them to each other.

To group:

Select the images you wish to group by clicking on and holding down your Shift key to select other images/drawings

→ Arrange

→ Group

To rotate:

Select the image you wish to rotate by clicking on it

→ Arrange

→ Rotate

To align:

Select the images you wish to align to each other by clicking on them and holding down the Shift key to select

→ Arrange

→ Align or Distribute

Tasks

Using the scenario of a new keep fit gym, select and use tools in desktop publishing to produce a document meeting the following specifications.

Pass

Pass-level candidates will need to:

- Produce a simple document of at least eight A4 pages, following your design brief and layout sketch.

- Use a desktop-publishing software package.

- Demonstrate (limited) use of desktop-publishing facilities: set margins; set column widths – column flow and page flow; apply at least three styles (e.g. heading, subheading, body text).

- Import text.

- Import images.

Merit

*Merit-level candidates will **also** need to:*

- Produce a detailed document of at least eight A4 pages.

- Meet the demands of design and layout brief, using a desktop-publishing software package.

- Demonstrate good use of desktop-publishing facilities – look at the range available and use *most* of the features.

Distinction

*Distinction-level candidates will **also** need to:*

● Meet *fully* the demands of the design and layout brief, using a desktop-publishing software package.

● Demonstrate good use of desktop-publishing facilities – look at the range available and use *all* the features.

Section 4: Use drawing tools

Assessment objective 4: *Use drawing tools included with DTP software to create basic shapes for inclusion in your completed publication* is covered in this section.

You have been asked to create a logo for the new sports facility. Using images, Clip Art and drawing tools, produce a suitable drawing.

Skills

In Microsoft® Publisher, there is a toolbar at the left of your screen that you can use to insert a variety of shapes and objects.

You have been asked to use a variety of drawing tools:

● 2D shapes;

● cut, paste, copy and crop;

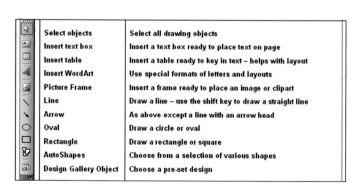

Select objects	Select all drawing objects
Insert text box	Insert a text box ready to place text on page
Insert table	Insert a table ready to key in text – helps with layout
Insert WordArt	Use special formats of letters and layouts
Picture Frame	Insert a frame ready to place an image or clipart
Line	Draw a line – use the shift key to draw a straight line
Arrow	As above except a line with an arrow head
Oval	Draw a circle or oval
Rectangle	Draw a rectangle or square
AutoShapes	Choose from a selection of various shapes
Design Gallery Object	Choose a pre-set design

Figure 5.12 – Toolbar

- monochrome and colour fill, and shading;
- different styles and colour of lines;
- layering of items to create a clear graphic;
- use a range of text styles and effects, including reverse and artistic text;
- use grouping of items.

How to cut, paste, copy and crop

Any item on the page can be cut, copied or pasted into a new location, using the toolbar or a key combination:

- Ctrl + x = cut;
- Ctrl + c = copy;
- Ctrl + v = paste.

To crop an image, you need to use the crop tool. You will find this on the Picture toolbar that appears when you insert and select an image on your page.

Select the crop tool

→ Your cursor changes when you get to one of the handles on your image

→ Click and drag

You can crop the image or expand the space the image takes up, without changing the size of the image.

Figure 5.13 – Crop tool used on image

How to fill and shade objects

Draw out a shape

→ Double-click on the shape, or

→ Right-click and Format AutoShape

The dialog box allows you to change the colour and style of the lines, the fill colour of the shape, the wrap options, and so on.

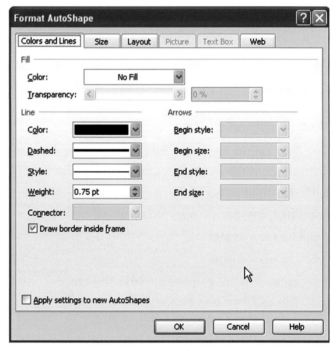

Figure 5.14 – Format AutoShape

How to create text styles and effects – reverse text and artistic text

See Section 3 for:

● dropped capitals;

● rotated text;

● coloured text.

Reverse text can be produced when a frame holding text is shaded, and the text is coloured white to show through the colour or greyscale of the frame.

Artistic text can be created using WordArt.

View

→ Toolbars

→ WordArt

→ Select the first icon

→ Select the style of text you wish to create (you can always change this later)

→ Key in your text

→ OK

● Using the edit text icon you can change your text, or simply double-click on the WordArt text on your page to edit.

● The gallery icon allows you to change the style of your WordArt text.

● The format icon allows you to change the style, colour, thickness, position, and so on, of the text.

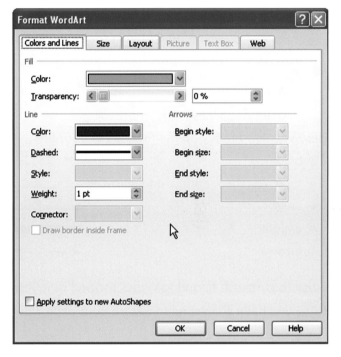

Figure 5.15 – Format WordArt

● The shape icon allows you to change the shape of the text.

● The text wrapping icon allows you to wrap text around the image, as with any other graphic.

How to draw shapes

Using the toolbar at the right of your screen, you can insert:

● lines;

● lines with arrowheads;

● oval;

● rectangle;

● AutoShapes.

Using the above shapes, you can create your own shape/drawing. Using the Format

→ AutoShapes menu, you can fill the shapes, colour them, resize, set text wrap options and place them on the page.

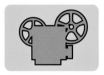

How to draw and format lines

Using the drawing toolbox, create a line.

Format menu

→ AutoShape

→ Color and Lines

Here you can modify all the features of your line:

- colour;
- type – dashed, dotted, and so on;
- style;
- weight;
- arrows.

How to arrange drawings and shapes in layers

Once you have shapes and lines on your page, you may wish to:

- group;
- rotate;
- align them to each other.

To group:

Select the shape/line you wish to group by clicking on and holding down your Shift key to select other images/drawings

→ Arrange

→ Group

To rotate:

Select the shape/line you wish to rotate by clicking on it

→ Arrange

→ Rotate

To align:

Select the shapes/lines you wish to align to each other by clicking on them and holding down the Shift key to select all

→ Arrange

→ Align or Distribute

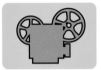

How to send back, bring forward (layering)

Select the object you wish to layer

→ Arrange

→ Order

You now have options to:

● Bring to Front;

● Send to Back;

● Bring Forward;

● Send Backward.

Each of the above has a different effect – practise on an image or drawing you have created.

Tasks

Using the scenario of a keep fit gym, you are required to create some basic shapes that will be incorporated into a logo design to be used on your publication. The shapes can be any combination of graphics and text, using the fill options and rotate options.

Pass

Pass-level candidates will need to:

● Create basic shapes to be included in your publication.

● Create a logo to be used on the front page of your publication – this can include text and graphics.

● Produce a drawing of a tennis court.

● Show evidence of layering.

Merit

*Merit-level candidates will **also** need to:*

● Create combined shapes to produce more complex shapes to be included in your publication.

- Create a map of the facility.

- Show evidence of layering and grouping.

- Show evidence of using the majority of facilities available.

- Produce accurate drawings.

Distinction

*Distinction-level candidates will **also** need to:*

- Provide a floor plan of the facility.

- Ensure that shapes created clearly meet the needs of the design brief and intended audience.

- Show evidence of lines and borders.

- Show evidence of using consistently the full range of facilities available.

Section 5: Prepare the publication for printing

Assessment objective 5: *Prepare publication for print* is covered in this section.

You will be working on the document you have created so far in Sections 3 and 4.

Skills

You need to review your work and make any changes. You will also need to produce a proof copy that will be sent to the client. You will need to produce a covering letter to the client, stating what you are including and what you require by way of printing, colours, numbers of copies, time by which you hope it will be ready and any other special instructions.

When reviewing your work, you should be checking for spelling errors by proofreading the document, as some spelling errors will be proper words mistyped (e.g. 'coy' when it should read 'copy').

You should correct any errors found in your document and print a proof copy. Finally, you should prepare your document as a final proof copy for print, using commercial print settings.

You should produce a report on the outcomes of your development at the different stages of your work, from the Tasks in Section 1 through to the Tasks in Section 4. You should also report on the processes of printing multiple copies of one document and the reasons for creating different print runs for different colours used within the document. The table shown here is an example report.

Section 1 Task	Section 2 Task	Section 3 Task	Section 4 Task
I found this easy once I had decided on the layout of my document. I set myself a deadline to complete the research and design, right through to the final document.	Creating the styles was a problem at the beginning, as I chose some fonts that were not appropriate. Once I realised that I could change the styles at a later stage, this was not a problem.	I decided on a three-column document, with images to balance the text throughout the document. I imported some text and the rest I keyed in.	I was unsure of what type of graphic to create, so experimented with the different drawing tools to create my own unique logo.

If a document is to be printed in more than one colour, this cannot be done by many printers, especially if the print run is for large numbers. To keep the costs down, commercial printers will run the document through using one colour, and then run it again using a different colour, building up the colours on the page. This may be a slower process than photocopying in colour, but it is more cost-effective. The proof copy will need marks on the page to enable the printer to align the page for each print run.

Sometimes in magazines, if this is not done correctly, the pictures and text can look out of focus or fuzzy, as the inks are not properly aligned.

How to spellcheck

Tools menu

→ Spelling

→ Spelling

The computer will read through your document and select words that are misspelt. Remember that the computer cannot check correctly spelt, but incorrect words – this must be done manually by you, when reading through your document.

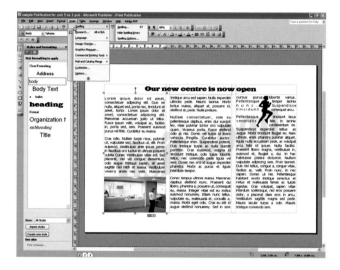

Figure 5.16 – Spelling

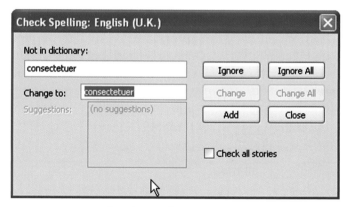

Figure 5.17 – Check Spelling

How to print

Once you are happy with your document, you need to print it.

Select File menu

→ Print

→ Choose options

→ OK

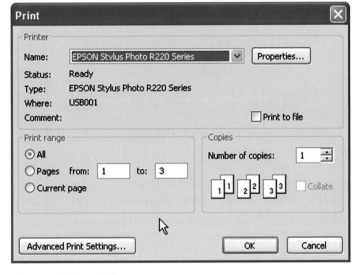

Figure 5.18 – Print

How to print commercially

This will depend on the printer you have available, but when setting up for commercial printing, you create one document that contains all the black text/objects and another that contains all the coloured text/objects.

When you are setting up for two-colour printing (when two colours have been used in a document), a two-page document will produce four pages – two pages will show only the black text/objects and two pages will show only the coloured text/objects.

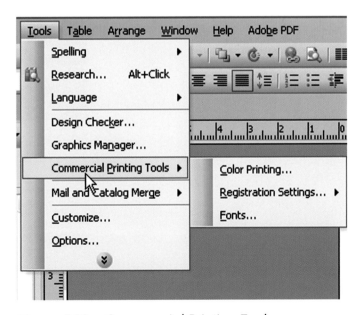

Figure 5.19 – Commercial Printing Tools

→ Process colors plus spot colors

→ OK

→ File menu

→ Print preview

→ Choose which options to print

● Composite – whole document with no different prints for colours;

● Black – just black parts of document;

● Spot – just one-colour parts of document.

You will need to show registration marks to enable printers to set up the print run, ensuring that the coloured print and the black print are aligned. The printers will pass the document through different colour options for each colour used in the document – this is why crop marks are necessary.

Figure 5.20 – Colour Printing

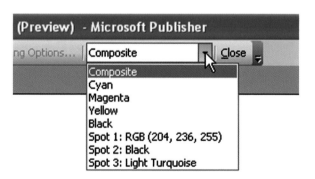

Figure 5.21 – Colour options

> **Registration marks:** graphics printed at the side and top of your document that provide a guide to a commercial printer of where to position the individual pages so as to align the print.
>
> **Crop marks:** give the publisher a guide as to where to cut or fold the document.
>
> **Colour bars:** provide the printer with the colours that are used in the document.

File menu

→ Print

→ Advanced Print Settings

→ Page settings tab

→ Select Registration marks, Crop marks and Color bars as a minimum

→ OK

→ OK

Figure 5.22 – Registration marks

Tasks

Using the work created in the Tasks from Sections 1 to 4, prepare your document for production of a final proof copy to be sent to the client. This final proof copy will be sent out with a covering letter, which you should also create.

You are also required to produce a report on the outcomes of your development at the different stages of your work, through the Tasks in Sections 1 to 4. You should also report on the processes of printing multiple copies of one document, and the reasons for creating different print runs for different colours used within the document.

Pass

Pass-level candidates will need to:

- Print an eight-page document as a proof copy.
- Produce a final copy (this may contain several errors).
- Provide final copy quality (this may not be of a business standard).
- Produce a covering letter.
- Produce a brief report of the final stages of producing multiple copies using commercial printing processes.

Merit

*Merit-level candidates will **also** need to:*

- Print an eight-page document as a final proof copy.
- Produce a final copy (this may contain some errors).
- Provide good final copy quality.
- Produce a report of the final stages of producing multiple copies using commercial printing processes.

Distinction

*Distinction-level candidates will **also** need to:*

- Produce a final copy (this will be mostly free from error).

- Provide final copy quality near to business standard.

- Produce a detailed report of the final stages of producing multiple copies using commercial printing processes.

Unit 6 Spreadsheets

Unit overview

This unit will help you to develop a thorough knowledge and understanding of how to create and use spreadsheets.

Examples in this unit are based on Microsoft Excel® 2003.

By working through the *Skills*, *How to* and *Tasks* sections in this unit, you will demonstrate all the skills required for Unit 6 and be able to:

- design a spreadsheet to meet the needs of an organisation;
- create a spreadsheet according to a design sketch, and format the spreadsheet;
- sort data and use simple filters;
- carry out modelling activities, using a spreadsheet;
- analyse data, using appropriate graphs/charts;
- create macros to automate procedures in a spreadsheet.

Section 1: Design a spreadsheet

Assessment objective 1: *Design a spreadsheet to meet the needs of an organisation* is covered in this section.

You have been asked to create a spreadsheet for the school tuck shop. Before you start keying anything into a Microsoft Excel® spreadsheet, you need to design the spreadsheet carefully by drawing a design sketch, to ensure that it is well laid out and covers all the requirements of the user and the organisation (the school). The tuck shop spreadsheet will need to show:

- a variety of products for sale;
- how many products are left in stock;
- the number of products sold;
- the retail (bought) cost of the products;
- the sale price;
- a calculation to show whether any products need to be reordered (*merit- and distinction-level candidates only*).

Your school/college has suggested that a tuck shop be opened during break-times to offer a range of confectionary items. However, the school assistant is unsure of how much to charge for the products. You have been asked to plan and create a spreadsheet for the tuck shop that will allow you to make predictions about the cost of the items to be sold, sort and filter some of the data, and create macros to automate tasks.

Skills

Design plan

You will need to draw a design sketch for the spreadsheet you are going to create. This plan should be a sketch diagram drawn by hand, to show the different features of the spreadsheet listed below. You will need to include a variety of formulae and functions, make predications, sort data and use filters, and create charts and macros to automate tasks. All these different features need to be included in the sketch that you draw. The sketch must include the purpose and audience of the spreadsheet, as detailed above, and show:

- the layout of the spreadsheet;

- user requirements for the spreadsheet;

- different cell formats (e.g. currency, date/time, text, decimal places);

- formulae to be used (e.g. + ? * / and [ ]);

- different functions.

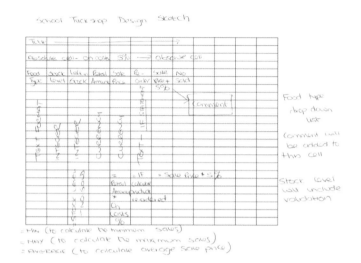

Figure 6.1 – School tuck shop design sketch

Functions

Within the spreadsheet design that you sketch and create in the next section, you will need to include some of the following functions.

Functions group 1

This includes arithmetic and statistical functions, such as SUM, AVERAGE, MAX, MIN, MEDIAN, MODE, COUNT, COUNTIF.

Tip: To add cells in a continuous row or column, you can use the AutoSum button on the toolbar (e.g. A1:A6). If data is not in a continuous row or column, you would use the =SUM formula.

- AVERAGE: this calculates an average across a number of cells – e.g. =AVERAGE(A1:B3).

- MAX: this returns the maximum value over a range of cells – e.g. =MAX(B1:C10).

- MIN: this returns the minimum value over a range of cells – e.g. =MIN(B1:C10).

- MEDIAN: this returns the MEDIAN or the number in the middle of a set of numbers e.g. =MEDIAN(B1:C10).

- MODE: this returns the MODE or the most frequently occurring, or repetitive, value in a range of data – e.g. =MODE(B1:C10).

- COUNT: counts numbers or dates – e.g. =COUNT(B1:C10).

  Tip: If you wish to count the number of text items in a range of cells, you would need to use the function =COUNTA(B1:C10).

- COUNTIF: counts the number of cells that meet a specific criteria, such as the number of items that need to be reordered – e.g. =COUNTIF(B6:B18, 10).

Functions group 2

This includes mathematical/trigonometric functions, such as SIN, COS, TAN, LOG, POWER, RND.

- SIN: returns the sine of the given angle.

- COS: returns the cosine of the given angle.

- TAN: returns the tangent of the given angle.

- LOG: returns the logarithm of a number to the base you specify – e.g. =LOG(10) – the logarithm of 10 (1).

- POWER: returns the result of a number raised to a power – e.g. =POWER(5,2) – this shows 5 squared, or 25.

- RND: rounds a number to a specific number of digits.

Functions group 3

This includes rounding functions, such as INTEGER, ROUNDUP and ROUNDDOWN, TRUNC.

- INTEGER: displays numbers as whole numbers (without any decimal places).

- ROUNDUP: rounds a number up, away from zero – e.g. =ROUNDUP(3.2,0) – this rounds 3.2 up to a whole number (in this case, 4).

- ROUNDDOWN: rounds a number down, towards zero – e.g. =ROUNDDOWN(3.2,0) – this rounds a number down to a whole number (in this case, 3).

- TRUNC: truncates a number to an integer by removing the fractional part of the number.

Functions group 4

This includes logical functions, such as IF, AND, OR, NOT, including nested IF statements.

- IF: returns one value if a condition you specify evaluates to TRUE, and another value if it evaluates to FALSE. Use IF to conduct conditional tests on values and formulae – e.g. in the tuck shop spreadsheet you may wish to use an IF to see whether any products need to be reordered.

- Nested IF: can include AND, IF, OR within the IF statement.

Functions group 5

This includes look-up functions, such as VLOOKUP, HLOOKUP, MATCH.

- VLOOKUP: searches for a value in the leftmost column of a table, and then returns a value in the same row from a column you specify in the table; the 'V' in VLOOKUP stands for 'vertical' – e.g. =VLOOKUP(2,A1:B3,2, True) – this looks up 2 in column A and then returns the value from column B in the same row.

- HLOOKUP: searches for a value in the top row of a table and then returns a value in the same column from a row you specify in the table – use HLOOKUP when your comparison values are located in a row across the top of a table of data, and you want to look down a specified number of rows; the 'H' in HLOOKUP stands for 'horizontal' – e.g. =HLOOKUP(2,A1:B3,2, True) – this looks up 2 in Row A and returns the value from Row B in the same row.

- MATCH: returns the position of an item in a table that matches a specified value in a specified order – use MATCH instead of one of the LOOKUP functions when you need the position of an item in a range instead of the item itself.

Functions group 6

This includes reference functions, such as ROW, COLUMN.

- ROW: returns the number of rows in a reference.

- COLUMN: returns the number of columns in a reference.

Functions group 7

This includes text functions, such as LEFT, MID, RIGHT, LEN, VALUE, TEXT, CONCATENATE, FIND.

- LEFT: returns the first character or characters in a text string, based on the number of characters specified.

- MID: returns a specific number of characters from a text string, starting at the position you specify, based on the number of characters specified.

- RIGHT: returns the last character or characters in a text string, based on the number of characters specified.

- LEN: returns the number of characters in a text string.

- VALUE: converts a text string that represents a number to a number.

- the text enclosed in quotation marks or a reference to a cell containing the text you want to convert – e.g. =VALUE("£500) shows the number equivalent to the string, which in this case which is 500.

- CONCATENATE: joins several text strings into one text string – e.g. =CONCATENATE (A1,B1); A1 could be First name, B1 could be Surname and these can then be joined as one item – e.g. First name and Surname together in a new cell.

- FIND: finds one text string (find_text) within another text string (within_text), and returns the number of the starting position of find_text from the first character of within_text.

Functions group 8

This includes date and time functions, such as TODAY, NOW, YEAR, MONTH, DAY.

- TODAY: returns the serial number of the current date (the serial number is the date-time code used by Microsoft Excel® for date and time calculations); if the cell format was General before the function was entered, the result is formatted as a date.

- NOW: returns the number of the current date and time; if the cell format was General before the function was entered, the result is formatted as a date – e.g. = NOW( ).

- YEAR: returns the year corresponding to a date; the year is returned as an integer in the range 1900–9999 – e.g. =YEAR (serial_number); serial_number is the date of the year you want to find; dates should be entered using the DATE function – e.g. use DATE(2008,5,23) for the 23rd day of May in the year 2008 (problems can occur if dates are entered as text).

- MONTH: returns the month of a date represented by a serial number; the month is given as an integer, ranging from 1 (January) to 12 (December) – e.g. =MONTH(serial_number).

- DAY: returns the day of a date, represented by a serial number; the day is given as an integer ranging from 1 to 31 – e.g. =DAY(serial_number).

Functions group 9

- Relative cell references: a relative cell is displayed in the spreadsheet formulae as A4, and when it is replicated down a column it becomes A5, A6, A7.

- Absolute cell references: an absolute cell is displayed in the spreadsheet formulae as A4, and the '$' makes both the column and the row reference within the cell absolute (i.e. it does not change) when it is replicated.

Tasks

Using the tuck shop scenario on page 216, you should draw a design sketch for the spreadsheet.

| Pass |

Pass-level candidates will need to:

- Include basic details of the layout of the spreadsheet in line with user requirements.

- Include cell formats.

- Use formulae, including two from the following: + ? * / and [ ].

- Use two different functions from at least two of the categories shown on pages 218–222 (these may not all be appropriate).

- Relative references may be appropriate.

- Not all relative references will be used.

| Merit |

*Merit-level candidates will **also** need to:*

- Produce a design sketch in line with identified user requirements, including more than one worksheet.

- Include different cell formats.

- Use all formulae (+ ? * / and [ ]).

- Use three different functions from at least three of the categories shown on pages 218–222 (most of these will be appropriate).

- Demonstrate use of relative or absolute cell references.

- Use at least one IF statement.

Distinction

*Distinction-level candidates will **also** need to:*

- Produce a detailed sketch in line with identified user requirements, including more than one worksheet.

- Use four different functions from at least four of the categories on pages 218–222 (all these will be appropriate).

- Demonstrate use of relative and absolute cell references.

- All choice will be appropriate.

Section 2: Create the spreadsheet

> **Assessment objective 2: *Create the spreadsheet according to the design and format it to make it user friendly* is covered in this section.**

Skills

You will need to create a spreadsheet based on the design sketch that you produced in Section 1. The spreadsheet must work and must include at least one worksheet.

Once you have created the spreadsheet, you will need to format and enhance it by changing the colours of text and backgrounds, and adding borders. An example completed spreadsheet (**tuckshop.xls**) is provided on the CD, to allow you to practise these skills.

How to add text/background colour/cell borders

To change the font of text within the spreadsheet:

Highlight the text you want to change

Format menu

> → Cells
>
> → Font
>
> → Choose suitable font, font style and size

To change the background colour of cells:

Highlight the cells to which the colour should be applied

> → Fill Color
>
> → The fill colour will colour the highlighted cells

To add cell borders:

Highlight the cells where a border is required

> → Click on the border icon
>
> → Select the type of border required (e.g. outside, inside, all)

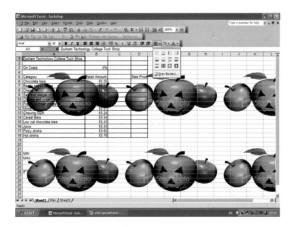

Figure 6.2 – Border icon

It is a good idea to apply different borders around different sections within the spreadsheet, so that different types of cells can be emphasised (e.g. a border around text cells, a different border around number cells and then an overarching thick border around all active cells).

How to adjust row height/column width

Sometimes when you key data directly into Microsoft Excel®, it is not always fully shown. To ensure that data in your spreadsheet is shown in full, you will need to adjust the row height/column width.

Format menu

> → Row/Column
>
> → Height
>
> → Key a number into the spreadsheet, or
>
> → Move the mouse pointer between the columns to expand the width/height

Tip: If you see #### in your cells, it means that the column needs to be widened to show the data.

How to merge cells

A heading, for example, can be merged and centred across a number of cells, to make it stand out or to ensure that the data is shown in full. To merge cells:

Highlight the cells to be merged

→ Click on the merge and center icon

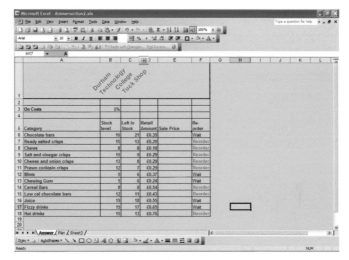

Figure 6.3 – Merge and Center icon

How to set the direction of text in a cell

Text in different cells can be rotated for emphasis or to save space within the spreadsheet. To set the direction of text in a cell:

Format menu

→ Cell

→ Alignment

→ 45°

→ OK

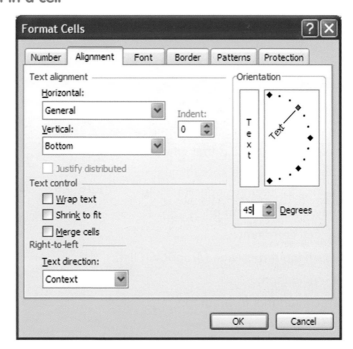

Figure 6.4 – Format Cells – change direction

How to wrap text

Text in cells can be 'wrapped', or displayed on more than one line. To wrap text in a cell:

Format menu

→ Cells

→ Alignment

→ Wrap text

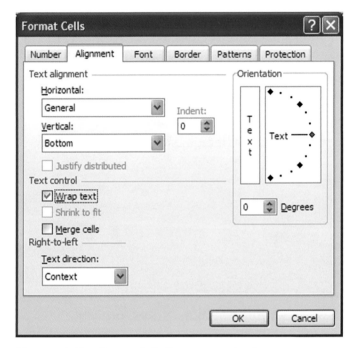

Figure 6.5 – Format Cells – wrap text

How to provide help for the user

Within the spreadsheet, you need to include at least one example of help for the user, so that when they are using the spreadsheet it is easy for them to operate. Help may be in the form of:

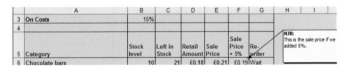

Figure 6.6 – Insert comment

- cell comments;
- an input message (dropdown list);
- validation;
- conditional formatting;
- protecting a workbook.

1   Cell comments: a comment is a note that you attach to a particular cell in a spreadsheet which can be used to provide feedback to users or as a reminder for yourself. To add a comment:

Select the cell where the comment is to be shown

→ Menu Insert

→ Comment

→ Add the text into the comment box

2 Input messages: an input message allows you to show a message to the user when they are using the spreadsheet. If they enter some data incorrectly, for example, you can advise the user that they can only enter decimal numbers of between 0.01 and 9.99 into these cells.

Click Data

→ Validation

→ Input Message tab

→ Make sure that you select the check box Show input message when cell is selected

Figure 6.7 – Input Message

→ Fill in the title and text for the message

3 Dropdown list: a dropdown list allows you to select information from a pre-defined list, without having to key in the data each time. To create a dropdown list, type the entries in a single column or row (do not include blank cells in the list). If the list is on a different worksheet, name the range of cells.

Select the range of cells to be named

→ Click the Name box

→ Type the name for the cells

→ Enter

→ Click Data

→ Validation

→ Settings

→ In the Allow box click List

→ Enter a reference to your list in the Source box (e.g. named cells)

In cell dropdown, select the check box

→ Specify whether the cell can be left blank: Select or clear the Ignore blank check box (you can also include input messages at this point)

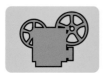

4 **Validation:** validation within the spreadsheet allows you to restrict the input of data into specific cells (e.g. only allow decimal numbers to be entered into a cost column). To set the validation:

Data

→ Validation

→ Select Allow Decimal

→ Select a minimum and maximum amount (e.g. 0.01 and 9.99)

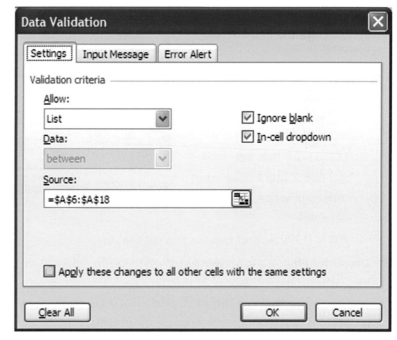

Figure 6.8 – Data Validation

5 **Conditional formatting**:
conditional formatting allows
you to change the format of
specific cells within a
worksheet if they meet a set
criteria – for example, you
might want to show cells in red
if the stock falls below a certain
number, but show them in green if they are above a particular stock level. To apply
conditional formatting:

Figure 6.9 – Conditional Formatting

Format menu

→ Conditional Formatting

→ Set the criteria

→ Click format

→ Change the cell colour to red

→ OK

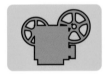

6 **Protecting a workbook**:

Tools menu

→ Protection

→ Protect Workbook

→ Enter password to protect the workbook

→ OK

Figure 6.10 – Protect Workbook

229

Tasks

Use the spreadsheet that you created in Section 1 for the tuck shop.

Pass

Pass-level candidates will need to:

● Create a functional spreadsheet, including text (this might contain only one sheet).

● Apply background colour to the worksheet by using fill cells.

● Apply a colour to the heading, a different colour to the column headings and a third colour to the remaining cells. Ensure that the colours are appropriate and make the spreadsheet look professional.

● Change the column heading direction to 45°.

● Adjust row height/column width to ensure that all data is shown in full on the spreadsheet.

● Merge cells.

● Create one example of help for the user, such as an instruction on the sheet, a cell comment, an input message or validation (this may not be of high quality).

Merit

*Merit-level candidates will **also** need to:*

● Include a second worksheet in the workbook to show yearly sales figures. Create a new worksheet to link the sales to a new monthly sales worksheet, which will record sales on a monthly basis. Calculate the sales per category item for the current month (January) and calculate the total sales during this month in terms of £/pence.

● Apply one border to all 'category' data and a separate border around the 'figures'.

● Hide one column within the workbook.

- Wrap some text in a cell so that it is displayed on more than one line.

- Add at least one cell comment and an appropriate validation in at least one row/column. Add a suitable input message.

- Use conditional formatting.

*Distinction-level candidates will **also** need to:*

Distinction

- Add sufficient help for the user to enable a beginner to use the spreadsheet with ease. This will include suitable cell comments and validation, with useful feedback to users.

- Input data from a dropdown list and use conditional formatting to make the output clearer.

- Protect the worksheet to prevent a user changing/deleting formulae.

Section 3: Create the spreadsheet

Assessment objective 3 – *Sort data and use simple filters* is covered in this section.

Skills

Data within a worksheet can be sorted in a number of ways, for example:

- alphabetically;
- numerically;
- by more than one column.

How to sort data

Highlight the data

→ Click Data

→ Sort

→ Select how the data is to be sorted (e.g. ascending/descending)

Tip: if you have not selected all the data in the worksheet to be included in the sort, or have only selected one column, Microsoft Excel® will ask you if your data selection is correct and whether you wish to continue.

Figure 6.11 – Sort

How to filter data

Filtering data is like running a query in a database. A filter looks at a range of data within the worksheet to check that it meets a certain criteria (e.g. crisps > 20p). Microsoft Excel® will then show you only the records that meet this criteria, and the remaining data in the worksheet is kept hidden. Data can be filtered using:

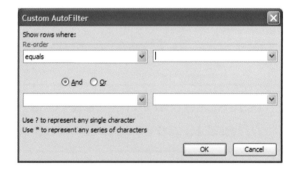

Figure 6.12 – Custom AutoFilter

- **AutoFilter:** filters the data using simple criteria (e.g. crisps);
- **Advanced Filter:** filters the data using more complex criteria (e.g. crisps > 20p).

To filter the data:

Highlight the data to be used in the filter

→ Click Data

→ Filter

→ (either AutoFilter or Advanced Filter)

A small arrow is then shown on the data to be filtered; click on this arrow and make your selection to be used in the filter (e.g. crisps).

To create an advanced filter:

Click Data

→ Filter

→ Advanced Filter

→ Key in the criterion for the search

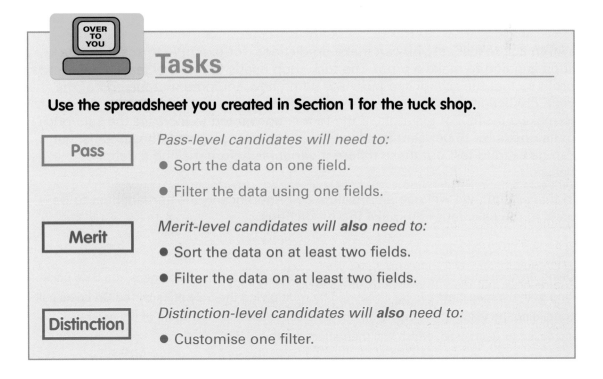

OVER TO YOU

Tasks

Use the spreadsheet you created in Section 1 for the tuck shop.

Pass

Pass-level candidates will need to:

● Sort the data on one field.

● Filter the data using one fields.

Merit

*Merit-level candidates will **also** need to:*

● Sort the data on at least two fields.

● Filter the data on at least two fields.

Distinction

*Distinction-level candidates will **also** need to:*

● Customise one filter.

Section 4: Change variables and make predictions

> **Assessment objective 4:** *Carry out modelling activities using a spreadsheet* is covered in this section.

Skills

Within a spreadsheet you can make predictions, for example to see if the tuck shop is going to make a profit. The tuck shop needs to make at least a small profit so that the school can purchase some new equipment at the end of the year. Predictions can be made of how much to charge for each product in order to make a profit. For example, if the tuck shop wanted to increase the sale price of its goods by 15 per cent to allow it to make a larger profit, the spreadsheet can be used to test out these different variables before making a definite decision.

In this section, we will use an absolute cell reference in the spreadsheet to be used in the calculation to make the predictions.

How to make predictions

Using the tuck shop spreadsheet to make a prediction about the sale prices, the **Sale price** field of the spreadsheet can be calculated by multiplying the **Sale price** by the **On costs** cell containing the value of 5%, using an absolute cell reference. This value of 5% can be increased or decreased, which will then affect the **Sale price**.

Once the **Sale price** has been multiplied by the **On costs** of 5%, you can change the figures by changing the **On costs** cell figure to 15% to see what happens to the data. To keep the 5% figures in the spreadsheet, you will need to insert a new column into your spreadsheet and give it the subheading label **Sale price +5%**. The figures can now be copied and pasted to a new part of the spreadsheet.

How to paste values to a new part of the spreadsheet

Highlight the data

→ Menu View

→ Paste special

→ Values

→ Paste the new values into a new column in the spreadsheet

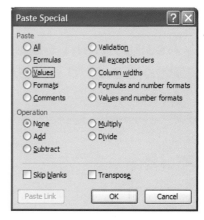

Figure 6.13 – Paste Special

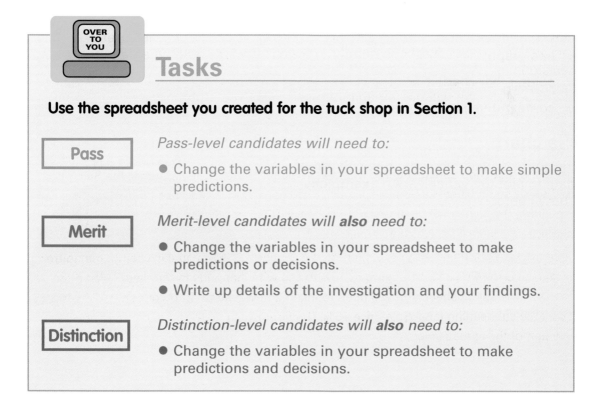

Tasks

Use the spreadsheet you created for the tuck shop in Section 1.

Pass

Pass-level candidates will need to:

● Change the variables in your spreadsheet to make simple predictions.

Merit

Merit-level candidates will also need to:

● Change the variables in your spreadsheet to make predictions or decisions.

● Write up details of the investigation and your findings.

Distinction

Distinction-level candidates will also need to:

● Change the variables in your spreadsheet to make predictions and decisions.

Section 5: Create a variety of charts

> **Assessment objective 5: *Analyse data using appropriate graphs/charts* is covered in this section.**

Skills

Charts

A variety of charts can be created in Microsoft Excel®. The following charts are the most common:

- pie chart;
- line graph;
- column/bar chart;
- comparative bar/line graph.

Pie chart

Pie charts usually use only one column of data to plot the variables. An example is shown here.

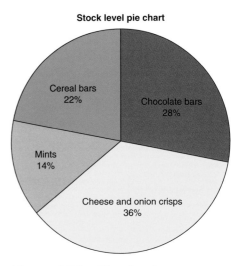

Figure 6.14 – Pie chart

Line graph

A line graph is used to plot independent and dependent variables (e.g. to show the frequency of data). An example is shown here.

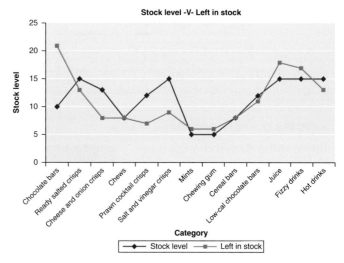

Figure 6.15 – Line graph

Comparative column/bar chart

A column/bar chart displays data in different categories or groups. An example is shown here.

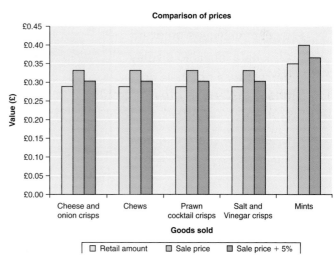

Figure 6.16 – Comparative column/bar chart

> **Continuous data:** data that can be measured on a scale (e.g. money, time, temperature).
>
> **Discrete data:** data where units of measurement cannot be split (e.g. there is nothing between one and two DVDs).

To create a chart/graph:

Highlight the data to be used in the chart

→ Click the chart wizard icon

→ Select chart type

→ Check that the data is displayed correctly in the preview window

→ Enter appropriate title and labels

→ Click legend to have the legend displayed on or off

→ Click data labels to display percentages or labels on different types of chart (e.g. pie)

→ Display the chart on a new sheet

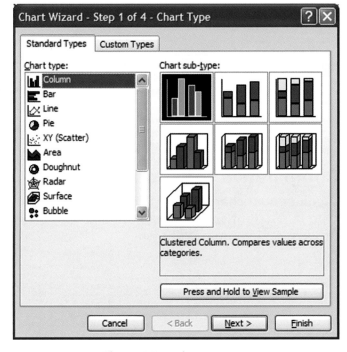

Figure 6.17 – Chart Wizard

Tasks

Use the spreadsheet you created for the tuck shop in Section 1.

Pass

Pass-level candidates will need to:

- Create at least two different types of graph/chart (these might not be the most appropriate type of chart for the data and might not be well labelled).

- Add an appropriate title to the charts and display appropriate legends, category names and percentage labels.

Merit

*Merit-level candidates will **also** need to:*

- Create at least one example of each type of graph, from line graph, bar chart and pie chart. At least one of these should compare values.

- Add appropriate titles and axis labels to the charts.

Distinction

*Distinction-level candidates will **also** need to:*

- Create at least one good example of each type of graph, from line graph, bar chart and pie chart.

Section 6: Record a simple macro

> **Assessment objective 6:** *Create macros to automate procedures in a spreadsheet* **is covered in this section.**

Skills

A macro automates a task or series of tasks. For example, if you regularly save and print your spreadsheet, you could record this as a macro, which would speed up the processing of this task – you would only need to click one button to save/print your spreadsheet instead of pressing two. The macro could also be used to recreate a worksheet on a monthly basis.

How to record a macro and a keyboard short cut

Tools menu

→   Macro

→   Record New Macro

→ Enter the macro name

→ In the Ctrl + box, enter letter/number that you will use to access the macro by using a keyboard short cut

→ Store Macro in: This Workbook

→ Click OK

→ Click on the Print icon

→ Stop the macro recording

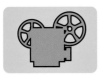

How to assign a button to the toolbar

View menu

→   Toolbars

→   Customize

→ Macros

→ Custom Button

→ Drag the custom button on to a toolbar

To assign a macro to this button:

Click on the button

→ Select the macro that you have created

→ OK

→ Test the macro to ensure that it works

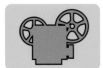

How to add a button to a sheet

Draw an object on the worksheet

→ Right-click to show the shortcut menu

→ Click Assign macro

→ Double-click Macro name

→ OK

How to format the object

Format

→ AutoShape

→ Color

→ Lines Tab

→ Fill

How to print out the macro code

To access the Visual Basic code that sits behind the macro:

Tools menu

→ Macro

→ Macros

→ Step into

→ The code is displayed and you can select print from here to print a copy of the code

Once you have printed out the code, this can be annotated by hand to show the contents of the macro you have created (e.g. highlight the code that says **ActiveWorkbook**. Save to show that the workbook has been saved as part of the macro).

Tasks

Use the spreadsheet you created for the tuck shop in Section 2.

Pass

Pass-level candidates will need to:

● Record a simple macro to automate at least one task and enable this macro to be run by either keyboard shortcut or a button on the sheet or on a toolbar.

● Access the macro code and print it out.

Merit

*Merit-level candidates will **also** need to:*

● Record a macro to automate a sequence of at least two tasks and enable this macro to be run by both keyboard shortcut and a button on the sheet or on the toolbar.

● Print out the code and annotate it to describe (in at least one sentence) what the macro does and how it can be run.

Distinction

*Distinction-level candidates will **also** need to:*

● Record two macros to automate a sequence of tasks and enable each of these macros to be run by both a keyboard shortcut and a button on the sheet or on the toolbar.

● Print out a copy of the code for each macro and annotate it to describe the function of at least three items of the macro code you have created.

Unit 7 Databases

Unit Overview

This unit will help you to develop a thorough knowledge and understanding of how to design, construct and interrogate a database.

Examples in this unit are based on Microsoft® Access™ 2003.

By working through the *Skills*, *How To* and *Tasks* sections in this unit, you will demonstrate all the skills required for Unit 7 and be able to:

- design a relational database to meet the needs of an organisation;
- construct a database according to a design;
- interrogate a database;
- create reports;
- create a user interface;
- test a database and make recommendations for improvements.

The How to sections in this unit are built around a party booking agency, and the Tasks sections are built around the customer details in a veterinary surgery.

Section 1: Design a relational database

Assessment objective 1: *Design a relational database to meet the needs of an organisation* is covered in this section.

You have been asked to create a relational database to record bookings for parties. The purpose of the database is for the Parties website to quickly book and organise themed parties, hosted by a party planner to ensure that the party runs smoothly. Parties can be booked via the Internet or by telephone, and the information needs to be stored in a relational database to prevent previous problems of overbooking. The database needs to include bookings, customers and party themes.

Before creating your database on the computer, it is best to plan the basic design of the database to ensure that it will suit your needs when you create it.

Skills

Design plan

You will need to draw up a sketch of a design plan for the relational database. This plan should include:

1 Table structure, which includes:

- primary keys;
- field names;
- field types;
- field lengths;
- validation rules;
- input masks.

2 Relationships between the different tables.

3 A data entry form, including combo boxes and customised forms.

See **designplanforpartydatabase.doc** on the CD

A relational database

A relational database stores information in one or more related tables. Related tables make querying the data easier, and this removes the need for duplicated data.

An entity relational diagram shows relationships to be created in the database. Different levels of relationships exist; these can be:

- one-to-one: both sides of the relationship only have a one-to-one relationship;
- one-to-many: one side has one and the other side has many variables;
- many-to-many: both sides of the relationship have many-to-many variables.

The diagrams shown here present an example of each type of relationship.

One-to-one relationship:

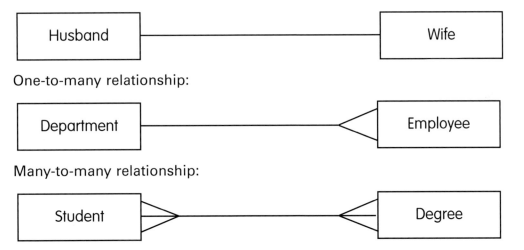

One-to-many relationship:

Many-to-many relationship:

This relational database avoids repeatedly entering the same data. For tables, single fields should only have a value for one thing. Take the example of a cars database, which might contain in one field 'blue Ford Focus'. This field contains three pieces of information – 'blue', 'Ford' and 'Focus', which will make it difficult later to query 'Ford cars'. It is therefore better to split this information into three fields.

Once you have drawn your design, you can create the database. The following information will help with this task.

Customer details table:

Customer details					
Cust ID	First Name	Last Name	Address1	Town	Postcode
501	John	Smith	1 The Grove	Chester	CB15 5XN
502	Alan	Clark	2 Bath Homes	Durham	DL16 6XN
503	Joanne	Davidson	3 Kings Road	Dundee	DL16 9RD
504	Janette	Dunkstable	4 Barrasford Road	Bristol	BS19 0DN
505	Matthew	Adams	5 Richmond Road	Cardiff	CR11 6FV
506	Natasha	Gasson	5 Canterbury Road	Leeds	LS21 1FF
507	Phillip	Gerry	7 Queens Drive	York	YO21 2FW
508	Graham	Edmondson	8 The Mansion	Durham	DH12 5NP
509	Ian	Hamilton	9 St James Road	Durham	DH13 5RR
510	Ryan	Tindale	10 Willowbank Road	Leeds	LS20 5NT
511	Samantha	Crabtree	11 The Denes	Chester	CB14 2NT
512	Sarah	Smith	12 Council Avenue	Liverpool	LS15 8RT
513	Steven	Wright	13 Sunderland Road	Manchester	MS13 2RF
514	Tom	Aisbitt	14 Chester Road	Durham	DL13 0JH
515	Tony	Clarkson	15 Durham Street	Durham	DL12 1JF
516	Phillipa	Jones	16 Rotary Way	Durham	DH14 3JN
517	Darrell	Hackett	17 Clive Road	York	YO03 7NZ
518	Darren	Jolley	18 Academy Road	Leeds	LS13 5HF
519	Elizabeth	Owen	19 Walkworth Avenue	Leeds	LS13 6PL
520	Andrew	Williams	20 Rothbury Road	Durham	DH13 5NT

Party themes table:

Party themes					
Party Theme	Suitable Age	Venue	Max Number	Min Number	Cost per head
Barbie	4	Durham	15	8	£7.50
Bob The Builder	3	Leeds	20	5	£6.95
Brides	18	Durham	30	10	£15.95
Pirates	3	Durham	15	6	£8.50
Vampires	18	York	30	10	£15.95

Party bookings table:

Party bookings							
Booking Ref	Cust ID	Date	Party Theme	Guests	Time	Party Cost	Employee ID
12573	501	01/12/2006	Pirates	5	18:00	£85.00	15
12590	502	02/12/2006	Bob The Builder	15	15:00	£75.00	16
12591	503	28/03/2007					0
12592	504	05/04/2007					0
12574	505	02/12/2006	Barbie	12	15:00	£75.00	16

You will need to add addional data to the Party themes and Party bookings tables to ensure that each table holds a minimum of 20 records.

How to add a primary key to a field within your database

Primary keys are used to identify the data in a database table that is dependent on a unique identifier. A primary key is one attribute (column) in a relation (table).

Open the customer details table in design view

→ Select the CustID field where the primary key is to be applied

→ Click the primary key button on the toolbar

Repeat this process for the other two tables.

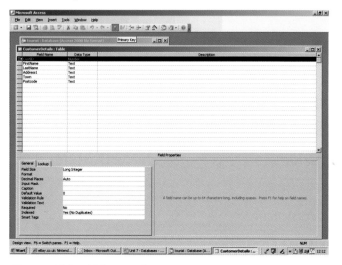

Figure 7.1 – Primary key

How to select field types

Appropriate field names should be included in the database (e.g. for surname you might use the field name 'LastName'). The three screen prints shown here show the field names selected for the Party bookings database and the field types set.

You can set different field types in Microsoft® Access™, such as date/time, text, number, currency, yes/no. This enables Microsoft® Access™ to set different characteristics, so that a number field can only hold numeric data. The following field types are available:

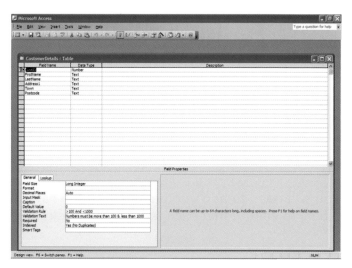

Figure 7.2 – Customer details table – selecting field types

- Text;
- Memo;
- Number;
- Date/Time;
- Currency;
- AutoNumber;
- Yes/No;
- OLE Object;
- Hyperlink;
- Lookup Wizard.

To change the field type:

Open the Customer details, Party bookings and Party themes tables

→ Click on the dropdown arrow in the data type column

→ Select the relevant characteristic

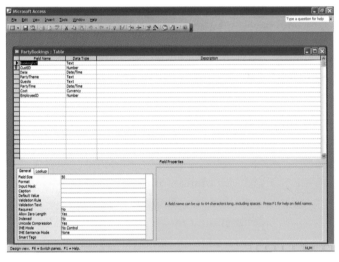

Figure 7.3 – Party bookings table – selecting field types

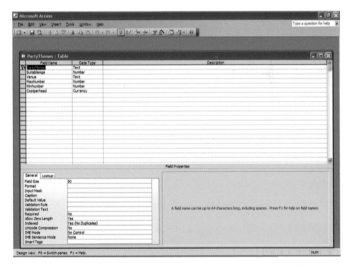

Figure 7.4 – Party themes table – selecting field types

How to change field lengths

Text usually defaults to a field length of 60; however, for shorter fields (e.g. Dr, Mr, Mrs), you might want to reduce the field size to allow a maximum of 5 characters. To change the field length:

Click in the Field Size towards the bottom of the design window

→ Key in the revised field size

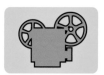

How to add validation rules and validation text

Validation of data within a database simply means that the data entered is checked to ensure that it makes sense to the computer (e.g. that a value such as age has been entered as a number). The following are examples of data validation:

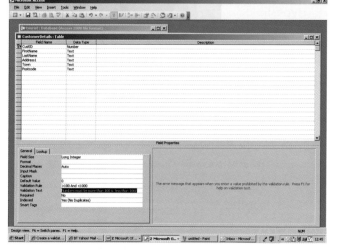

Figure 7.5 – Validation rule and text

- presence check: data has not been left blank;
- type check: age as a number;
- length check: surname is no more than 12 characters;
- range check: entered value falls within a range (e.g. £0–£1,250);
- format check: particular format (e.g. TS1 3DF);
- check digit: last digit at end of string is a check digit (e.g. ISBN number).

Just like input masks, you can create validation rules and messages to specify data input into specific fields. When data entered violates the validation rule, you can display validation text with a message for the user. For example:

Rule: Enter only Mr, Mrs would read: 'Mr' Or 'Mrs'

Message: Invalid entry

To create a validation rule:

Open the Customer details table in Design View

→ Key in the following details in the validation rule box towards the bottom of the page: >100 and <1000

→ Click in the validation text

→ Key in: Numbers must be more than 100 and less than 1000

How to create an input mask

In database tables/queries, input masks are used in fields to control the values that may be entered. Some examples of input masks from www.microsoft.com are shown in the table.

Input mask definition	Examples of values
(000) 000-0000	(206) 555-0248
(999) 999-9999!	(206) 555-0248 ( ) 555-0248
(000) AAA-AAAA	(206) 555-TELE
#999	-20 2000
>L????L?000L0	GREENGR339M3 MAY R 452B7
>L0L 0L0	T2F 8M4
00000-9999	98115- 98115-3007
>L<??????????????	Maria Pierre
ISBN 0-&&&&&&&&&-0	ISBN 1-55615-507-7 ISBN 0-13-964262-5
>LL00000-0000	DB51392-0493

To create an input mask on the Customer details table:

Open the table and select the postcode field

→ Click on the button at the end of the input mask

→ Next

→ Next

→ Choose the symbols in the mask (e.g. with and without the space)

→ Next

→ Finish

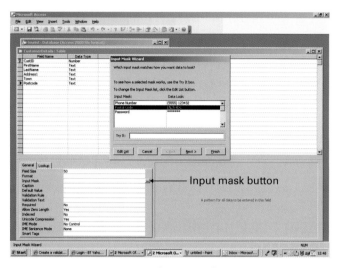

Input mask button

Figure 7.6 – Input Mask Wizard

How to create relationships between the different tables

This sets the relationship between tables in the database. The tables are linked by the unique identifier in each table. To create relationships:

Open the relationship window by clicking on the toolbar button

→ Drag the primary key field from the Customer details table (CustID) to the same named field in the Party bookings table (foreign key)

→ Relationship is created

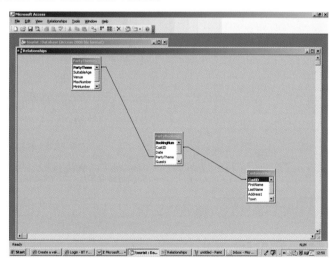

Figure 7.7 – Relationships

How to create a data entry form

A data entry form can be used to enter the details into a form instead of directly into a table. The form can include combo boxes (dropdown lists) to make the data selection easier, and the form can be customised.

Data entry forms offer a more user-friendly way of entering data into database tables. To create a form:

Click forms

- → New
- → Form Wizard
- → Select the Party bookings table for which the form is to be created
- → OK
- → Select all the fields to be displayed in the form
- → Next
- → Select the layout type (e.g. justified)
- → Next
- → Select the background (e.g. rice paper)
- → Next
- → Add a title for the form **Party bookings**
- → Finish

How to create a combo box on the form

Open the Party bookings form in Design View

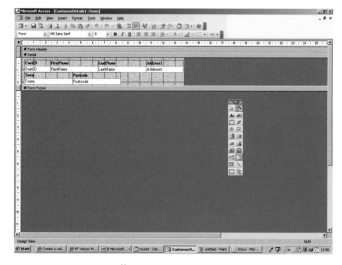

Figure 7.8 – Toolbox

→ Create a dropdown box by selecting the Combo Box icon from the Toolbox (see **Combo box button** on CD)

Draw the shape of your box onto your form, and decide whether you want to type the values in as a list or look up the values in a table or query.

Combo Box Wizard

Select: 'I will type in the values that I want'

→ Next

→ Select Party Themes table

→ Select Party Themes field

→ Next

→ (apply any sort)

→ Next

→ Store that value in this field and select Party Theme

→ Next

→ Finish

Figure 7.9 – Combo Box Wizard

Place on form so no text overlaid

Ensure that the form still has a consistent layout (e.g. font, style). Select Party Theme for each of the bookings in the database to check that your combo box works.

Tasks

You have been employed by the local veterinary surgery, ANIVETS, and asked to create a database to record the customer details. The surgery requires a database to hold the details of the patients, their owners and any treatments that have been carried out, so that invoices and letters can be despatched systematically. The database needs to be a relational database and hold a minimum of three tables. The tables can be:

- pets;

- owners;

- treatments.

Appropriate field names, field types, validation rules and input masks should be designed and created.

The vet requires reports to be run showing the owner's details, the pet's details and any treatments carried out, so that invoices can be issued following any treatment, and mailshots offering new products sent to customers.

Some data for your database is shown here; however, you may want to search the Internet to find suitable data to create your database tables. You will need to ensure each table holds a minimum of 20 records.

Owners' table:

Owners' details					
Cust ID	First Name	Last Name	Address1	Town	Postcode
306A1	John	Tindale	1 The Grove	York	YO21 2FW
306A2	Alan	Smith	2 Bath Homes	Leeds	LS21 1FF
306A3	Joanne	Hamilton	3 Kings Road	Leeds	LS20 5NT
306A4	Janette	Gerry	4 Barrasford Road	Durham	DL16 6XN
306A5	Matthew	Gasson	5 Richmond Road	Durham	DH12 5NP
306A6	Natasha	Edmondson	5 Canterbury Road	Durham	DH13 5RR
306A7	Phillip	Dunkstable	7 Queens Drive	Dundee	DL16 9RD
306A8	Graham	Davidson	8 The Mansion	Chester	CB15 5XN
306A9	Ian	Crabtree	9 St James Road	Chester	CB14 2NT
306A10	Ryan	Clark	10 Willowbank Road	Cardiff	CR11 6FV
306A11	Samantha	Adams	11 The Denes	Bristol	BS19 0DN
306A12	Sarah	Wright	12 Council Avenue	York	YO03 7NZ
306A13	Steven	Williams	13 Sunderland Road	Manchester	MS13 2RF
306A14	Tom	Smith	14 Chester Road	Liverpool	LS15 8RT
306A15	Tony	Owen	15 Durham Street	Leeds	LS13 5HF
306A16	Phillipa	Jones	16 Rotary Way	Leeds	LS13 6PL
306A17	Darrell	Jolley	17 Clive Road	Durham	DL13 0JH
306A18	Darren	Hackett	18 Academy Road	Durham	DL12 1JF
306A19	Elizabeth	Clarkson	19 Walkworth Avenue	Durham	DH14 3JN
306A20	Andrew	Aisbitt	20 Rothbury Road	Durham	DH13 5NT

Pets' table:

Pet Name	Pet Type	CustID	Age	Notes
Barbie	Cat	306A9	5	Lost sight in one eye
Vixon	Dog	306A11	0.6	
Sooty	Dog	306A3	2	Broken ankle
Mickey	Rabbit	306A7	0.3	Left hind leg missing
Tom	Cat	306A12	3	

Treatment table:

CustID	Treatment Date	Treatment Type	Cost	Paid
306A9	01/03/06	Dental care	£50	Y
306A11	01/04/07	Eye care	£60	N
306A3	31/05/06	Diabetes	£35	N
306A7	28/11/06	Neutering	£125	N
306A12	20/05/06	Worming	£25	N

> **Pass**

Pass-level candidates will need to:

- Draw a design sketch of a relational database, which will need to include table structure (primary keys, field names, field types, field lengths).
- Show the relationships between the tables.
- Create at least one form template.

<table>
<tr><td>**Merit**</td><td>*Merit-level candidates will **also** need to include:*</td></tr>
</table>

- Validation rules and combo boxes in the design.
- Forms for each of the tables created.

<table>
<tr><td>**Distinction**</td><td>*Distinction-level candidates will **also** need to include:*</td></tr>
</table>

- At least one input mask.
- Customised forms for each table.
- All choices will be appropriate.

Section 2: Create the database

Assessment objective 2: *Create a functioning database of at least 20 records in each table* **is covered in this section.**

Skills

You will need to create your database based on the design plan that you drew in Section 1 of this unit. The database must work and must include at least three tables, with 20 records in each table. Make up some party bookings or look at the examples in the screen prints shown here.

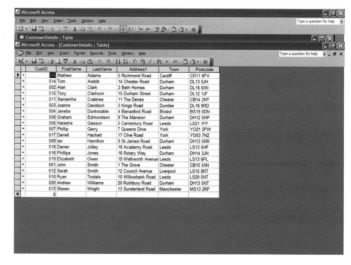

Figure 7.10 – Customer details table

Using the data from Section 1, you are going to create your three tables for the Party bookings database, and set the field types, lengths, any validation rules and input masks to match the design plan. Then you will need to create the relationships between each table. Your database tables should be similar to those shown here but will contain at least 20 records.

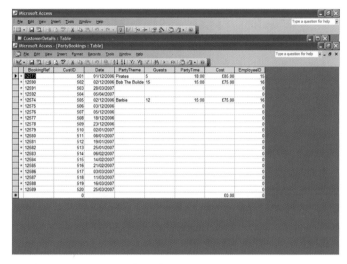

Figure 7.11 – Party bookings

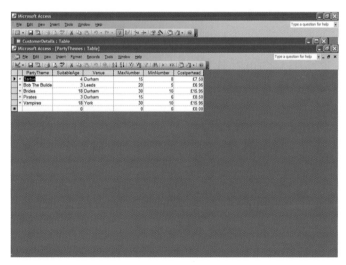

Figure 7.12 – Party themes table

How to create a form

Click Form

→ New

→ Form Wizard

→ Select the Party bookings table

→ Select all fields

→ Next

→ Select layout

→ Next

→ Choose a style

→ Next

→ Enter a title for the form **Party bookings**

→ Finish

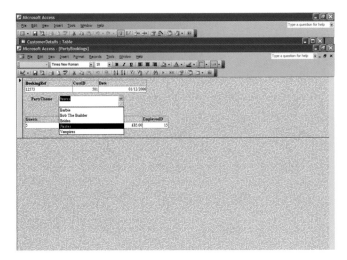

Figure 7.13 – Create a form (this shows drop-down lists for Party Themes)

How to customise a form

Once the form has been created, you can customise it by adding pictures, changing the font styles/sizes and changing the background colour.

Insert pictures into a form:

Open the form by clicking on the design button on the toolbar

→ Insert menu

→ Picture

→ Select a picture to be inserted on the background

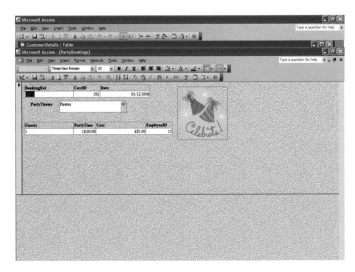

Figure 7.14 – Insert pictures into a form

Change font styles/sizes:

Open the form by clicking on the design button on the toolbar

- → Select the BookingRef, CustID and Date text boxes
- → Click on the font selection box and change the font style to Arial Rounded size 12
- → Repeat for all text boxes on the form
- → Ensure that all the data is still shown in full

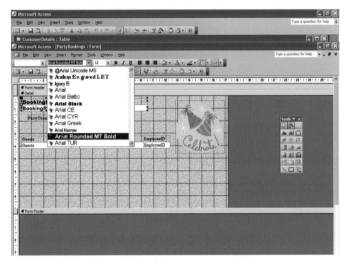

Figure 7.15 – Change front styles/sizes

Change background colour:

Open the form by clicking on the design button on the toolbar

- → Right-click in the main part of the form (Detail)
- → Click the fill/back colour button

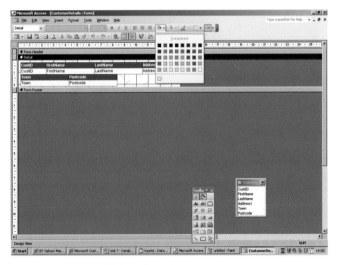

Figure 7.16 – Fill/back colour

Tasks

Use the veterinary scenario on page 255, or use your own scenario and the plan you created in Section 1 of this unit, Create a Database.

| Pass |

Pass-level candidates will need to:

- Create a relational database that includes three tables and a minimum of 20 records in each table.
- Create a form for at least one of the tables, to help with data entry, and create 20 bookings that are related.

| Merit |

*Merit-level candidates will **also** need to:*

- Create a form for each of the tables created.
- Ensure that the database reflects the design work undertaken.

| Distinction |

*Distinction-level candidates will **also** need to:*

- Customise the forms created for each table (e.g. change the font styles/sizes, insert pictures and change the colour schemes).
- Ensure that the database matches exactly the design work undertaken.

Section 3: Interrogate the database

> **Assessment objective 3:** *Interrogate the database* is covered in this section.

Skills

The data within the database can be sorted in a number of ways, for example:

- alphabetically;
- numerically;
- by more than one column.

Simple queries

Simple queries can be created within the database to search for and find specific results which match a given criteria; for example, you might want to search for all 'red' cars in a database. Microsoft® Access™ then returns the results showing all the 'red' cars.

Multiple queries can be created to find more than one item within a database; for example, you could search for 'Ford' and 'red' to return the results showing all 'red Ford' cars. However, you can also use multiple queries in the same field (e.g. 'Ford' and 'BMW') and Microsoft® Access™ will return the results showing all 'Ford' and 'BMW' cars.

Complex queries (not, between, and)

Complex queries look at more than one field. They are made up of two or more simple queries joined together by logical operators, such as AND, OR and NOT; for example, 'Ford' AND 'BMW'.

The table shown here sets out the logical operators which can be used in Microsoft® Access™.

NOT	WHERE **NOT** (Author = Jones) This will search for all records where the author is NOT Jones.
AND	WHERE Author = Jones **AND** Date = 1999 This will search for all records where the author is Jones AND who had a book published in 1999.
OR	WHERE Author = Jones **OR** Date = 1999 This will search for all records where the author is Jones OR who had a book published in 1999.

Example range operators to be used in queries

The table below shows the range operators that can be used in Microsoft® Access™.

Operators	Description
>	Greater than
<	Less than
>=	Greater than or equal to
<=	Less than or equal to
<>	Not equal to

Wildcard or like queries

The asterisk (*), per cent sign (%), question mark (?), underscore character (_), number sign (#), exclamation mark (!), hyphen (-) and brackets ([ ]) are wildcard characters. These can be used in queries and expressions to include all records, filenames or other items that begin with specific characters or match a certain pattern.

Queries from linked tables

Both simple and complex criteria can be used in single or linked tables. More than one table can be added to the query design and then data selected from both tables.

How to sort data in the table

Open the Customer details table and highlight the CustID column

→ Click A–Z for ascending or Z–A for descending

To sort on more than one field in the database, it is a good idea to create a query and sort the data into ascending or descending order within the query.

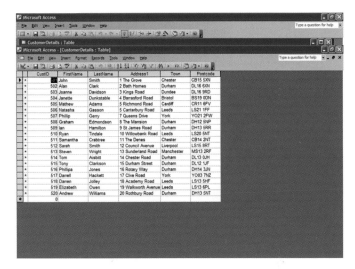

Figure 7.17 – Sort data

How to create a query to sort two columns of data

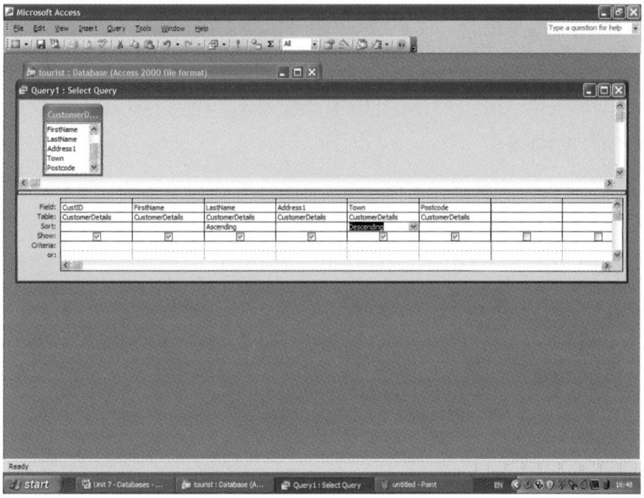

Query menu

→ New

→ Design View

→ OK

→ Select the Customer details table

→ Add

→ Close

→ Transfer all the required fields to the bottom half of the database screen by double-clicking on each field name

Figure 7.18 – Sort query

Sort the **LastName** field into ascending order and **Town** into descending order, as shown in the screen print.

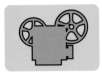

How to create a simple query

The party
bookings
organiser wants
to find all the customers who live
in Durham. The most efficient way
to do this is to create a new query.

Query menu

→ New

→ Design View

→ OK

→ Select the Customer details
  table

→ Add

→ Close

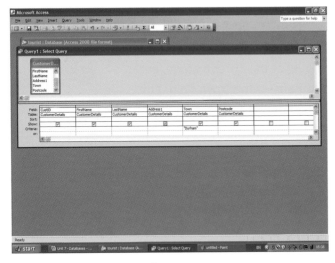

Figure 7.19 – Criteria for a query

→ Transfer all the fields to the bottom half of the database screen by double-clicking
  on each field name

Enter the criteria (e.g. Durham, as shown in the screen print), then click on the red
exclamation mark on the toolbar and run the query – the details of all the customers
who live in Durham will be displayed. Save this query as **Durham**.

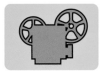

How to create a multiple query on more than one field

Create the query as indicated above; at the criteria stage, enter 'Durham' in the Town field, and '*road' in the Address1 field. All customers who have 'road' and 'Durham' in their address records will be returned by Microsoft® Access™. Save this query as **Durham Road**.

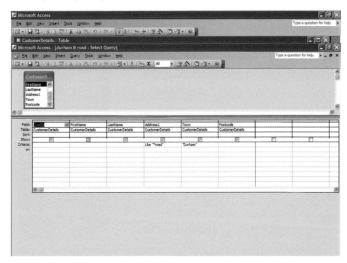

Figure 7.20 – Multiple query on more than one field

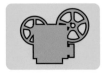

How to create a multiple query within the same field

Create the query as indicated above; at the criteria stage, enter **Durham** OR **Leeds** in the Town field. Those customers who live in either Durham or Leeds will now be displayed.

Tip: If you enter **Durham** AND **Leeds** instead of **Durham** OR **Leeds**, no records will be shown – this would mean someone would have to live in two places!

Save this query as **Durham and Leeds**.

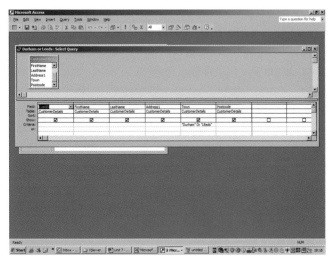

Figure 7.21 – Multiple query within the same field

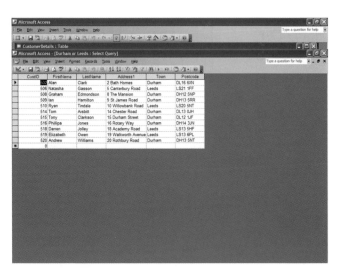

Figure 7.22 – Records from multiple query within the same field

How to create a complex query on linked tables

Add all three tables to the database query and select the following fields:

- Customer details table (CustID, First Name, Last Name, Address1, Town, Postcode);
- Party bookings table (PartyTheme).

Find those bookings where the party theme is Barbie and the party is booked during December 2006.

Save this query as **Barbie – 12-06**.

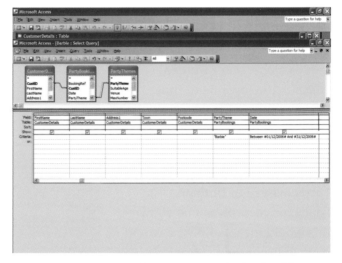

Figure 7.23 – Complex query on linked tables

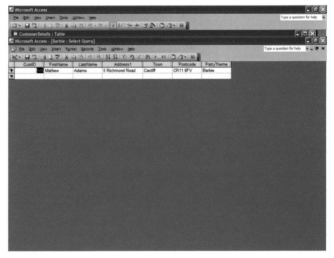

Figure 7.24 – Results from complex query on linked tables

Describe the purpose of the queries

Once you have run all your queries, you will need to explain to the examiner/moderator what you have done and describe the purpose of the queries; for example, the party organiser wants to find out which party themes are the most popular.

Tasks

Use the veterinary scenario on page 255.

| Pass |

Pass-level candidates will need to:

- Sort one table.
- Carry out one query using simple criteria.
- Carry out one query using multiple criteria on linked tables.
- Print out each query and annotate each printout, describing the purpose of each query.

| Merit |

*Merit-level candidates will **also** need to:*

- Carry out a sort on more than one field.
- Carry out one query using complex criteria on linked tables.
- Print out each query and annotate each printout, explaining the range of queries used.

| Distinction |

*Distinction-level candidates will **also** need to:*

- Carry out two complex queries on linked tables.
- Print out each query and annotate each printout, fully justifying the range of queries used.

Section 4: Create reports

> **Assessment objective 4:** *Create reports* **is covered in this section.**

Skills

Microsoft® Access™ allows you to create a variety of reports to display the information from your tables and/or queries more effectively. The reports you produce should include a range of standard templates, and for the merit- and distinction-level candidates the report templates should be customised.

How to create a standard report

Create a report based on the query you created in Section 3 for customers who live in Durham.

Click on the reports

- → New
- → Report Wizard
- → Select the query **Durham**
- → OK
- → Select all the fields to be displayed in the report
- → Next
- → Select any fields to be sorted
- → Next
- → Decide on the layout of the report
- → Next
- → Choose a style
- → Add a title
- → Finish

Your completed report will now be displayed.

You can customise this report to display the details more effectively, by changing the fonts and background colours, and ensuring that all the data is shown in full.

How to create a customised report

Click on design to open the report **Durham** in Design View

→ Right-click on an area within the design (e.g. details)

→ Choose a fill colour to change the background colour

→ Change the font style/size by selecting the text boxes and then changing the font style/size

→ Save and preview the report

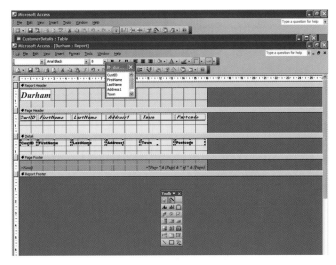

Figure 7.25 – Customised report

Tasks

Use the veterinary scenario on page 255.

Pass

Pass-level candidates will need to:

● Produce a report for each of the queries created.

● Choose a range of different templates to display these reports.

Merit

*Merit-level candidates will **also** need to:*

● Customise one of the reports.

Distinction

*Distinction-level candidates will **also** need to:*

● Customise each of the reports using different customisation (e.g. colour, fonts, adding pictures).

Section 5: Create a user interface

Assessment objective 5: *Create a user interface* is covered in this section.

Skills

A user interface or switchboard can be created, which gives users access to different sections of the database; for example:

- forms;
- queries;
- reports.

The interface should make use of a range of macros, which can improve efficiency for the user and allows the novice user to run complex queries/reports without having advanced knowledge/understanding of Microsoft® Access™ databases.

You can create a switchboard to make it easier for the user to operate the database. This switchboard would include the following buttons:

- linking to the forms;
- linking to the queries;
- linking to the different reports.

The first thing you need to do is create the macros for the menu and then create the command buttons.

How to create a macro

You are going to create a macro to open the Party bookings form.

Click on Macros

- → New
- → Click on the Action dropdown menu and select Open Form
- → At the bottom of the screen, click on Form Name and select Party bookings

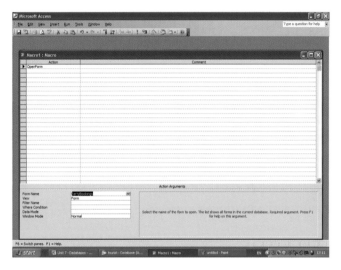

Figure 7.26 – Party bookings form

How to create a macro to run a query, print preview and print out the query

A macro can be created that runs a query and then displays a completed report for the user.

Click on Macros

- → New
- → Open Query – Durham or Leeds
- → Select Open Report – Durham or Leeds
- → Change view to Print Preview
- → Select Printout from underneath Open Query

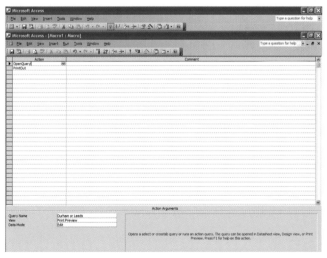

Figure 7.27 – Create a macro

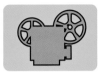

How to create a switchboard

The switchboard you create will contain a number of buttons, allowing the user to easily click on a button to open and run queries and reports.

Click on Forms

→ New

→ Design View

→ OK (you do not need to choose any tables/queries, as this form will not be bound to a table or query)

→ A blank form appears

→ Maximise the window and resize the form (approximately 12 × 6 cm)

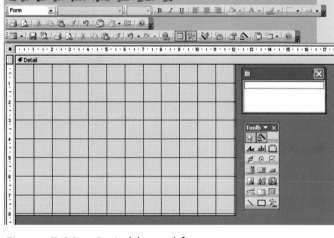

Figure 7.28 – Switchboard form

Draw a box with the label tool across the width of your page

→ Type in the box **Party themes menu**

→ Increase the font size and centre the text within the box

→ Draw a command button and place it in your form, towards the left margin

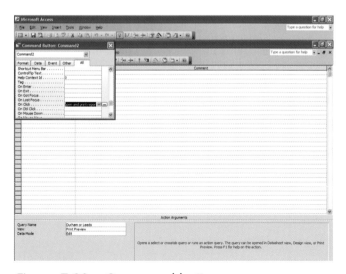

Figure 7.29 – Command button

→ The wizard will start

→ Click Cancel (we will assign our own macro to this button)

→ Change the text 'Command2' to read 'Add Customer Details'

Now that the buttons have been created, you need to tell each button what to do to open the relevant forms.

Right-click on the button, select Properties

→ In the On Click box, click on the dropdown arrow and select the correct macro for each button (e.g. to open the members form, select the Openpartybookings macro)

→ Close this window and repeat for your second box

Create a button to run the **Durham or Leeds** query and report – you can copy and paste one of the buttons you created earlier, and rename the button and change the properties, as shown in the screen print.

How to customise the switchboard

Now that you have created your switchboard and buttons, you can customise the display by changing the background colours, colour of buttons, fonts, and so on.

Right-click in the form and select Properties

→ Select Format to change the background colour

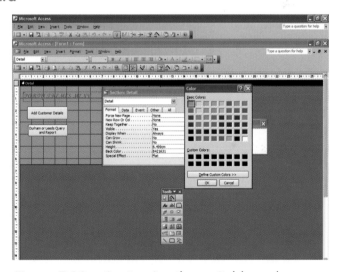

Figure 7.30 – Customise the switchboard

How to make your switchboard load

To create a switchboard to load at the start-up of the database:

Click Tools

→ Startup

→ Select Switchboard from the dropdown menu Display Form/Page

Test that the switchboard works on opening.

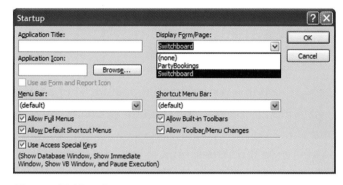

Figure 7.31 – Startup

Alternatively, you can create a shortcut on the desktop to the switchboard form, so that when the database is opened, the switchboard is the only screen the user can see:

In the database object window, right-click on the switchboard form

→ Select Create shortcut to the desktop

→ The form will be shown on the desktop

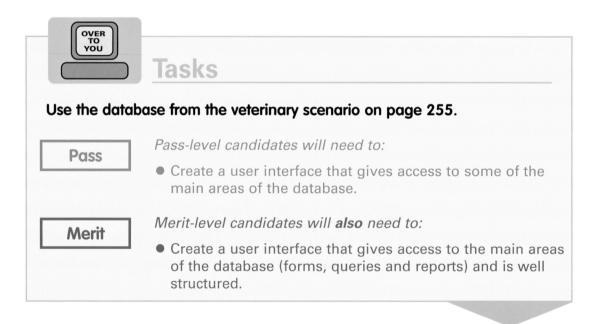

Tasks

Use the database from the veterinary scenario on page 255.

Pass

Pass-level candidates will need to:

● Create a user interface that gives access to some of the main areas of the database.

Merit

*Merit-level candidates will **also** need to:*

● Create a user interface that gives access to the main areas of the database (forms, queries and reports) and is well structured.

*Distinction-level candidates will **also** need to:*

● Create a fully customised and easy-to-use user interface, giving access to the main areas of the database.

Section 6: Test the database

Assessment objective 6: *Test the database* is covered in this section.

Skills

Once the database has been created, you will need to create a test plan to show the areas of the database to be tested (e.g. accessing the database from the user interface). The test plan will need to be carried out and evidence produced through completion of the test plan, or by using a checklist to show the testing that has been carried out. If any issues arise from the testing (e.g. one of the macros to access the form does not work), you will need to amend your database to ensure that it is fully functioning.

Here is an example test plan.

Test	Test purpose	Test data to be used	Expected result	Actual result
A	Check that the postcodes have been entered using the validation rules/input mask	DH1 8JH	Rejected	
B	Check that the CustID field only accepts whole numbers	1.20	Rejected	

Tasks

Use the database from the veterinary scenario on page 255.

Pass

Pass-level candidates will need to:

- Create a test plan that covers some elements of the database, and check that a query runs correctly.
- Follow the test plan to identify any changes to be made to the database.
- Indicate on the test plan the outcomes of the testing.
- If any improvements are required, carry out these improvements in the database.
- Provide evidence in the form of screenshots showing the improvements made.

Merit

*Merit-level candidates will **also** need to:*

- Create a test plan that covers the main elements of the database.

Distinction

*Distinction-level candidates will **also** need to:*

- Create a test plan that covers all the main elements of the database.

Unit 19 Application of data logging

Unit overview

This unit will help you to develop knowledge and understanding of how data logging can be used in a variety of situations. Data are raw figures used to produce information, such as that used by shops to monitor your buying habits via a bonus card, allowing them to target marketing to your purchasing trends, hoping you will spend more with them in the future.

By working through the *Skills*, *How to* and *Tasks* sections in this unit, you will demonstrate all the skills required for Unit 19 and be able to:

- investigate an application of data logging;
- investigate the hardware used in data logging;
- set up and carry out an investigation(s) using data logging;
- evaluate data-logging activities.

The How to and Tasks sections for Sections 1 and 2 in this unit are built around a supermarket checkout.

The How to and Tasks sections for Sections 3 and 4 are built around a classroom/laboratory experiment.

Section 1: Investigate an application of data logging

> **Assessment objective 1:** *Investigate an application of data logging* is covered in this section.

Data has to be captured using some form of data capture (e.g. barcodes, questionnaires or sensors). Once data has been collected, it needs to be logged. Data logging involves collecting different readings, using sensors and processing this data using a computer. Today it is even possible to capture medical data at a distance, using sensors, rather than using sticky pads to monitor heart rates.

Skills

There are a variety of different data-logging applications, including:

- **environmental monitoring** (e.g. monitoring the temperature, hours of sunshine);
- **logistics tracking** (e.g. tracking parcels);
- **sports training** (e.g. cardiovascular rate);
- **security monitoring** (e.g. infrared sensors for detecting intruders);
- **medical applications** (e.g. blood pressure monitors).

Investigation

You will need to carry out an investigation into data logging within an organisation you are familiar with or have access to, and produce a written report or illustrated talk. Sources of information for your report or illustrated talk could be:

- visits to the organisation that you are investigating;
- company reports;

- product catalogues;
- product manuals;
- installation instructions.

An important source of information for any of these is the Internet, and it is probably worthwhile to create a 'Data logging' folder in your Bookmarks or Favorites folder in your Internet browser.

How to set up your bookmarks folder in the Mozilla Firefox® web browser

Other browsers, such as Opera or Microsoft Internet Explorer®, offer much the same facilities, though Microsoft Internet Explorer® uses the term Favorites for what the others call bookmarks.

Open the browser
- → Click on Bookmarks in the menu at the top of the window
- → Choose Organise Bookmarks

Figure 19.1 – Organise Bookmarks

Choose New Folder
- → Give your new folder a meaningful name and (optional) description

Figure 19.2 – Properties for 'New Folder'

Click on Bookmarks again

→ Select your new folder – you will see that it is empty

Navigate to a web page that interests you

→ Click on Bookmark This Page (or press Control + D)

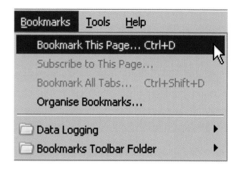

Figure 19.3 – Bookmark This Page

Choose to add your new bookmark to your new folder

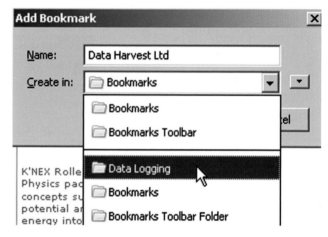

Figure 19.4 – Add Bookmark

Click OK

→ Check that the bookmark has been added to the new folder

Repeat for each website in this category.

Figure 19.5 – Bookmark in new folder

Skills

Your report or illustrated talk should describe:

- the purpose of the application;
- the hardware and software used;
- description of the application in use;
- data logging carried out;
- advantages and disadvantages of the application.

The purpose of the application

If you think of a supermarket checkout, the shop will want to record:

- prices and quantities of goods sold;
- time of day;
- number of items per customer;
- the effect of 'special offers' or other promotions on sales;
- customer details linked to purchasing decisions through an optional 'loyalty card'.

When carrying out your investigation, you will need to include the purpose of the application of data logging.

The hardware and software used

When carrying out your investigation, you should observe the computer hardware and software used for the data-logging operation. For example, equipment at a typical checkout will probably include:

- barcode scanner (built in to the till);
- a handheld barcode scanner for large or difficult items;
- magnetic card reader for some loyalty cards;
- smart-card reader for chip-and-pin cards, such as credit and debit cards;
- scales for loose goods sold by weight (note the need for calibration of these);
- software – probably proprietary and supplied with the hardware as a package.

Description of the application in use

Consider how the data logging in the supermarket is carried out in real life. How is the data collected? What happens if there is an equipment failure, such as a broken sensor, or even something as simple as a damaged price tag?

Data logging carried out

Everyone using the supermarket has to pass through the checkout and all goods sold are recorded. If payment is made by any form of card, the card has to be validated to make sure that it is genuine and, if it is, the purchases recorded. The record of these transactions also becomes part of the data recorded by the card issuer. Where the customer presents a loyalty card, their spending can be linked directly to them as an individual, and the supermarket can use this information to make targeted special offers to both individuals and groups of consumers. Information that is collected in real time to calculate the customer's itemised bill is also stored for later analysis. It may also be used to update stock records and may feed into the wider logistics systems of the company.

Advantages and disadvantages of the application

Some of the advantages of using data-logging equipment are:

- sensor readings (barcodes or scales in this case) are faster than a till operator keying in data derived from product labels;

- there is less scope for human error – the data logging requires little human input;

- as members of the public become more familiar with the technology of self-service tills (where the shopper does the scanning) and other data logging, data collection costs will be reduced even further;

- price and quantity data would have to be collected anyway; data logging records data in a way that makes it easy to derive further information, such as spending patterns though time or peak hours for shopping, by calculating these variables from the raw data.

Some of the disadvantages of using data-logging software are:

- the equipment is expensive and therefore represents an overhead to the company using it;

- the equipment is complex and needs a well-organised technical support operation to keep it running;

- the cost of the equipment is such that smaller companies may be excluded from using it, so there may be a social cost in terms of decreased competition;

- both staff and customers may feel alienated by the impersonality of the system – consider the resistance that many customers express towards self-service tills, where they do the data logging themselves and there is no human contact in the course of the transaction;

- equipment failures can disrupt the whole operation – a single missing barcode can cause a delay, which rapidly results in a tailback of customers waiting for service;

- a large-scale failure – such as loss of mains power – can close the operation down instantly and without warning, possibly for several hours.

Tasks

Carry out an investigation into an organisation that you are familiar with or have access to. The investigation can be carried out by visiting the organisation, carrying out interviews or researching information from company reports or the Internet. Your investigation could look at monitoring traffic or environmental changes, or you could link this unit into any science coursework.

You will need to produce a talk or short report.

Pass

Pass-level candidates will need to:

- State the purpose of a data-logging application.
- Describe the main hardware and software used.
- Provide a description of the application in use.
- Explain how data logging is carried out.
- Describe what data is collected.

- Explain how data is stored.
- Analyse the data.
- Describe the advantages of data logging in this situation.

A table could also be completed, like the one shown below.

Activity	Purpose of application	Hardware and software used	Application in use	How data logging is carried out	What data is collected	How data is stored	Analysis of data	Advantages

Merit

*Merit-level candidates will **also** need to:*

- Explain the advantages and disadvantages of data logging in this situation.

Distinction

*Distinction-level candidates will **also** need to:*

- Describe how sensors are used.
- Explain the advantages and disadvantages and the limitations of using data logging to meet the needs of the situation, making clear comparisons with alternative methods.

As an alternative to the table method of organising your findings, you could use each of the table headings to produce a continuous narrative report along the lines of:

Heading (e.g. 'What data is collected?')

- item one;

- item two;

- item three.

Then add a few sentences to summarise the items in the bulleted list.

Remember to use any pictures, diagrams or graphs that you think are appropriate to your report.

Section 2: Investigate hardware and software used in data logging

Assessment objective 2: *Investigate the hardware and software used in data logging* **is covered in this section.**

Skills

You will now need to investigate the hardware and software used in data-logging applications. Some of this information could come from the investigation you carried out in Section 1.

You will then need to broaden your enquiry to ensure that it covers both types of data-logging systems (i.e. dedicated data-logging devices and devices that are attached to a computer through one of its ports). You will also need to investigate a wider range of sensors. The range of sensors can include:

- infrared sensors, which can be used in rooms as part of a burglar alarm system;

- push-switch sensors, which are used in computers, TVs and monitors;

- light sensors, which measure low light and bright light to turn lights on and off in houses;

- light 'gates' or switches, which turn on or off as an object moves past them;
- heat sensors, which turn the central heating on and off when the temperature gets to a certain level within a house.

Some Internet research will be sufficient to provide some examples. For example, using the search terms 'data-logging sensors' or 'data-logging applications' in a search engine such as AltaVista will produce masses of information. Your problem is more likely to be the sheer amount of information available, rather than any lack of it. Many commercial sites provide manuals and product catalogues which you can download for further use. Some sites that are worth looking at are:

www.signatrol.com

www.omniinstruments.co.uk

www.peaksensors.co.uk

www.dataharvest.com

www.howstuffworks.com

There is a search facility on the site and the problem is, once again, not a lack of information, but rather the large volume you will need to evaluate in order to decide what is useful to you.

In addition, you should locate other sites and extract the information that you find for use in your report.

Calibration

Once a sensor has been installed it must be calibrated, which means that it needs to be tested and adjusted; for example, if a weight sensor is being used, the scale needs to be checked and adjusted to zero if there is nothing on it. If you used the supermarket example in Section 1, you could refer back to the scales used in a typical checkout operation.

Types of data-logging systems

There are different types of data-logging systems, for example;

- Dedicated data loggers: these collect the data and then have to be connected to a PC so that the data can be transferred from the data logger to the PC.

● Sensors attached to PCs through an interface: data is collected by the sensor and then automatically transferred to a PC via a phone or radio link.

Manufacturers' websites can be a good source of information on these systems.

Description of types of data-logging systems to include

You will need to write a short paragraph about the main differences between two types identified. It would be useful to include a specific example of each type, and you could refer to your investigation in Section 1, as well as any product information from manufacturers' websites, product catalogues, product manuals, and so on.

Identify and describe different types of sensors

You must identify and describe at least four different types of sensors. Some examples of sensors are:

● digital sensors (e.g. switches/gates);

● dissolved oxygen;

● humidity;

● light;

● magnetic field strength (Hall probe);

● pH;

● pressure;

● sound;

● temperature.

You will need to write about:

● How the sensor works (i.e. how does it collect the data?). For example, you may want to look at how a light gate works. This is usually a U-shaped piece of hardware with an infrared emitter and detector. They come in different sizes (anything from 75 millimetres to 1 metre) and can be used to measure accurately the time taken for an object – anything from a toy car to a person – to pass between the transmitter and the receiver ends of the gate.

● What software application is used and how the is data transferred to a PC. You will need to describe how the data captured by a device is used. How is the data transferred from the logging device? Is it via a cable to a PC port or a wireless link? Or does a dedicated logging device record the data internally and then transmit it as a batch job later?

(*Tip:* You will find that some sound meters support both methods of collection, storage and transmission.)

Another consideration is the software used to analyse and present the information. Many data loggers use proprietary software and file formats that are specific to that application. Others will allow you to export the data in a file type such as comma separated value (CSV). This format can be imported into a spreadsheet application such as Open Office Calc or Microsoft Excel®. Another more modern format for this purpose is Extensible Markup Language (XML), and there are utilities available to convert between the two.

● Whether the user needs to calibrate the sensor, and what calibration is required. Some sensors, such as the U-shaped light gate, do not need to be calibrated; the two measuring points are a fixed distance apart. A scale, on the other hand, needs to start weighing from zero, and will need to be set up (calibrated) to ensure that it starts from zero and measures accurately.

● Reason for calibration (*for one sensor only*). You will need to take one sensor as an example and explain why it needs to be calibrated. For example, a scale used in a laboratory experiment must start from zero and weigh accurately through its range. If it did not do this, any experiment that used it would be based on unreliable data and its conclusions would be invalid. In terms of the supermarket example in Section 1, for example, the accuracy of scales is regulated by law and may be checked from time to time by local government inspectors.

● How to calibrate (*for one sensor only*). You need to describe how to calibrate one particular sensor, and this can be done be looking at the manual for a device that you have access to, or even on the manufacturer's website. For example, the Oxygen Sensor from Data Harvest has a downloadable manual – in Adobe® Portable Document Format (PDF) – which gives details of how to calibrate that particular device. The Data Harvest website (www.data-harvest.co.uk) has a search facility, allowing you to search for the term 'oxygen sensor' to find the information you want.

Tasks

Carry out some research on the Internet or by visiting different organisations, and then produce a talk.

Pass

Pass-level candidates will need to:

- Show the main differences between dedicated data loggers and sensors attached to PCs through interfaces, and describe one example of each.

- Describe examples of at least four different types of sensor and provide an example of an application where each might be used, stating clearly the purpose of the application and the data being monitored.

Merit

*Merit-level candidates will **also** need to:*

- Describe examples of at least five different types of sensor, and for each one:

    1 give a brief overview of how the sensor works;

    2 describe one application where the sensor might be used, stating clearly the purpose of the application and the data being monitored;

    3 state whether or not the sensor needs to be calibrated by the user.

Distinction

*Distinction-level candidates will **also** need to:*

- Compare the advantages and disadvantages of the two types of system.

- Describe examples of at least six different types of sensor, and for each one:

    1 give a description of how the sensor works;

2 describe one application where the sensor might be used, stating clearly the purpose of the application and the data being monitored;

3 state whether or not the sensor needs to be calibrated by the user.

● Explain the purpose and processes of calibration and describe how at least one type of sensor can be calibrated.

Section 3: Set up and carry out an investigation using data logging

Assessment objective 3: *Set up and carry out an investigation (or investigations) using data logging is covered in this section.*

Skills

You are now required to carry out some data-logging activities. Think about activities that you carry out within science/geography subjects. You will need to find a problem to investigate and choose more than one sensor that could be used to collect the data. You will then be required to choose one sensor. Exactly how you go about this will depend to some extent on the equipment available to you. However, the generic 'rules' of setting up your data-logging experiments are the same. You will need to:

● define the purpose of the investigation;

● list the equipment required (including equipment needed to record or display your results);

● set up the required equipment;

● perform any calibration needed for at least one of your chosen sensors.

You will also need to consider the effects on the accuracy of your results when handling and positioning sensors, and when deciding when to take readings. Your portfolio will need to contain evidence of your results and these must be analysed and a report produced, describing the purpose of the investigation, the methods employed and the results. Recording your results accurately – whether through photographs of equipment; saving data to some permanent store, such as a hard disk for later analysis; or formatting for display on screen or on a printer – means that you need to check this 'secondary' equipment with as much care as you exercise in choosing your data-logging hardware and software. Recording your results accurately and in a form that can be retrieved later is an essential part of your investigation.

Merit- and distinction-level candidates will need to use more than one type of sensor so that they can monitor more than one physical variable (e.g. temperature, light, acidity). This may be done in one complex experiment or as a number of smaller, separate experiments. These candidates will present their results using charts/graphs and tables, explain how they analysed their results and provide detailed explanations.

Example experiments might be to monitor:

- reaction rates of fellow students in your group;
- temperature inside and outside a room;
- daylight times – day/night;
- a toy car rolling down a slope;
- how steady your breathing is during a variety of activities;
- the speed of cars;
- your pulse.

Your experiment will need to cover the following, however, not all are necessary for all grade-level candidates:

1 Conducting one or more investigations, choosing appropriate hardware:
- data logger or computer with interface;
- appropriate sensors.

2 Setting up equipment:
- connect equipment;

- calibrate sensors where necessary;
- set period and interval of logging.

3 Obtaining and storing results:

- carry out data logging;
- store results.

4 Analysing the results:

- use specialist software or transfer to generic application (e.g. Microsoft Excel® spreadsheet to present the results using graphs/charts);
- summarise the results of the investigation.

5 Produce a report:

- purpose of investigation;
- describe the methods used;
- describe the results (e.g. charts/graphs and tables, list of raw data).

In order to illustrate the approach outlined above, we will walk through a simple experiment, using a single sensor type to record a single variable. For this outline experiment we are using two light gates, one at the top and one at the bottom of the slope. The light gates start and stop timing as the card attached to the car breaks the beam. If we (or, more importantly, perhaps, the computer) know the distance between the light gates, then the speed of the car as it rolls down the slope can be calculated.

In the course of your investigation you should also consider alternative means of obtaining your data – what other sensors might you be able to use? You may also like to consider how you might do this using manual observation and a stopwatch. What are the implications of your choice of equipment and method for the accuracy of your results?

For this illustrative example, we will measure the speed of a toy car running down a ramp using a pair of simple, single-ended light gates (or switches) to capture the data.

Just as a recipe for a meal consists of a list of ingredients, an outline of the cooking methods and some serving suggestions, our experiment will be broken down into manageable steps.

Purpose of the investigation

In this case, to measure the speed of a toy car running down a ramp.

Equipment

- Toy car – either rectangular in outline or with a rectangular object fixed to it (see diagram);
- Ramp;
- Data logger;
- 2 × light gates;
- Clamps to secure the equipment (especially the light gates), to ensure accurate and consistent readings;
- Guides to keep the trolley on track;
- Blu-tack™ (or similar) for securing things;

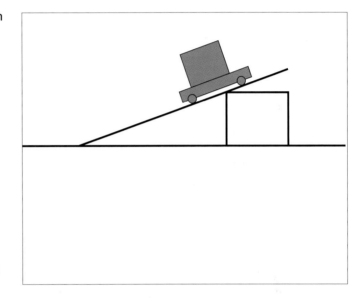

Figure 19.6 – Toy car and ramp experiment

- Bean bag (or similar) to stop the trolley after it has rolled off the end of the ramp.

In addition, you may want to have a camera to record your set-up and a printer to print out your results. Neither of these items is critical to the experiment, but they can be useful in assembling your portfolio of evidence later.

Your set-up might look something like that shown here.

Method – setting up

- Check that you have *all* your equipment and that it is working – batteries, in particular, seem to have a habit of failing at inconvenient moments.
- Set up the ramp, using a pair of metre rules (or other straight edges) to ensure that the car runs accurately – you can fix them in place with Blu-tack™.

- Place a bean bag so that it will stop the car after it has passed the second sensor.
- Without taking any measurements, run the car down the ramp a couple of times and make any adjustments that may be needed to ensure that it is working smoothly.
- Fix your sensors in place. Choose a suitable distance between them and use clamps to be sure that they cannot move in the course of the experiment.
- Attach the sensors to the data-logging equipment – you will need to consult the manual for the particular equipment that you are using. Turn it on and check that it is working.
- Enter the distance between the sensors into the data logger – it needs this to calculate distance travelled and time, in order to calculate the speed of the car.
- Check that you have any secondary equipment, such as a camera, a printer, a PC, to receive data from the logging application for storage and later analysis. The exact list will depend on what you are doing and the equipment available.

Method – doing the experiment

With all your equipment tested, in place and running, the actual experiment is quite straightforward:

- Run the car down the slope, recording the results.
- Repeat several times – no fewer than three.
- Save the data.

If you are using a dedicated data logger, you may also want to export the data in a suitable format (such as CSV) for later analysis with software such as a spreadsheet, which will allow you to format the data for presentation and to create charts or graphs of your results.

In the course of your experiment(s), you should note and, if necessary, take measurements to deal with any health and safety issues that you encounter – this is a requirement for Assessment objective 4 in this unit. These need not be life-and-death issues – quite simple things like identifying a trip hazard from badly placed cables and doing something about it is sufficient to demonstrate your awareness of the importance of health and safety at all times.

Tasks

Pass

Pass-level candidates will need to:

- Choose an appropriate problem to solve and select at least one appropriate sensor to carry out a simple investigation.
- Connect the equipment.
- Set the period and interval of logging.
- Obtain some results.
- State the purpose of the investigation.
- Write about the method used.
- Comment on the results found.
- Explain your choice of sensor for the experiment.
- Display the results as a list of raw data.

Merit

*Merit-level candidates will **also** need to:*

- Choose appropriate sensors to carry out an investigation monitoring at least two different physical variables (either through two separate experiments or a single, more complex experiment).
- Save your results.
- Carry out some analyses to summarise your findings.
- Describe the purpose of the investigation(s).
- Explain how the investigation(s) was carried out,
- Explain how you analysed and described the results.

Distinction

*Distinction-level candidates will **also** need to:*

- Choose appropriate sensors to carry out a complex investigation or several simpler investigations, monitoring at least three different physical variables.

- Set up and connect the equipment, and check the calibration of at least one sensor to ensure accuracy.

- Save your results and carry out a detailed analysis to summarise your findings.

- Describe in detail the purpose of the investigation(s).

- Describe how you analysed the results.

- Describe how the investigation(s) was carried out and include details of procedures followed to ensure precision and reliability of results.

- Produce a report, illustrated with charts/graphs and tables, detailing your findings.

Section 4: Evaluate data-logging activities

Assessment objective 4: *Evaluate data-logging activities* is covered in this section.

Skills

Evaluation

Once you have completed your data-logging activity in Section 3, you will have to evaluate the usefulness of data logging. This should be a *critical* evaluation of what you did and why you did it that way, and an assessment of the accuracy of your results. You will also need to comment on health and safety concerns.

If, for example, you used the 'car on the ramp' experiment, you would need to give at least one advantage of using data-logging equipment to obtain your results. In this instance, you could compare the accuracy of the results of using data-logging equipment with the alternative method of using a handheld stopwatch to obtain your data. A really good answer along these lines would use a manual collection method to generate comparable data as a separate experiment, so that you could compare the accuracy of your results. You might conclude that the difference between the results was caused by the reaction time of the person holding the stopwatch. This, in turn, suggests some possible further experiments in measuring reaction times. With this in mind, you might even want to go back to Section 3 and build these experiments into your overall project.

You will also need to state one of the disadvantages of using data-logging equipment in your experiment. Given that the data produced by using logging equipment is probably more accurate, it may be possible, for example, to assess the increased reliability of the data as insufficient to justify the time, trouble and expense of acquiring it that way.

You will need to comment on the accuracy of your findings. If you used the 'car on the ramp' experiment, for example, you should have data for a number of different 'runs'. Given that the physical phenomena you measured would not be expected to vary greatly, divergences from the mean value of your readings are probably the result of experimental error. If you also gathered data by manual means (i.e. rolling the car down the ramp and using a stopwatch), you would have a different set of readings to compare. What is their divergence from the mean? What does it tell us about the accuracy of this method of obtaining the data? What is the degree of accuracy of the two methods? Are your two sets of data strictly comparable in this way?

Your report will also need to consider measures that you had to take to ensure health and safety. This could relate to the laboratory in which you carried out the work. Did everyone need to be briefed about fire exits, evacuation procedures, the location of the nearest fire extinguisher of a type approved for use with electrical equipment? The health and safety considerations could apply equally to the experiments themselves. Any experiment involving heat or chemicals might make it necessary to wear suitable protective clothing such as gloves or goggles, for example. Manufacturers' websites can be a source of information on health and safety considerations for their products. You can also search the Internet for a Material Safety Data Sheet for any product (these sheets are required by US law, but are available everywhere). There is similar legislation in the UK under the Control of Substances Hazardous to Health (COSHH) Regulations.

While it is not actually a requirement for this section, remember how valuable visual presentation of results can be. Graphs, charts or pictures can all enhance your report. A graph that shows the results of many measurements can be taken in at a glance – unlike the table of figures from which it is derived. A good report, of course, will provide both – the graph for its instant impact and the table to back it up.

Merit- and distinction-level candidates will need to provide a report along the lines outlined above, but with more examples and more detail. Whatever the level of your report, however, the key thing to bear in mind is that this is an exercise in *evaluation*: what you did, why you did it, the alternatives and the overall reliability of your results.

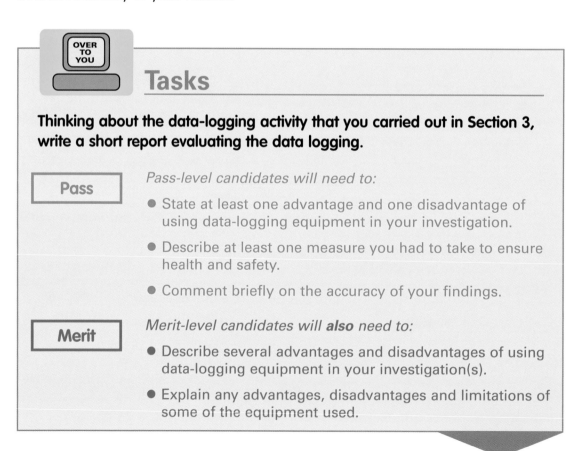

Tasks

Thinking about the data-logging activity that you carried out in Section 3, write a short report evaluating the data logging.

| **Pass** |

Pass-level candidates will need to:

- State at least one advantage and one disadvantage of using data-logging equipment in your investigation.

- Describe at least one measure you had to take to ensure health and safety.

- Comment briefly on the accuracy of your findings.

| **Merit** |

*Merit-level candidates will **also** need to:*

- Describe several advantages and disadvantages of using data-logging equipment in your investigation(s).

- Explain any advantages, disadvantages and limitations of some of the equipment used.

- Comment on the accuracy and reliability of your findings.
- Describe clearly any health and safety issues you had to consider while carrying out the investigation(s), and any measures you took in response to those issues.

Distinction

*Distinction-level candidates will **also** need to:*

- Provide a comprehensive evaluation of using data-logging equipment in your investigation(s).
- Include a consideration of the purpose of each investigation.
- Describe alternative methods that could have been used.
- Provide an evaluation of the accuracy and reliability of your findings.
- Explain any health and safety issues you had to consider while carrying out the investigation.

Unit 20
Creating animation for the WWW using ICT

Unit overview

This unit will help you develop the knowledge, skills and understanding of how to design, produce and test a short animation which is fit for purpose.

By working through the *Skills*, *How to* and *Tasks* sections in this unit, you will demonstrate all the skills required for Unit 20 and be able to:

- review several existing animations;
- design an animation;
- create an animation;
- test the animation.

Examples in this unit are based on Macromedia Flash® and Adobe Photoshop®.

For this unit you will need to create:

- a report reviewing several existing animations;
- an animation at least 15–30 seconds long.

There should be evidence of:

- reviewing several existing animations;
- design;
- testing – using a test plan;
- creating an animation.

The animation you create will need to be presented in a suitable format; this might be:

- a web page;
- printouts.

You will need to demonstrate the following skills:

- researching, collecting and describing a range of animations already in use on websites;
- designing an animation, describing the aim and audience;
- creating an animation at least 15–30 seconds long, using a variety of software tools;
- presenting the work using a suitable format.

Section 1: Research, collect and describe existing animations

Assessment objective 1: *Review several existing animations* is covered in this section.

You are going to create animations to promote a new sports facility that has just opened. The sports facility will have a website, a presentation that will run within the complex and a variety of media, both electronic and paper-based.

You have been asked to research, collect and report on at least two different existing animations, as provided or viewed on the Internet.

Skills

The easiest form of collating information on animations you view is to create a simple table to record this data.

Animation	Date	Source	Type	Aim of animation	If aim not met, why not	Good features	Not so good features	Possible improve-ments
1		www. hud.ac.uk	Flash	To stand out from static information – eye-catching and encouraging viewer to click on for more info	Became boring after seen once	Not too overcrowded with info	Change of colour scheme	Modify colour scheme to be in line with rest of page
2								

The types of animation you could select are:

- animated GIFs;
- Flash media;
- Adobe Shockwave® media;
- animated web banners.

Visit the following websites to see a range of the above types of animation:

www.gifs.net/gif/
www.trendyflash.com/tdcsb/samples/sample10/index.html (click on 'free radicals')
www.trendyflash.com/tdcsb/samples/sample19/index.html
www.ugoplayer.com/games/applehunt.html
www.gnc-web-creations.com/banners-custom.htm

Tasks

Using the scenario of a keep fit gym, research a range of materials to evaluate what is already published for this type of venue. The best place to review other people's work is on the Internet. Using Google, search for websites about sports complexes, sports arenas or gym facilities.

Pass

Pass-level candidates will need to:

- List the good and not so good features of at least two different animations.

- Produce a table to collect this information.

Merit

*Merit-level candidates will **also** need to:*

- Identify the aim of the animation.

- Give a *detailed* explanation of the good and not so good features of at least two different animations.

- Suggest possible improvements to the animations.

Distinction

*Distinction-level candidates will **also** need to:*

- Give a *thorough* explanation of the good and not so good features of at least two different animations.

- Suggest a range of valid improvements to each animation, to help the animation to meet its aims.

Section 2: Design an animation

Assessment objective 2: *Design an animation* **is covered in this section.**

Skills

Like all media, it is best to create a storyboard design before starting to work on the computer.

The storyboard will show detail of the actual drawing of the frames in the animation. You will also identify how you are going to produce the animation (which software you are going to use). The storyboard will appear like a series of comic strips, with individual drawings that make up the animation. The drawings will only be early ideas – these will develop when you create the artwork.

You should consider the following animations:

SATURDAY SPORTS DAY – RELAY RACES

Runner from start position to final winning post as an animation

Text advertising the event in a banner with the runner in the background running across the banner

- The aim of the animation – is to encourage people to attend the sports day
- How it will be created – using Flash
- Who it is for – students, parents and the local community
- What elements are to be used – <u>tweening</u> between frames to give the appearance of movement of the runner

Figure 20.1 – Storyboard

- Tweening: this is smooth transition from one frame to another – adding more steps between frames.

- Frame by frame: there can be a staggered step between frames – this depends on the number of frames you have in your set.

- Transitions: this is how one frame moves to another.

- Effects: frames fade in, fade out, move one way or another.

- Video: adding video clips can make the animation more interesting.

- Timings: these ensure that there is enough time for the viewer to read or take in the message.

You can download elements to make up your animation; you do not need to create every stage yourself. These elements may be:

- text;

- images;

- sound;

- video.

You will need to produce a report to accompany your storyboard, telling the reader:

- the aim of the animation;

- how it will be created;

- who it is for;

- what elements are to be used.

You may wish to use a table like the one shown here to report on your work.

Date	Source	Aim	How it was created	Audience	Elements used	Animation effects used
10 Oct	www.trendy flash.com/ tdcsb/ samples/ sample10/ index.html	To advertise a PR company	Using Flash and images	People wishing to use a PR company for advertising	Text Graphics Sound recording	Tweening Transitions Effects Timings

Tasks

You are now going to design your animation for a keep fit gym. Using your research, create a storyboard for your animation.

Using Photoshop Image Ready, you can choose whether to use frame-by-frame animation or tweening to smooth out your animation.

You may wish to create a table (like the example above) to collate the information, in addition to your storyboard.

Pass	*Pass-level candidates will need to:*
	● Describe the aim of the animation.
	● Produce a storyboard covering the main elements.

Merit	*Merit-level candidates will **also** need to:*
	● Describe the target audience for the animation.
	● Ensure that the design has a clear structure.

Distinction	*Distinction-level candidates will **also** need to:*
	● Provide a thorough description of the aim of the animation.
	● Produce a storyboard covering *all* the elements.
	● Ensure that the design is well structured.

Section 3: Create an animation

> **Assessment objective 3: *Create an animation* is covered in this section.**

You are now going to produce an animation to advertise the new sports facilities – you can use all the elements you have collected in Sections 1 and 2, or create an entirely new animation.

Skills

Photoshop has a package called Image Ready, which allows you to create animations or animated GIF files.

Macromedia has a software package called Flash, which allows users to create an electronic storyboard, with stages set and unfolded. Effectively, you make a movie of events to form an animation.

There are also numerous animated GIFs on the Internet that are free to download and use; these could be combined within your own design, giving more emphasis to your advertising campaign.

Your animation should be between 15 and 30 seconds long, and show that a variety of animation techniques have been used:

- basic graphic techniques (e.g. drawing/editing shapes, use of colour, lines, text, importing objects – refer to Units 3 and 21);
- cutting, copying and pasting (refer to Units 3 and 21);
- tweening or frame by frame;
- frame rates;
- motion guides;
- looping.

You should also show that you understand that the animation should:

- run smoothly;
- be fit for purpose;
- be exported in a suitable format;
- be optimised for use on the Internet.

The above will be demonstrated by use of screenshots, printouts or an electronic portfolio.

How to create frame-by-frame animation

Open Photoshop

File menu

    → Jump to

→ Image Ready

→ File

→ New

→ Select your image size – 500 × 200

→ Select paint fill from the drawing toolbox

→ Select foreground colour

→ Click on background of image to fill with colour

Open image **run.bmp**

→ Remove or fill background

→ Copy and paste into new image

→ Use the type tool to create text near the top centre of the banner: **Sports**.

→ Create text in the middle off-centre of the banner: **Gala**.

→ Create text at the bottom right of the banner: **Today**.

If the Animation dialog box is not displayed

→ View menu

→ Animation

→ Your image will appear in the first frame of the animation

→ Click on the duplicate frames icon at the bottom of the Animation dialog box

→ Duplicate the frame

→ Do this twice

→ You should have three frames

In the layer palette all the layers are displayed

→ Click on the first frame

→ Deselect the layers **Gala** and **Today**

→ The visible layers should only be showing the runner and the word **Sports**

→ Click on the second frame

→ Select the layer with the runner and move the runner down your banner

→ Reselect the word **Gala**

→ Click on the third frame

→ Select the layer with the runner and move the runner to the right of your banner

→ Reselect the words **Gala** and **Today**

Set the timing of your animation

→ Click on the first frame

→ Change 0 sec at the bottom of the frame to 0.5 sec by clicking and selecting from the list

→ Repeat for each of the other frames, setting each frame at 0.5 sec

You have now created an animated graphic

→ Use the tools at the bottom of the animation dialog box (they work just like a DVD player)

→ Select the first frame

→ Press Play

At the bottom of the Animation dialog box, you can choose whether your frames run Once or Forever (looped)

→ On this occasion, choose Once

Save your file as an animated GIF file

File menu

→ Save Optimized as

→ As a GIF format

How to improve transitions between slides using tweening

Tweening comes from the word 'between' – the software creates frames between each frame you have created, to give a smoother appearance to your animation.

Select frames 1 and 2 by holding down Ctrl and clicking

→ Select the tweening tool at the bottom of the Animation dialog box

→ Frames to add

→ 5

→ OK

→ Repeat this with frames 7 and 8

→ Frames to add

→ 5

→ OK

→ Set your timings to each frame and run the animation again (see the difference)

→ Save your animation as **filename.gif**

UNIT 20 | Creating animation for the WWW using ICT

How to use Flash to produce an animation

Flash shows many features on the screen as you are using it – these will be referred to in the following instructions.

- At the top of your screen is the Layers and Scene panel.
- In the middle is your Stage.
- Down the left side of the screen is the Tools panel.
- At the bottom of the screen is the Properties panel.
- To the right of the screen is your Library and any other panels you open. If this is not visible:

  Open your Align panel

  → Window

  → Align

  Your screen should now look like the screenshot shown here.

Figure 20.2 – Flash screen

Figure 20.3 – Properties panel

Figure 20.4 – Toolbox

How to set the frame rate

In the Properties panel you can set the frame rate. The number of frames displayed one after another per second of animation creates the illusion of movement – the higher the frame rate, the smoother the movement.

The default frame rate for web production is 12; for television and other media it can go as high as 30 frames per second. For Flash animation for use on the web, 12 is correct; this gives a consistent flow of movement, but does not increase your file size.

- Set your stage size to 300 × 200
    - → Properties panel
    - → Change the Size
- Set the colours on your Tools panel
    - → Stroke color (the pen) red
    - → Fill color (the bucket) yellow

    At Frame 1, using the oval tool, create a circle in the middle of your stage
    - → Click in frame 50
    - → Right-click
    - → Select Insert Blank Key Frame
    - → Using the text tool, key in the text **SPORT**
- Convert the text into a shape
    - → Your oval is one shape – you cannot tween between a shape and text, so you need to convert your text
    - → Modify
    - → Break Apart (or Ctrl + B) and repeat this (the first time it converts your text to individual letters; the second time it converts your text to a shape)
- Click in the middle of your timeline
    - → 25

    In the Properties panel
    - → Tween
    - → Change to Shape
- Click in your timeline at the beginning
    - → Press Enter to run your morph
- Your shape should change to the text

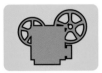

How to use motion guides and looping

> **Motion guides:** allow you to track your image across the stage; using the runner image, for example, you can make the runner move across the stage in any direction you wish by simply drawing a random line.

- Place a graphic on the stage

  File menu

    → Import

    → Import to stage

    → Select image

- Rename the layer to the name of your graphic

    → Double-click on the layer word at the top left of your stage

    → Key in the name of your layer

- Add a Keyframe at Frame 40

- With your image layer selected, right-click and select Add Motion Guide from the dropdown menu

- The guide layer is now set – you know this because it says Guide, and this guide has the same name as your layer

- On the Guide layer, using the pencil tool, draw out a line of any shape or length (this will be the path the graphic follows)

- The colour and size of this line will not be visible when you publish your movie

- Double-check that the Snap (magnet on the toolbox on the left) is turned on

    → Drag the graphic over to the start of the path (your line)

- A small circle will appear as you place your graphic at the beginning of your line (this is the part that will snap to the guide)

    → If the circle does not appear, move your graphic until it does

- Go to Keyframe 40 where you inserted the other Keyframe

    → Move your graphic to the other end of the motion path

    → Make sure it snaps to the guide

- You have now created the starting point and the ending point (just like in normal motion tweening)
- While you have the graphic layer selected, click anywhere along the timeline between Keyframe 1 and Keyframe 40
    - → Frames panel at the bottom of your screen
    - → Select Motion
- Save the graphic as a movie

    File menu

    - → Export
    - → Export as movie

This option of tweening also produces a loop effect (i.e. your graphic motion will restart once it gets to the end).

Tasks

You are now going to produce an animation to advertise the keep fit gym – you can use all the elements you collected in Sections 1 and 2 earlier, add to them or create new ones.

Pass

Pass-level candidates will need to:

- Make sure that the animation is at least 15 seconds long.
- Make use of basic graphic techniques and tweening, or frame-by-frame animation (some elements may not work as intended).
- Export the animation in a suitable file format (e.g. animated GIF or movie).

Merit

*Merit-level candidates will **also** need to:*

- Make sure that the animation is at least 30 seconds long.

- Ensure that the animation is appropriate.

- Make good use of basic graphic techniques and tweening, or frame-by-frame animation, frame rates and looping (most elements will work as intended).

*Distinction-level candidates will **also** need to:*

- Make sure that the animation meets the identified aims.

- Ensure that the animation is optimised and all elements work as intended.

Section 4: Test the animation

> **Assessment objective 4:** *Test the animation* is covered in this section.

For this section you are required to produce a test plan, showing that you have tested your animation fully.

Skills

The evidence here could be a checklist, with evidence of the outcomes of the testing and suggestions for improvement. Merit- and distinction-level candidates will need to carry out some of the suggested improvements.

		Suggested improvements	Date tested/ initials
Suitable content	Graphics worked well, but needed more colour	Add colour	
Correct message relayed	Showed running, could have shown other events	Add another event	
Frame rate	A little quick – viewer did not have time to take in before the image started again	Slow down	
Correct timing	No – see above	Slow down	
Correct loops	Looked a little wooden – jerked along rather than a smooth movement	Add more steps	
Suitable format	Worked in Microsoft Internet Explorer®	No problems	

Tasks

For this section you are required to produce a test plan, showing that you have fully tested your animation. Use a table to produce your results, such as the example shown above.

Pass

Pass-level candidates will need to:

● Test the animation using a test table – including four appropriate tests.

● Identify areas for improvement.

Merit

*Merit-level candidates will **also** need to:*

● Test the animation using a test table – including five appropriate tests, covering the main areas of the animation.

● Identify areas for improvement and take action on one of the areas.

Distinction

*Distinction-level candidates will **also** need to:*

● Test the animation using a test table – including six appropriate tests, covering all main areas of the animation.

● Ensure that the testing is appropriate.

● Identify areas for improvement and take action on most of the areas.

Unit 21 Computer graphics

Unit overview

This unit will help you to develop knowledge of the different types of computer graphics that can be used in web pages.

By working through the *Skills*, *How to* and *Tasks* sections in this unit, you will demonstrate all the skills required for Unit 21 and be able to:

- research, collect and describe a range of existing graphics/images for use in web pages;
- plan the production of a range of graphic images for a client, to be used on their website;
- create a navigation bar or menu bar;
- create a set of navigation buttons;
- create an advertising banner;
- present your work to a client for a specific purpose, using a suitable format for display.

Examples in this unit are based on Adobe Photoshop® and Macromedia Dreamweaver®.

For this unit you will need to create:

- a navigation bar or menu bar;
- a set of navigation buttons;
- an advertising banner.

There should be evidence of:

- research;
- planning;
- design.

The images you create will need to be presented in a suitable format. This might be:

- a web page;
- a slide presentation;
- printouts.

Section 1: Research, collect and describe existing graphics/images

Assessment objective 1: *Research, collect and describe a range of existing graphics/images for use in web pages* **is covered in this section.**

You have been asked to create a navigation bar or menu bar, a set of navigation buttons and an advertising banner to be used in a variety of media advertising a new sports facility. Before you start producing any images, you need to research a variety of websites, looking at the basic make-up.

Skills

You will need to collect and display examples of graphics from at least two different websites. You must describe the purpose, giving both negative and positive aspects, of the use of these graphics. The best way to report on the graphics sourced is with a simple table, like the one shown here.
Merit- and distinction-level candidates will also need to:

- visit more than two websites;
- discuss the graphics' suitability;
- discuss the impact of the graphics;
- give details of the physical size of the graphics.

Date	Website	Item	Purpose	Negative	Positive	Graphic or graphic filename	Graphic's suitability	Impact	Physical size
25 Jan	www. hodder. co.uk	Navigation menu – left side	Take the user to other areas of the website	Unless you know what you are looking for, it may be difficult to find	You can go straight to the correct depart-ment – the menu is clear		Does what it should – but not sure I got where I wanted to go very quickly	Dark back-ground and white text very visible	Good size – takes up less than 1/3 of the page

How to save a graphic from a website

Locate the website

→ Right-click on the image

→ Select Save picture as

→ Give the picture a name

Tasks

You have been asked to create a navigation bar or menu bar, a set of navigation buttons and an advertising banner to be used in a variety of media advertising a keep fit gym. Before you start producing any images, you need to research, collect and store a variety of websites, looking at the basic make-up.

Create a table to collate and report on your findings, using the following headings:

- **Date;**
- **Website;**
- **Item;**
- **Purpose;**
- **Negative;**
- **Positive;**
- **Graphic or graphic filename;**
- **Graphic's suitability;**
- **Impact;**
- **Physical size.**

Produce a presentation with screenshots, or download the graphics into an electronic portfolio or folder.

| Pass |

Pass-level candidates will need to:

- Collect/display example graphics from at least two different websites.

- Describe the purpose of the graphics.

- Comment on the features – both positive and negative.

| Merit |

*Merit-level candidates will **also** need to:*

- Collect/display example graphics from at least three different websites.

- Discuss the suitability of the graphics.

- Give details on the size of the graphics, and discuss.

- Comment on the features – both positive and negative – giving reasons.

| Distinction |

*Distinction-level candidates will **also** need to:*

- Collect/display example graphics from at least four different websites.

- Discuss the impact of the graphics.

- Comment on the features – both positive and negative – giving valid reasons.

Section 2: Plan to produce a range of graphics/images

> **Assessment objective 2:** *Plan the production of a range of graphic images for a client, to be used on their website* is covered in this section.

Skills

For this section, you will need to plan and produce sketch diagrams of three different types of graphics to be used on a client's website. These sketches should represent:

- a navigation bar or menu bar;
- a set of navigation buttons;
- an advertising banner.

sketch.doc

You will also need to report on the following:

- the target audience;
- the purpose of the design;
- a house style to be used;
- the size of the graphics – both physical and file size.

This might be by means of a table, like the one shown here.

Date	Graphic filename or website	Target audience	Purpose of design	House style used	Physical size	File size

Tasks

You need to plan and produce sketch diagrams of three different types of graphics to be used on a client's website.

You should use the research collected in Section 1 as ideas for your designs, and for discussion of audience suitability and purpose of design. You may use parts of graphics found on websites and adapt them for your purpose. If you use parts of other website graphics within your own design, you **MUST** provide evidence as screenshots or witness testimonies, along with detailed information of where the graphics came from (the website address).

Pass	

Pass-level candidates will need to:

- Produce a basic sketch for three different types of graphics.
- Describe the target audience for the graphics.
- Describe the purpose of the graphics.

Merit	

*Merit-level candidates will **also** need to:*

- Produce a detailed sketch for three different types of graphics.
- Use a house style.
- Take into consideration the size of the graphics, and discuss.

Distinction	

*Distinction-level candidates will **also** need to:*

- Give details of what graphics you intend to create, and discuss.
- Produce a comprehensive detailed sketch for three different types of graphics.

Section 3: Create a navigation bar or menu bar

Assessment objective 3: *Create a navigation bar or menu bar* **is covered in this section.**

In Sections 1 and 2 you have researched and designed your own website graphics. Now you are to create the first graphic element of a navigation bar or menu bar.

Skills

You must consider the following:

- date;
- navigation bar or menu bar – was this produced using:

  1 tables?

  2 icons?

  3 dropdown menus?

  4 expanding/collapsing menus?

- suitability for purpose;
- suitability for audience;
- whether the colour contrasts are correct.

You should save your work and produce a printout.

Navigation bar: a horizontal or vertical menu of multiple words, pictographs or buttons, each being a link to some internal or external web page, part of a page or other website. 'Nav bars' typically occupy the left edge, near the top or bottom of the web page.

Menu bar: a sequence of menus across the top of the web page.

Using Dreamweaver, you are going to create a navigation bar. This will then be used as a navigation method, taking the viewer of the website from one page to another.

The use of tables for content layout in Dreamweaver

Tables are used to lay out the page content.

- They grow with content.
- Images can be positioned more accurately.
- Navigation systems can be created to a standard width and height (where images of different sizes are used).

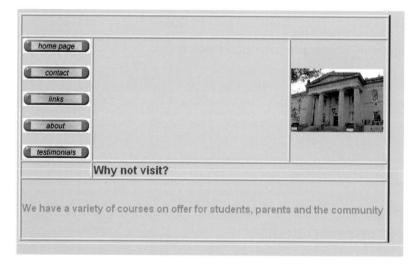

Figure 21.1 – Table layout 1

PENS4U

About Us

Products

Spiral notebooks
A4 ruled paper pads
Assorted A4 coloured card
Pens
Pencils
Envelopes
Binders and files

	POSTAGE COSTS (SINGLE ORDERS)		
	BRUNEI	**U.S.A.**	**REST OF WORLD**
			AIRMAIL	**SURFACE MAIL**
	US$5.50	US$6.50	US$8.00	US$5.00

On-line services
Pens
Pencils
Envelopes
Binders and files

Figure 21.2 – Table layout 2

Gymnastic

ABOUT US

PRODUCTS

TREADMILL
EXERCISE BIKE
HOME GYM
ROW
MAC
STEP
INCLINE PRESS
ELLIPTICAL

WE DELIVER TO:

BRUNEI
GREECE
ITALY
MALAYSIA
PRAGUE

WE HAVE
BRANCHES
AROUND THE
WORLD AND WE
CAN DELIVER
WHEREVER WE
HAVE A BRANCH.
YOU CAN ALSO
CALL IN AND
PICK UP YOUR EQUIPMENT.

WHAT WE DO	We sell both commercial and home use gym equipment at a reasonable price.	
HOW WE DO THIS	Because we run several companies within various countries we are able to purchase the equipment we sell at a discount price. The saving we make we pass on to our customers.	
WHERE WE ARE BASED	Our Head Office is in Greece, but we have outlets in Brunei, Greece, Italy, Malaysia and Prague.	
HOW YOU CAN ORDER	You can order on-line through our website or by phone or fax. We also produce a comprehensive catalogue listing all our products.	

Figure 2.14.bmp
Type: BMP File
Size: 1.44 MB
Dimension: 684 x 739 pixels

Figure 21.3 – Table layout 3

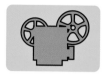

How to insert tables into Dreamweaver

In the Layout bar, select the Table tab

Select the number of rows and columns you wish to display (you can always change this later if it is not right)

Figure 21.4 – Table tab

→ Select the overall size of your table (again, this can be changed later)

→ Select the border thickness and any cell padding (internal margin) and spacing (between each cell)

→ OK

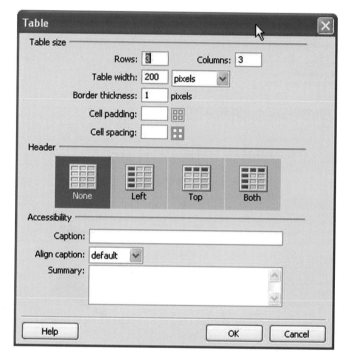

Figure 21.5 – Table dialog box

How to insert content into your table

You can insert images, text, navigation buttons and links.

This is a very simple process:

Insert menu

→ Image

→ Select image

→ OK

→ Key in text, or

Insert menu

→ File

→ Select text file

→ OK

Insert menu

→ Image

→ Select navigation button stored

→ OK

→ Key in text to be used for link

→ If image or text is to be used as a link, select image or text

→ In the Properties panel at the bottom of the screen, key in or select the link in the Link dialog box

How to create a navigation system, including hyperlinks

- On a new blank page in Dreamweaver, insert a table of one row and five columns.

Figure 21.6 – Navigation bar setup

- Add the image **homeb.gif** to your web page in the second row of the table in column one.

- Add the image **aboutb.gif** to your web page in the third row of the table in column one.

- Continue adding the following images in the first column, moving between columns by pressing the Tab key: **contactb.gif**, **linksb.gif**, **testimonb.gif**.

- Select the first button in the Properties panel at the bottom of your screen – Link: key in **index.html**; Alt: key in **Home page**.

- Continue adding the links and alternative text to each of the navigation buttons:

    aboutb.html – About us

    contactb.html – Contact us

    linksb.html – Various links

    testb.html – Testimonials.

- Save this web page as **index**.

You have now created a navigation system with hyperlinks. At this stage you may not have created all the pages, but as you do so, these will link to the home page.

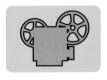

How to create a navigation bar in Dreamweaver

You have been provided with six graphic files:

home.jpg

home2.jpg

info.jpg

info2.jpg

sport.jpg

sport2.jpg

These files will be used to create the normal state and the over state for each menu item.

Open Dreamweaver

Insert menu

→ Image Objects

→ Navigation Bar

→ A navigation bar dialog box will open

→ At the bottom of the dialog box, select Vertical bar

→ In the Element Name section, key in **home**

→ Choose the image **home.jpg** for the Up image

→ Choose the image **home2.jpg** for the Over image

→ You will be given options to save the images in your default web page directory

→ Alongside the option Alternative text, key in **home page**

→ Alongside the option When clicked, Go to URL, key in the web page for this element: **home.htm**

Continue adding the two further elements until the navigation bar is complete. Click on the + for each element you want to add:

Image – Alt text – URL

Info – information page – info.htm

Sport – sports available – sport.htm

Exit the navigation bar dialog box

> → Save
>
> → File
>
> → Preview in browser to test your graphics

Figure 21.8 – Behaviours dropdown

How to add dropdown menus

At the right side of your screen

> → Panels

→ CSS

→ Application

→ Tag

→ Files

→ Select

→ Tag panel group is not expanded

→ Click on the arrow to expand it, if not already expanded

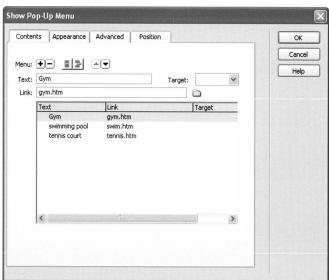

Figure 21.9 – Show Pop-Up Menu

→ Click on the Behaviors tab

→ Select your third button – Sport – in the Behaviors panel

→ Select onMouseOver

→ Click the + menu

→ Choose Show Pop-Up Menu

→ A new window opens, allowing you to create your pop-up menu for the navigation bar element

Content tab:

Text: **Gym**

Link: **gym.htm**

Add new element using **+**

Text: **Swimming pool**

Link: **swim.htm**

Add new element **+**

Text: **Tennis court**

Link: **tennis.htm**

Appearance tab:

Amend the Font to a suitable format and size

Up state – Text: **Red**; Cell: **Yellow**

Over state – Text: **Yellow**; Cell: **Red**

Advanced tab:

Check Pop-Up borders

Border colour: Red

Position tab:

Choose a relevant position

Click OK

→ Save your web page

→ Test your menu

Figure 21.10 – Menu dropdown

→ File

→ Preview in Browser

You have now created a navigation bar with dropdown menus.

You can edit the menu you have created as follows:

Click on the button of the menu you wish to edit

→ Look at the Behavior tab in the Tag panel

→ Double-click on Show Pop-Up Menu

→ This brings up the pop-up menu which controls all menu choices

How to add expanding/collapsing menus

The easiest way to create these menus is to download free code from the Internet and add it to your website.

Visit one of the following sites:

http://f-source.com/buy/adobeMenu/

www.a4menubuilder.com/

www.antssoft.com/ultramenu/index.htm?ref=google&group=2

Tasks

In Sections 1 and 2, you have researched and designed your own website graphics. Now you are going to create the first graphic element of a navigation bar or menu bar.

You should consider the following:

Date	Navigation bar or menu bar – was this saved as produced using: tables? icons? dropdown menus? expanding/collapsing menus?	Suitability for purpose	Suitability for audience	Colour contrasts correct?	Printout produced Filename

You will need to produce printouts as evidence of your work. You may also save the navigation bar or menu bar to be viewed online.

Pass

Pass-level candidates will need to:

- Produce a basic navigation bar/menu bar, using some colour.
- Ensure that the navigation bar/menu bar is suitable for the purpose, and discuss.
- Use a table.

Merit

*Merit-level candidates will **also** need to:*

- Produce a navigation bar/menu bar using colour appropriately.
- Use some graphics and text, combined appropriately.
- Ensure that the navigation bar/menu bar is suitable for the target audience, and discuss.

Distinction

*Distinction-level candidates will **also** need to:*

- Produce an effective navigation bar/menu bar, making good use of colour.

- Use some dropdown boxes or expanding/collapsing menus.

- Ensure that the navigation bar/menu bar is fit for purpose, and discuss.

Section 4: Create navigation buttons

Assessment objective 4: *Create a set of navigation buttons* **is covered in this section.**

Using Photoshop and Image Ready, you are going to create graphic buttons that will be used in Dreamweaver as a navigation method.

Skills

Using Photoshop and the associated program Image Ready, you can create a button menu with interactive elements such as rollovers. The program also creates the JavaScript for your web page, at the same time as producing the graphic.

Navigation button: usually located across the top, down the left side or at the bottom of the web page, this can be text, images or a combination of both.

> **Rollover:** also called a mouseover, this can be used in creating a navigation method for a website. It is a technique using JavaScript that allows you to change a button/graphic element when the user rolls the mouse over the item (a word or graphic image) on the web page. The term 'rollover' came from the ball in a mouse which rolls on a surface to guide the mouse across the web page.

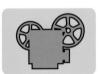

How to create navigation bar buttons

- Open a new document, 650 × 250 pixels, with a white background.
- Decide on your colour scheme – here we will choose red and yellow.
- At the left of the screen is the drawing toolbox – at the bottom of the toolbox, select the background and foreground colour options.
- Click on the foreground and choose red; click on the background and choose yellow.
- Select the rectangle tool – if the rectangle is not showing, use the triangle at the bottom left of the tool.
- Click and drag a long thin rectangle across most of the width of your image canvas – once you let go of the mouse button, your foreground colour should appear in the rectangle.
- In the Layers panel at the bottom right of your screen:

  Layers

  → The top layer will be your new shape
  → Right-click
  → Rasterise layer
  → Double-click on the shape 1 Layer
  → Layer Style dialog box
  → Tick box Stroke
  → OK

- You should now have an Effects list:

  Double-click the Stroke option

→ Layer Style dialog box

→ Choose the formatting option of your stroke effect

→ You can also select your second colour

● You are now going to split your rectangle into three sections to create your menu bar:
Select the small triangle at the corner of the rectangle tool in the drawing toolbox

→ Select the line tool

→ Choose your yellow colour

→ Draw a straight line down the rectangle about a third of the way down (leave a small space at the top and bottom of the rectangle – do not draw the line from the very top to the very bottom)

→ Rasterise this shape

→ Right-click on the shape 2 layer in the Layer Style dialog box

→ Select Duplicate layer

→ In the drawing toolbox, choose the move tool

→ Click and drag the second line to the correct position on your coloured rectangle

→ Select the Layer menu from the dropdown menus

→ Choose Merge down

→ Repeat this so that you only show shape 1

→ When you are happy with your layout, choose Layers menu

→ Merge Visible

How to add text to your nav bar

In the drawing toolbox

→ Text tool

→ Click, and from the menu options at the top of your screen, choose a font, size and colour (yellow) to place text on the first section of your navigation bar

→ Click in the first section of your nav bar and type the word **home**

→ Click on the next section and type the word **info**

→ Click in the final section of your nav bar and type the word **sport**

→ Align your text within your nav bar image

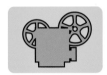

How to use Image Ready

File menu

→ Jump to

→ Image Ready

→ In the drawing toolbox, select the slice tool

→ Click and drag a rectangle around your first button and text on your nav bar (home) – do not include the line separator

→ Repeat this for each of the three buttons (you are defining the button area)

→ You should now see each slice listed at the right

→ Select the first slice by double-clicking in the bottom slice in the Web Content panel

→ Name this slice **index.htm**

→ Repeat for the other two slices:

Slice 2: info – **info.htm**

Slice 3: sport – **sports.htm**

How to add rollover interactivity to the buttons

Right-click on the **home** slice in the Web Content dialog box

→ Add Rollover State

→ Select Over state

→ In the Layer Option tab, select Color Overlay

→ Change the opacity to 50%

→ Repeat for the other two slices

→ Once you have added your effect to all the slices, save it as **navbar**

→ Check using the Preview in Browser button in the toolbox

JavaScript has been created for you using Photoshop and Image Ready.

Figure 21.11 – Buttons plus script

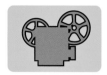

How to add to your web page

File menu

→ Save Optimized As, choose a target directory

→ Filename

→ **index.htm**

→ Open your index.htm file in your browser and view your navigation bar

To use on other pages you create:

Copy the whole code from index.htm

→ Create your new web page

→ Paste your code onto this new page

→ Save the new page in the target directory where index.htm is saved

Tasks

Using Photoshop and Image Ready, you are going to create graphic buttons that will be used in Dreamweaver as a navigation method. You will need to save these navigation buttons in a suitable format and produce printouts showing all states.

The buttons only need to contain a minimum amount of text, but you may wish to include icons or graphics, or a combination of text and graphics.

Pass

Pass-level candidates will need to:

● Produce three buttons – these can be new graphics, ready-made templates or adaptations of graphics that already exist.

Merit

*Merit-level candidates will **also** need to:*

● Produce three interactive buttons – these can be customised, ready-made templates or created from scratch.

- Ensure that the buttons are fit for purpose, and discuss.

| Distinction |

*Distinction-level candidates will **also** need to:*

- Ensure that the buttons are suitable for the target audience, and discuss.

Section 5: Create an advertising banner

Assessment objective 5: *Create an advertising banner* **is covered in this section.**

Skills

Web pages can contain areas holding advertisements. These may be for other company products or services, but can also be used to advertise a special offer by the company that owns the web page. These forms of advertising generally take up a small rectangle of space on the web page and are known as advertising banners. These banners can be static (not moving) or animated. They can contain images, text, links, and so on.

You should consider the following aspects when creating your banner:

- suitability of purpose;
- suitability for audience;
- interactivity;
- animation;
- combination of text and graphics.

You will be required to report on the above; you may wish to produce a table to record this information.

In the screenshot shown here, there is an advertisement for the ICT Nationals – this box has an area containing a link to take the viewer to another location to read more.

Figure 21.12 – Advertising banner

How to create frame-by-frame animation

Open Photoshop

File menu

> → Jump to

> → Image Ready

File menu

> → New

> → Select your image size – 500 × 200

> → Select paint fill from the drawing toolbox

> → Select foreground colour

> → Click on background of image to fill with colour

Open image **run.bmp**

> → Remove or fill background

> → Copy and paste into new image

> → Use the type tool to create text – **Sports** – near the top centre of the banner

> → Create text – **Gala** – in the middle off-centre of the banner

> → Create text – **Today** – at the bottom right of the banner

If the Animation dialog box is not displayed

View menu

> → Animation

→ Your image will appear in the first frame of the animation

→ Click on the duplicate frames icon at the bottom of the Animation dialog box

→ Duplicate the frame

→ Do this twice

→ You should have three frames

In the layer palette all the layers are displayed

→ Click on the first frame

→ Deselect the layers **Gala** and **Today**

→ The visible layers should only be showing the runner and the word **Sports**

→ Click on the second frame

→ Select the layer with the runner and move the runner down your banner

→ Reselect the word **Gala**

→ Click on the third frame

→ Select the layer with the runner and move the runner to the right of your banner

→ Reselect the words **Gala** and **Today**

Set the timing of your animation

→ Click on the first frame

→ Change 0 sec at the bottom of the frame to 0.5 sec by clicking and selecting from the list

→ Repeat for each of the other frames, setting each frame at 0.5 sec

You have now created an animated graphic

→ Use the tools at the bottom of the animation dialog box (they work just like a DVD player)

→ Select the first frame

→ Press Play

At the bottom of the Animation dialog box, you can choose whether your frames run Once or Forever (looped)

→ On this occasion, choose Once

Save your file as an animated GIF file

File menu

→ Save Optimized as

→ As a GIF format

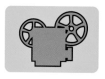

How to improve transitions between slides using tweening

The word 'tweening' comes from the meaning of between, as the software creates frames between each frame you have created, in order to give a smoother appearance to your animation.

Select frames 1 and 2 by holding down Ctrl and clicking

→ Select the tweening tool at the bottom of the Animation dialog box

→ Frames to add

→ 5

→ OK

→ Repeat this with frames 7 and 8

→ Frames to add

→ 5

→ OK

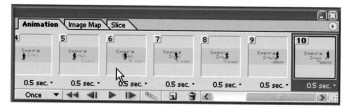

Figure 21.13 – Tweening

→ Set your timings to each frame and run the animation again – see the difference

→ Save your animation as a GIF file format

Tasks

Produce an advertising banner for your client's website. This banner should have both text and graphics and be suitable for purpose.

You should consider the following and produce your comments in a table:

● **filename;**

● **suitability of purpose;**

● **suitability for audience;**

- **interactivity;**
- **animation;**
- **combination of text and graphics.**

Pass

Pass-level candidates will need to:

- Produce a static advertising banner.
- Combine text and graphics.

Merit

*Merit-level candidates will **also** need to:*

- Produce an advertising banner that has user interaction.
- Ensure that the banner is fit for purpose, and discuss.

Distinction

*Distinction-level candidates will **also** need to:*

- Produce an animated/moving advertising banner.
- Ensure that the banner is suitable for the target audience, and discuss.

Section 6: Present your work to the client

Assessment objective 6: *Present work to a client for a specific purpose, using a suitable format for display* **is covered in this section.**

Skills

You are required to produce your work in a suitable format to display your graphics to a client. This format could be electronic or paper-based. The best option would be to create a simple web page and display your graphics there.

Another format would be to present your work in a slide presentation. You will need to produce printouts of your work.

There is no ideal method for showing your artwork – you may choose a combination of paper-based and electronic (web page using a browser or software-based).

The image you create will need to be optimised for the Internet (i.e. size and colour and saved in a suitable format). Large file size images cost the user money and time. They require significant storage space (if you store them) and bandwidth (to download them). A web page that takes more than 10 seconds to load will turn your visitors away. You can optimise your images for the Web. Your images should be in either GIF or JPEG formats (GIF works best for logos and navigation buttons, while JPEG works best for photographs). The idea is to reduce the size of your graphics so that they take as few KB as possible, while retaining acceptable quality.

How to optimise graphics for the Internet

Choose the correct file format:

GIF loses no pixel data when it is compressed, whereas JPEG formats lose some pixel data in order to make the file size smaller. Therefore, JPEGs offer smaller file size, but a lower-quality image.

File menu

> → Save as
>
> → Choose the file format

Choose the correct colour depth:

The more colours in your graphics, the more file space for the colour information. GIF files can use as many as 256 colours (8-bit colour) or as few as 2 colours (1-bit colour). In addition, 256-colour images can be 24-bit colour images – this is when you need to reduce down to 8-bit colour. Taking the colour down can reduce the file size by one-third.

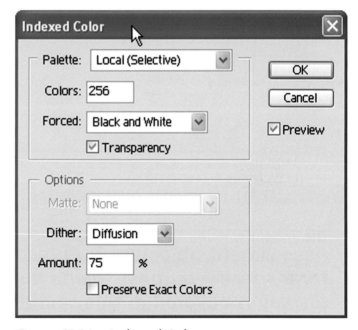

Figure 21.14 – Indexed Color

File menu

> → Save as

> → Choose GIF format

> → The next dialog box gives you an option to set the colour depth

Choosing the correct resolution:

If you are producing a graphic to be used solely on a computer, you can use a lower resolution as computer screens display at 72 dpi – you will get just the same result for lower resolution and therefore a smaller file size.

Image

> → Image size

> → Choose the resolution

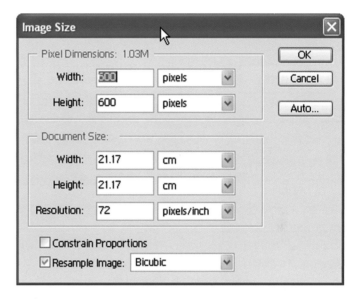

Figure 21.15 – Image Size

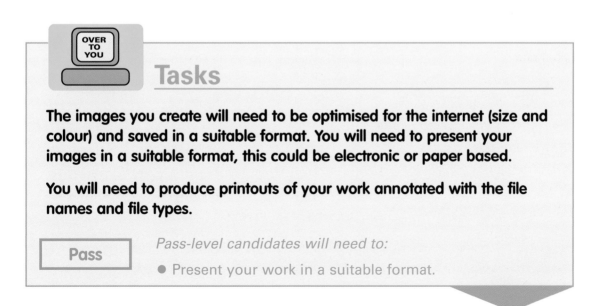

Tasks

The images you create will need to be optimised for the internet (size and colour) and saved in a suitable format. You will need to present your images in a suitable format, this could be electronic or paper based.

You will need to produce printouts of your work annotated with the file names and file types.

Pass

Pass-level candidates will need to:

● Present your work in a suitable format.

Merit

*Merit-level candidates will **also** need to:*

- Present your work properly and in a suitable format.
- Demonstrate the use of suitable file types.

Distinction

*Distinction-level candidates will **also** need to:*

- Present your work effectively in a suitable format.
- Optimise all graphics used for use on the Web.

Unit 22 Sound

Section 1: Review several existing audio clips

Assessment objective 1: *Review several existing audio clips* is covered in this section.

Before you start editing or creating your own clip, it is useful to review existing audio clips to evaluate what works well and what does not work so well, so that you can consider these factors when creating your own clip.

Skills

You are required to review two different audio clips (e.g. radio advert, soundtrack from a film trailer, music clip or music file downloaded from the Internet) and produce a review that covers:

- the good and not so good features of the audio clip (when listening to the clip, think about the rhythm, contrast, pitch, changing tempo, using voices, using instruments);

- the aim of the audio clip (e.g. to make a car chase in a film more dramatic);

- how the aims of the audio clip are met (e.g. if you have chosen to review a soundtrack for a film, think about how the music makes an impact without words – is the music a form of expression?);

- if the aims are not met, why not?

- possible improvements to the two different audio clips in terms of the features listed above.

Note that the sound clip does not have to be very long – you might only wish to listen to a clip which is no more than 90 seconds in length.

The website www.filmtracks.com has some good reviews of film soundtracks since 1996. Other useful websites include:

www.adtunes.com
www.napster.co.uk
www.itunes.com

Load Microsoft Internet Explorer®, visit a website and find at least two audio clips that are interesting to you. Listen to the sound clip and then complete the table shown here.

Sound clip	Date	Source	Good features of audio clip	Not so good features of audio clip	Aim of the audio clip	How the aims are met	How the aims are not met	Possible improvements
1	1 Jan	www. napster. co.uk	Superb mix and balance between dialogue score and effects; the soundtrack had some good choral elements	There was an aggressive use of base and this was overpowering at times	The aim of the clip was to be used during a dramatic car chase in the film	The aims were met – the music score fitted well with the moving images	N/A	The aggressive use of the surrounds and the pumping out of the bass could be lessened
2	2 Jan	www. napster. co.uk	This was an inspiring soundtrack and included some good electronic elements; you could hear the gunfire and the surround speakers	The track was complicated in places and sometimes included a rumbling bass	The aim of the audio clip was part of a film clip and was used when no one was speaking	N/A	I do not think the aims were met – the soundtrack was rather muted for such a massive Hollywood blockbuster film	Make the track less complicated and more inspiring by including a more balanced mix between the score and effects

Tasks

Pass

Pass-level candidates will need to:

- Find two different audio clips.
- List the good and not so good features of these two audio clips, in the form of a short written paragraph or a table (like the one shown here).

Sound clip	Date	Source	Good features of audio clip	Not so good features of audio clip
1				
2				

Merit

*Merit-level candidates will **also** need to:*

- Identify the aim of the audio clips.
- Provide a detailed explanation of the good and not so good features of the audio clips.
- Suggest possible improvements, using the table shown here.

Sound clip	Date	Source	Good features of audio clip	Not so good features of audio clip	Possible improve-ment
1					
2					

*Distinction-level candidates will **also** need to:*

- Provide a thorough explanation of the good and not so good features of the audio clips.
- Suggest a range of valid improvements to help the audio clip meets its aims, using the table shown here.

Sound clip	Date	Source	Good features of audio clip	Not so good features of audio clip	Aim of the audio clip	How the aims are met	How the aims are not met	Possible improve-ments
1								
2								

Section 2: Design an audio clip

Assessment objective 2: *Design an audio clip* is covered in this section.

Skills

You are required to plan the creation of an audio clip. The audio clip that you are going to create can be added to the zoo video clip in Unit 23 or can be played in a powerpoint presentation.

Produce design documentation

Before you start creating the audio clip, you need to produce a design plan. The audio clip that you create should be at least 45 seconds in length. The design plan will need to include:

- a description of the aim of the audio clip (e.g. the aim of the NicAnn zoo audio clip is to enhance the video clip shown on the NicAnn Zoo website, and to provide details of the elephants at the zoo);

- a description of the intended audience for the audio clip (e.g. visitors to the zoo who want to know more about the elephants);

- the software to be used (in our case, this will be Adobe Audition).

Produce a storyboard

A storyboard is a visual representation of how the audio clip will be created. The storyboard will need to show the detail relating to the audio clip and:

- the content of the clip;

- the timeline (the timeframe for the clip from the first to last frames);

- fading (e.g. to fade in and out the first and last frames within the clip);

- use of silence (e.g. inserting pauses and removing non-essential noises);

- volume;

- mono or stereo (a monophonic signal contains only one sound source; stereo contains dual sound sources, from left and right channels);

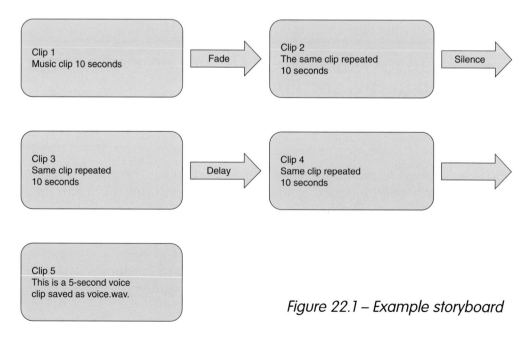

Figure 22.1 – Example storyboard

- special effects (e.g. amplitude, delay effects, filters, noise reduction, distortion, change the pitch, mute).

The aim of this audio clip is to produce a 45-second clip that can be played alongside a video clip of elephants for NicAnn Zoo, which can be uploaded to the Internet. The storyboard must match the audio created in the next section.

The timeline is shown in the screenshot.

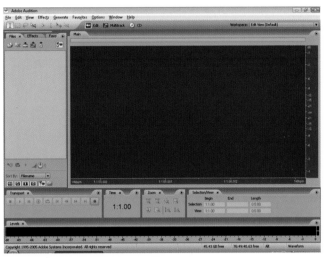

Figure 22.2 – Opening a window in Audition

Tasks

You have been asked to create a sound clip to go with an anti-bullying video clip for the school website. The sound clip should be appropriate for the audience and should be at least 45 seconds in length. This can include sound and narration, either created by you or imported from other software.

Pass

Pass-level candidates will need to:

- Describe the aim of the audio clip you are about to create.
- Create a simple storyboard, covering the main elements of the audio clip.

Merit

*Merit-level candidates will **also** need to:*

- Describe the intended audience for the audio clip.

*Distinction-level candidates will **also** need to:*

● Describe thoroughly the aim of the audio clip and the intended audience.

Section 3: Create an audio clip

Assessment objective 3 – *Create an audio clip* is covered in this section.

Skills

Having designed your audio clip in the previous section, you can now create the clip. Remember that it must be at least 45 seconds in length. The audio clip will need to include the following audio editing techniques:

● importing components (music, sound, speech);

● cutting, copying, pasting;

● splitting and trimming clips;

● silencing and fading;

● effects;

● exporting in a suitable file format.

Adobe Audition allows you to import files from a CD, Microsoft Windows Media® Player or from recorded speech.

Remember that you need to consider copyright before copying files from a CD. Some files is included for you to practise with (**voice.wav, Clip1.wav, Clip2.wav, Clip3.wav, Clip4.wav, Clip5.wav**).

How to copy a file from CD

Click on the Copy from CD button

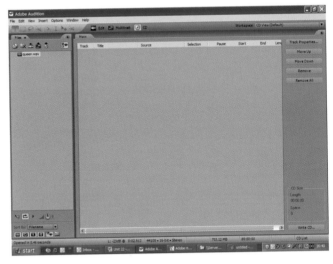

Figure 22.3 – Copy from CD

Insert the CD into the CD drive

→ Click File, Open CD List

→ Select the track

→ Click open – the imported clip is now shown

Figure 22.4 – Open track

Figure 22.5 – Imported CD track

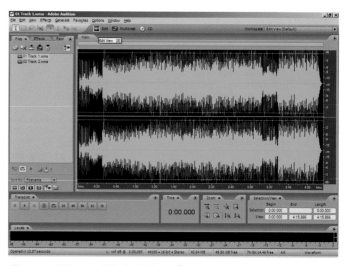

Figure 22.6 – CD in Waveform

How to record your voice

Find a quiet area and then switch to Waveform (edit) – this displays the audio clip across time.

Press the red record button and select your sample type (e.g. 44100 mono 16)

> → OK
> → When you finish recording, click Stop
> → Save the file by clicking File menu
> → Save As
> → Enter a filename

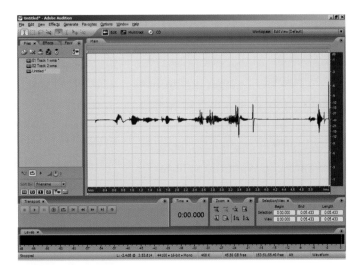

Figure 22.7 – Voice recording

How to cut, copy, paste

Select the audio clip you want to cut/copy/paste.

To copy audio data to the active clipboard:

Edit menu

> → Copy

To copy and paste the audio data into a newly created file in one step:

Edit menu

> → Copy To New

To remove audio data from the current waveform and copy it to the active clipboard:

Edit menu

> → Cut

This can now be pasted into a new clip or deleted.

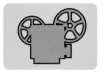

How to split and trim clips

In Multitrack View on the toolbar, select the time selection tool or the hybrid tool. Do either of the following:

- To split the clip in two, click where you want the split to occur.
- To split the clip into three, drag across it to specify two split points (one at the beginning of the selection, and one at the end).

Choose Clip

→ Split

Alternatively, if you want to trim the clip to 10 seconds, choose a beginning and end time of 10 seconds and the clip will be trimmed to 10 seconds.

Highlight the clip to 10 seconds

Edit menu

→ Cut

→ File

→ New

Edit menu

→ Paste to show your new trimmed clip of 10 seconds

Alternatively, right click and select 'trim'

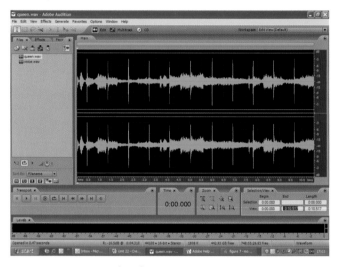

Figure 22.8 – Split clip

Figure 22.9 – Trimmed clip

How to create a multitrack

You have been provided with a number of clips. Create a new session in Audition and open the following:

clip1.wav

clip2.wav

clip3.wav

clip4.wav

clip5.wav

voice.wav

Click Multitrack

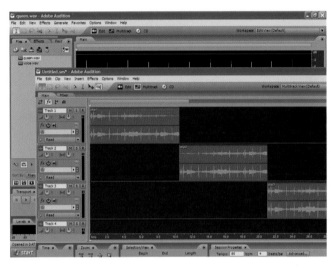

→ Insert

→ clip1

Figure 22.10 – Multitrack

→ Repeat by clicking in track2 and insert clip2 at the 10-second start point

→ Repeat until all four clips and the voice file have been inserted, as shown in the screenshot.

How to add silencing and fading

Select the first clip

→ Select the last seconds of this clip

→ Highlight this by holding down the Shift key and pressing the left arrow on the keyboard along the clip

→ Click FX button arrow and select Amplitude

→ Amplify

→ Amplify and then drag the arrows to just before –36. Click on the close icon to close this window

→ Fadeout

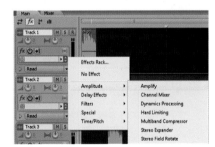

Figure 22.11 – Fadeout

Repeat for the second clip, but instead of moving the arrows to –36, move them to almost +15, and this will add a fade-in.

Alternatively, to add silencing and fading:

Make sure you are in Edit view and click where you want the fading to start

→ Click Favorites

→ Fadeout

Effects menu

→ Amplify/Fade process

→ Fadeout

→ OK

→ Test the clip to ensure that it fades out

To generate silence:

Click where you want the silence to start

→ Click effects tab image on CD

→ Vocal remove

→ Generate

→ Silence

→ 3 seconds

How to add fade/amplification

Select part of the clip to be amended

Effects menu

→ Amplitude

→ Amplify/Fade

→ The Amplify/Fade window will appear

→ Click on the Fade tab and choose one of the options

→ Check that the Enable Preroll and Postroll Preview checkbox is selected

→ Click Preview

→ OK

To create a faster fadeout:

Press F2 on the keyboard

Choose Edit menu

→ Repeat last command

→ Click OK to apply the fade again

How to add special effects

To apply noise reduction:

Select one of the clips

Effects menu

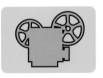

→ Restoration

→ Capture Noise Reduction Profile

→ OK

→ Click anywhere in the waveform to clear the current selection

Figure 22.12 – Noise Reduction

→ Home Key

→ Double-click (Noise Reduction process)

→ A new window is displayed

→ Preview

→ Move the Noise Reduction Level slider to 50%

→ Spectral Decay Rate field

→ 50

→ Bypass option

→ Bypass again

→ Any background noise should now be reduced

→ Try some of the other effects from the effects tab

How to save the file into a suitable format

To save the file in Adobe Audition:

File menu

→ Save session as

→ Choose a suitable location and save the file with the name **test**

→ Save all the amended files in this new folder

To save as a .wav file, so that it can be played on different software:

File menu

→ Export

→ Audio Mix Down

→ In the Mix Down Options section, select Embed Edit Original Link Data

→ Filename (test) and select WAV format

→ Save

→ Test the clip to ensure it is 43 seconds in length

Tasks

Use the anti-bullying scenario on page 359 to create an audio clip that matches the plan you created in Section 2.

| **Pass** | *Pass-level candidates will need to:* |

- Create an audio clip of at least 45 seconds in length.
- Import components (music, sound, speech).
- Import a speech file or record your own voice-over.
- Cut and copy parts of the audio clip so that it becomes seamless.
- Add special effects.
- Export the file into a suitable format.

| **Merit** | *Merit-level candidates will **also** need to:* |

- Split/trim the audio clip.

| **Distinction** | *Distinction-level candidates will **also** need to:* |

- Add silencing/fading.

Section 4: Testing

> **Assessment objective 4:** *Test the audio clip* is covered in this section.

Skills

Now that you have created your audio clip, you will need to test it to ensure that it works. The most efficient way to do this is to draw up a test plan, carry out the tests and provide evidence of the testing in the form of a completed test plan or a checklist.

Create a test plan

The test plan will need to be created in relation to the audio clip created in Section 3. The test plan needs to address the following:

- How suitable is the content?
- How have you conveyed the correct message?
- How long does the clip run for?
- How suitable are the effects?
- How suitable is the file format?

An example test plan is shown in the following table.

Test number	Area to be tested	Expected result	Actual result
1	Timeline	45 seconds	
2	Imported components	Sound Speech file	
3	Special effect	Noise reduction	
4	File format	Exported to suitable file format	

Tasks

Use the audio clip you created in Section 3.

Pass

Pass-level candidates will need to:

- Create a test table containing three tests.
- Identify areas of improvement.

Merit

*Merit-level candidates will **also** need to:*

- Include four tests.
- Action one of the areas for improvement.

Distinction

*Distinction-level candidates will **also** need to:*

- Include five tests.
- Action most of the areas for improvement.

Unit 23 Creating video

Unit overview

This unit will help you develop knowledge and understanding of how to review, design, create and test a short video clip.

Examples in this unit are based on Pinnacle Studio Version 9.0, a video capture and editing program.

By working through the *Skills*, *How To* and *Tasks* sections in this unit, you will demonstrate all the skills required for Unit 23 and be able to:

● review several existing video clips;

● design a video clip;

● create a video clip;

● test the video clip.

The How to sections are built around NicAnn Zoo and the tasks are built around banning bullying at school. You will need to collect content for your own video clips to create this project, download suitable content from the Internet or you may be provided with files.

Section 1: Review existing video clips

Assessment objective 1: *Review several existing video clips* is covered in this section.

You have been asked to create a video clip that will be incorporated into a website for NicAnn Zoo. You have been provided with a video file **zoo.mpg**, showing some African elephants, which you can edit and upload to your website.

Before you start, it is good idea to have a look at several different video clips and review these – this will help you when designing and creating your own video clip.

Skills

Review video clips

You will need to review at least two different video clips from the following list:

- TV advert;
- movie trailer;
- music video;
- promotional video;
- online media clips.

For each of the video clips reviewed, you will need to:

- identify the good and not so good features;
- identify the aims of the clip;
- comment on how the aims are met;
- if the aims are not met, explain why not;
- suggest possible improvements.

You could visit the following websites, which have example video clips available:

www.youtube.com
www.bbc.co.uk/videonation
www.movie-list.com

It is a good idea to visit each of these websites. You could pick an online media clip from www.youtube.com or a movie trailer from www.movie-list.com. Once you have found suitable clips, you will need to review these. The review should take the form of written evidence, covering the points set out above. Note that the video clip doesn't have to be very long – you might wish to view a clip which is only 90 seconds in length. You could use a table like the example provided here.

Video clip	Date	Source	Type	Aim of video clip	Aims met?	If aims not met, why not?	Good/not so good features	Possible improvements
1	1 Feb	www.youtube.com	Media clip	To highlight anti-bullying in schools	Yes – the video clip included animation and text	N/A	Good: The clip included sharp/detailed pictures and it was good the way the title zoomed in and out. Not so good: The clip was black and white and could have been enhanced with colour. The contrast/shadow was too dark in places	Colour could have been used to enhance this clip and there could have been less contrast/shadow used on the black-and-white clips, as this made some of the animation text difficult to read
2	3 Feb	www.movie-list.com	Movie trailer	To show some of the features of the upcoming movie	Yes – the trailer showed just enough detail so you could tell whether you wanted to go and watch this movie or not	N/A	Good: The title zooms back in after it zoomed out and the clip showed clear, detailed pictures. Not so good: There appeared to be flecks of dirt throughout the clip	The movie maker should revisit a number of the scenes and remove any of the flecks of dirt from the clip to ensure that it is clear and clean throughout

Tasks

You will need to review at least two different video clips from the following list:

- **TV advert;**
- **movie trailer;**
- **music video;**
- **promotional video;**
- **online media clips.**

Pass

Pass-level candidates will need to:

- List the good and not so good features of the clips, using the table shown here.

Video	Date	Source	Type	Good features	Not so good features
1					
2					

Merit

*Merit-level candidates will **also** need to:*

- Provide a detailed explanation of the good and not so good features of the clips.
- Explain in detail the aims of the video clip.
- Suggest possible improvements.

Again, this can be set out in a table, like the one below.

Video	Date	Source	Type	Good features	Not so good features	Aims of video clip	Possible improve-ments
1							
2							

Distinction

*Distinction-level candidates will **also** need to:*

- Provide a thorough explanation of the good and not so good features of the clips.

- Comment on how the aims are met.

- If the aims are not met, explain why not.

Again, this can be set out in a table, like the one below.

Video	Date	Source	Type	Aims of video	How the aims are met	If aims are not met, why not	Possible improve-ments
1							
2							

Section 2: Design a video clip

> **Assessment objective 2:** *Design a video clip* is covered in this section.

Skills

Now that you have reviewed a number of clips, you need to produce a design plan that includes:

- the aim of the video clip;
- the audience for the video clip;
- the software to be used;
- a storyboard showing, for example:

  1 the content of the video clip;

  2 timeline;

  3 text (titles and credits);

  4 images/animations;

  5 sound;

  6 video;

  7 transitions;

  8 special effects.

You have been provided with a video file, **zoo.mpg**, which has been captured from a video camera, showing some elephants at a zoo. You can use this file to practise the techniques used in this unit. Your plan will therefore need to relate to the zoo. The video clip will be uploaded and viewed as part of the website for prospective visitors to the zoo. The video clip will need to be at least 45 seconds in length. A sound file is also included on the CD and this can be added to the video clip however you can source your own elements.

The software to be used is Pinnacle Studio Version 9.0.

Storyboard

A storyboard walks you through the plan of the video clip and includes a number of pictures/diagrams, showing how the clip will look when completed.

The storyboard will need to include:

- the content of the video clip (e.g. the video will contain a title, some clips of elephants, some transitions, a final transition once the clip has come to an end, an imported sound file and special effects);

- timeline – this shows the timeframe for the video clip, from the first to last frames;

- text (e.g. a title frame and credits frame at the end);

- images/animations (e.g. any still images to be included, such as photos);

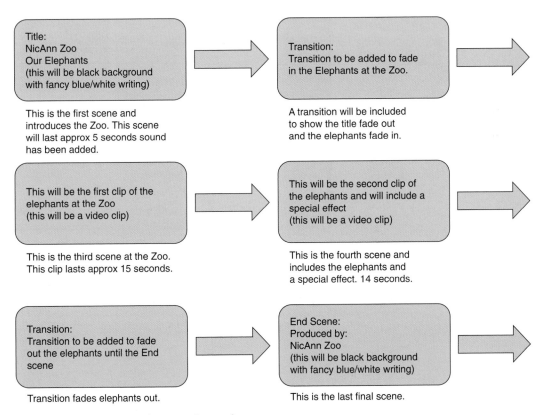

Figure 23.1 – Example storyboard

- sound (e.g. a sound file can be recorded or imported);
- video (e.g. an MPEG file which shows some elephants at a zoo);
- transitions (e.g. descriptions of how one frame is replaced by the next one) – transitions can include fading in and fading out to make the edited video clip run smoothly;
- special effects (e.g. cleaning effects, time effects, fun effects and style effects).

The aim of this video clip is to produce a 45-second clip of elephants for NicAnn Zoo which can be uploaded to the Internet. A sound file has been added and plays for the full 45 seconds.

The timeline is shown in the screenshot.

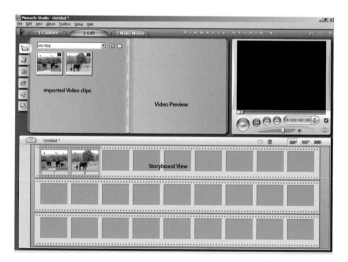

Figure 23.2 – Storyboard view

Tasks

You have been commissioned to produce an anti-bullying campaign within your school/college. The Principal has asked you to create a 45-second media clip which can be uploaded to the website, highlighting what bullying is and what the school is doing to combat it. You can carry out research on the Internet to obtain any copyright-free clips/animations to be used within your movie, or you can capture the movie yourself using a suitable video camera. Alternatively your teacher may provide these.

Pass

Pass-level candidates will need to:

● Produce a short written statement, which includes:

   1 the aim of the video clip;

   2 the software to be used.

● Produce a storyboard of the video clip you are to create, which shows:

   1 the content of the video clip;

   2 a timeline;

   3 text (titles and credits);

   4 images/animations;

   5 sound;

   6 video;

   7 transitions;

   8 special effects.

Note that Pass-level candidates do not need to include eight items in the storyboard. See p397 for requirements

Merit

*Merit- and distinction-level candidates will **also** need to:*

● Describe the intended audience for the video clip.

- Produce a storyboard which includes:

  1 titles and credits;

  2 effects.

| Distinction |

*Distinction-level candidates will **also** need to:*

- Provide a thorough explanation of aim and audience
- Produce a storyboard which also includes sound/narration.

Section 3: Create a video clip

Assessment objective 3: *Create a video clip* is covered in this section.

Skills

Based on the NicAnn Zoo scenario, you now need to create the video clip. The clip will need to be at least 45 seconds in length. The video will need to include the following editing techniques (depending on the grade level you are working towards):

- import components (images, animations, video, sound);
- edit clips;
- split and trim clips;
- transitions and effects;
- add titles;
- add soundtrack;
- add narration;
- export the video into a suitable file format.

How to import a video clip

Load Studio

→ Click on the Edit tab

→ Open the project and file
zoo.mpg

Figure 23.3 – Open file

Four scene clips are shown – these need to be dragged onto the storyboard. The third clip does not need to be included in our movie, so drag and drop clips 1, 2 and 4 onto the storyboard.

Storyboard view allows you to play your images and review these to ensure that they are in the correct places.

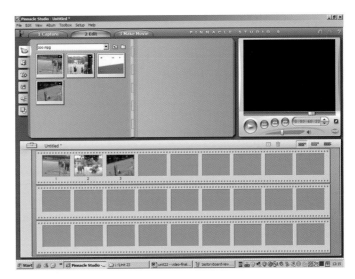

Figure 23.4 – Storyboard view

The timeline allows you to cut/crop and move images.

Figure 23.5 – Timeline for scenes

Click on the Play button to see if the clip has imported correctly. The clip is approximately 25 seconds in length.

The first clip is 33 seconds in length and the second one 24 seconds in length. Trim the second clip so that it is only 15 seconds in length.

Figure 23.6 – Press the Play button to check the clip

How to trim/split a clip

Click on the open/close video toolbox button, just above the timeline, next to the briefcase

Select the second clip

→ Trim it by 1.14 seconds, by dragging the clip from the start to remove the people, until after the first tree on the clip, or

→ Click on the start of the clip in the timeline and drag the cursor to the right

→ As the arrow changes to two heads, the preview shows how much has been clipped

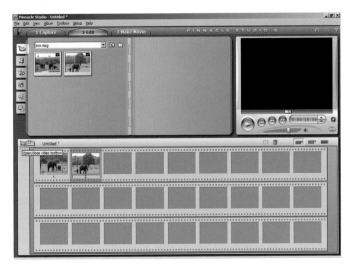

Figure 23.7 – Open/close video toolbox

Figure 23.8 – Trimming a clip

To cut the clip in half:

Select the last clip

→ Drag the arrow to the part that you wish to divide into two

→ Click on the blade icon to cut the clip into two

Figure 23.9 – Splitting

Play the trimmed clip to ensure that it has been trimmed, the people have been removed and the last clip has been cut in two. Close the toolbox.

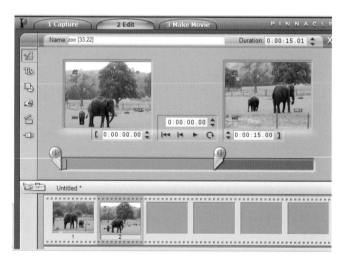

Figure 23.10 – Trimming

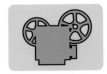

How to add a title overlay

To create an opening title screen, click on the storyboard icon

→ Click the Titles tab

→ Select one of the designs

→ Drag the design to the timeline in front of the first elephant clip

Figure 23.11 – Titles

Double-click on the title in the timeline

→ Click Edit Title

→ Change the text to: NicAnn Zoo – Our Elephants

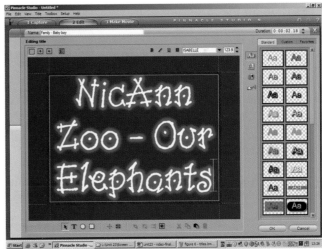

Figure 23.12 – Edit title

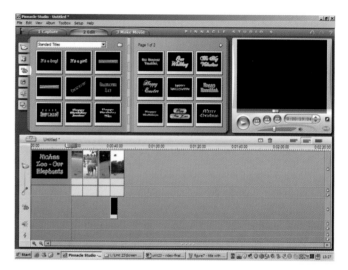

Figure 23.13 – Title with timeline

Apply any of the effects
- → Change the timing of this clip to 6 seconds
- → Click OK

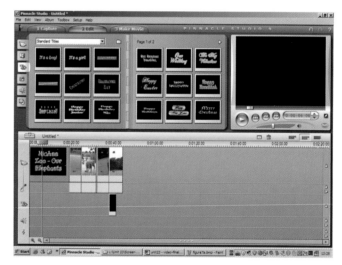

Figure 23.14 – Change the timing of the clip

Click on the background icon to change the background of the title overlay.

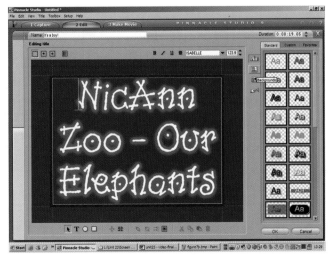

Figure 23.15 – Change background

Add a final overlay which shows:

Produced by: (your name)

Change the time of this frame to 10 seconds and change the background to match the title slide.

To add a scrolling last credit slide, double-click the last slide

→ Click Roll and close this screen

→ Play to see the rolling credits

→ Save the file as **zoo1**

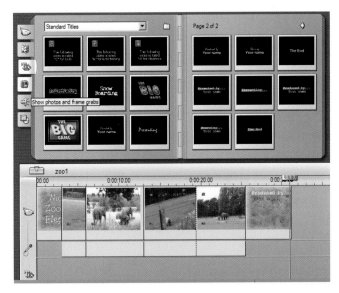

Figure 23.16 – Creating a final overlay

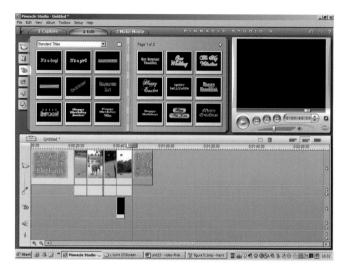

Figure 23.17 – Final overlay

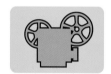

How to import a photograph

You have been provided with three pictures of elephants:

Figure 23.18 – Import a photograph

elephants1.jpg

elephants2.jpg

elephants3.jpg

Click on the camera icon

→ Find a suitable photo to import to the project

→ Select the folder that contains the pictures

→ Click open

→ Drag the first and last photos onto the timeline

→ The first photo should be dragged to after the title overlay and the last photograph should be dragged to before the end title overlay

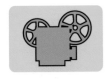

How to add music from CD

You can add music from a CD or you can add a voice-over.

Click Setup

→ Choose CD and voice-over

Figure 23.19 – CD and voice-over

Select the drive letter of the CD drive

→ Click on the Edit tab

→ Click on the open/close audio toolbox

→ Click on the CD icon

→ Add background from Audio CD

→ Choose a track

→ Click Add to Movie

Figure 23.20 – Setup Options

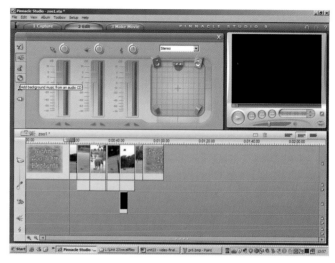

Figure 23.21 – Add background noise

Insert a CD into your computer

→ Select the track

→ Click on Add to movie

The sound clip is much longer than the video clip. Drag the sound clip from the right to the left to ensure that it is the same length as the video clip.

Save the file as **zoo2**.

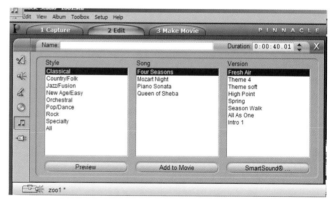

Figure 23.22 – Add to movie

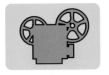

How to add music/audio

Click on the Create background music automatically button

→ Choose a song according to style, song and version

→ Change the length of the clip again in the timeline to ensure that the sound clip is no longer than the video clip

Figure 23.23 – Create background music automatically

Figure 23.24 – Style, song and version

How to add voice-over

Click Choose record a voice-over narration

→ Connect a microphone to your computer through an audio input

→ Click Record

→ Record your voice narration

→ Click stop when the recording is complete

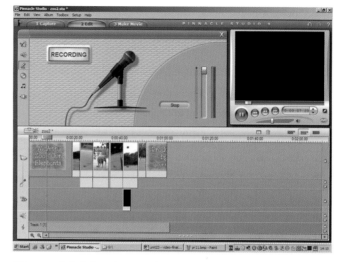

Figure 23.25 – Record your voice narration

How to use transition effects

Transitions provide a break in the scenes and can add pacing, closures and openings to the video clips.

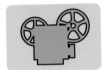

Figure 23.26 – Show transitions

Click on Show transitions

→ Find an appropriate transition effect

→ In storyboard mode, drag and drop the transitions between each of the clips

Double-click on the transition effect on your storyboard to show how long each transition lasts

→ Click Play to check each of the transitions within your presentation

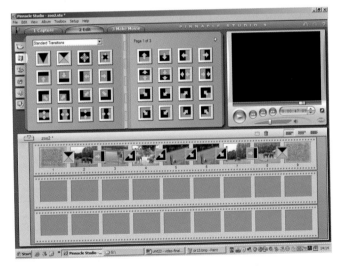

Figure 23.27 – Drag and drop transitions

How to use special effects

Click on the first clip

→ Click on the video toolbox

→ Click Add an effect to a video clip

Figure 23.28 – Add an effect to a video clip

Select Style Effects

→ Emboss

→ Repeat this for the credits clip, but choose a different effect

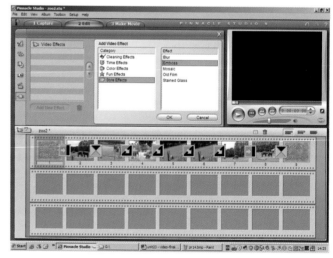

Figure 23.29 – Special effects

Check that your clip is at least 45 seconds in length and that all aspects work correctly.

Save as **zoo3**.

Figure 23.30 – Check your clip

How to make a movie

Once you have completed editing all the components of the video, you can make a movie.

Click on the make movie button

→ Select MPEG

→ Create MPEG file

Create a movie

→ Give the file a suitable filename, saving it either onto your computer or to a CD/DVD

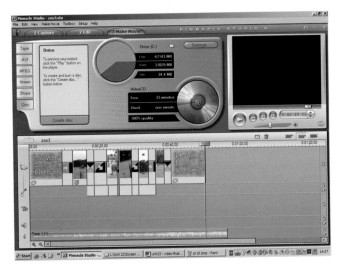

Figure 23.31 – Make Movie

Tasks

Pass

Pass-level candidates will need to:

- Create a video clip, which must be at least 45 seconds in length, for the anti-bullying campaign.
- Import some other components (e.g. still images).
- Edit the clips.
- Add transitions.
- Add a soundtrack.
- Create a movie by exporting the file into a suitable format.

Merit

*Merit-level candidates will **also** need to:*

- Add titles.
- Add special effects.

Distinction

*Distinction-level candidates will **also** need to:*

- Split/trim a clip.
- Add either a soundtrack or narration.

Section 4: Test the video clip

> **Assessment objective 4:** *Test the video clip* is covered in this section.

Skills

Now that the video clip has been created, you need to test it to ensure that it is working. You will need to create a test plan. Once the test plan has been created, you will need to carry out the tasks listed on the test plan and provide evidence of this through a completed test plan or checklist. Once you have completed the tests, any suggestions for improvements must be made.

The test plan will need to include suitable content and answer the following questions:

● Is the correct message conveyed?

● Is the time allocation suitable for each component?

● Does the video clip run for the correct length of time?

● Have suitable effects/transitions been applied?

● Has the video clip been saved in a suitable format?

Make the improvements based on the testing outcomes.

An example test plan is shown in the table here.

Test number	Area to be tested	Expected result	Actual result
1	Timeline	45 seconds	
2	Transitions	3 included – smooth?	
3	Soundtrack	Working soundtrack	
4	Content	Does the video include suitable content relevant to the zoo?	

Tasks

Pass

Pass-level candidates will need to:

- Create a test table which includes at least four tests.
- Test your video against the test table.
- Identify areas for improvement.

Merit

*Merit-level candidates will **also** need to:*

- Create a test table which includes at least five tests.
- Action one of the areas for improvement.

Distinction

*Distinction-level candidates will **also** need to:*

- Create a test table which includes at least six tests.
- Action most of the areas for improvement.

INDEX